What Time is the 9:20 Bus?

A Journey to a Meaningful Life, Disability and All

Lucinda Hage

Peterborough 2014

ISBN 978-0-9936526-0-8

Library and Archives Canada Cataloguing in Publication

Hage, Lucinda, 1950-, author
    What time is the 9:20 bus? : a journey to a meaningful life, disability and all / Lucinda Hage.

Includes bibliographical references.
ISBN 978-0-9936526-0-8 (pbk.)

    1. Tiller, Paul--Health. 2. Hage, Lucinda, 1950-. 3. Mothers and sons--Ontario--Peterborough. 4. Tuberous sclerosis--Patients--Ontario--Peterborough--Biography. 5. Parents of children with disabilities--Ontario--Peterborough--Biography. I. Title.

RJ496.T8H35 2014   616.85'8840092   C2013-908589-0

4rd Printing 2017

Lucinda Hage
www.inclusionforlife.com

"It is because we belong with others and see them as brothers and sisters in humanity that we learn not only to accept them as they are, with different gifts and capacities, but to see each one as a person with a vulnerable heart. It is in belonging that people discover what it means to be human."

– Jean Vanier, Becoming Human

For my son Paul Conrad Tiller
and all the people who help him shine

Foreward

I was delighted to be asked by Lucinda, on behalf of Paul, to provide a brief introduction to this very important book. When Paul was diagnosed with Tuberous Sclerosis, there was much less known about this disorder and its genetics, and we were very concerned for the family as they faced such devastating news regarding their newly adopted son. Lucinda's description of those early days in hospital certainly focuses on the horror that parents' experience when seeing their child in such a different and uncontrollable environment.

Lucinda and Paul have been on a very long journey and the book portrays a much happier outcome than I would have predicted when I first met Paul. It is indicative of an extraordinary resilience shown by Lucinda, and is clearly mirrored in Paul despite his vulnerabilities.

I think this book should be read by medical caregivers – not just neurologists and neurological nurses – but all those who deal with families whose children are seriously ill. It is often hard when you work in a hospital setting, literally on a 24/7 basis, to appreciate that most families have strength and courage. Certainly in Paul's case, his life has been infused with a tremendous amount of love and caring and his outcome reflects all of this.

Daune MacGregor MD, DCH, PBDM FRCP(C),
Professor of Pediatrics (Neurology),
University of Toronto,
Staff Neurologist
The Hospital for Sick Children,
Toronto, Ontario

PART ONE

IN THE BEGINNING

"YOU MEAN PAUL, YOUR PAUL, is living in his own apartment? By himself?" one of my son's former high school teachers asked, as she shook her head in disbelief. "It's so hard to imagine."

I nodded and smiled, basking in the glow of Paul's accomplishment.

"Sometimes we don't expect enough of these kids," she continued.

"You're so right," I replied.

It was June 2010, and I was visiting the school where Paul, now 25, had completed his high school education four years earlier, in the Learning and Life Skills (LLS) program. It was for students with special needs, who were grouped together by their developmental level to learn basic life skills rather than academics.

I had been invited to attend the art show produced by this year's senior class. Paul began his education in a segregated public school classroom at the age of seven and had been in an LLS class for students with "behaviours" throughout high school. It was too bad he wasn't with me today; he would have enjoyed being congratulated on how much he had achieved since his teachers last saw him.

Our journey – actually, more of an expedition – to a life of meaning and independence for Paul didn't come easily. His intellectual disability seriously impacted his comprehension, speech and behaviour. It plunged me into a life I didn't expect and certainly didn't want, with heartaches I couldn't have imagined.

It took a mother's love, a good measure of faith and courage and a large dose of persistence for Paul to achieve his current level of independence.

EVEN AS A CHILD, I SAW MYSELF AS A MOTHER. I grew up playing with dolls, lovingly dressing them and tucking them into their cradles each night. In my 20s and early 30s, I became an aunt seven times over and a godmother to four.

But my own arms were empty, even though I'd been married for eight years. I would look longingly at pregnant women crossing the street when I was downtown, wishing I was one of them. When friends and family members got pregnant and gave birth, I would smile and buy baby gifts, but cry myself to sleep.

My biological clock was ticking so loudly, it was drowning out rational thought. There were times I was so distraught I'd sit on the couch in the evening with a bottle of sweet vermouth and a plate of peanut butter sandwiches. My stomach definitely got bigger, but for the wrong reason.

In 1979, at the age of 29, I admitted to my family doctor that I needed help, and was referred to a gynaecologist. As an infertility patient, I opened myself with hopefulness to each invasive and often painful test. My husband John, then 35, was asked to provide a sperm sample to test his motility, which he did, albeit reluctantly.

He wanted to have children, but objected to having our private life made public. "Only once a week?" asked the gynaecologist as he peered at me over the top of his black-rimmed glasses. I sank into the chair with my head down, vowing to lie the next time the topic of our sex life was scrutinized.

The test results were inconclusive, so I travelled to two teaching hospitals looking for answers; one of them put me on a fertility pill. With each invasive procedure, I liked my body less. I felt like a failure as a woman, but was too ashamed to talk about it.

After eight months of tests and treatment, I was given no specific reason why I couldn't get pregnant. I kept working and pretending everything was fine, but I was blown apart inside.

A year later, when the Children's Aid Society had an information meeting for childless couples wishing to adopt, John and I eagerly went to the session. A middle-aged woman covered the adoption process in some detail, and then announced it would take at least five years to adopt a baby.

"If any of you are turning forty before then, forget it. You are too old," she said reminding me of the Wicked Witch of the North.

The silence in the room was broken by the man sitting beside me. "Why the hell did we even bother coming?" He stormed out of the meeting with his wife in tow, and we weren't far behind. Another dream had been shattered.

My way of coping was to throw myself into a letter-writing campaign, pleading our case for private adoption to doctors across the country. I specifically targeted Prince Edward Island. Abortions were illegal in that province, and I thought that might increase our chances. I didn't receive any replies.

I was used to working hard to get what I wanted, and for the first time in my life, I couldn't simply apply myself and produce the desired results. I had to accept that there were some things not even I, the smiling, blue-eyed achiever, could control. This was to become a more important lesson than I could ever have imagined.

—∞—

I had no control over my body, but my brain still worked, so I enrolled in a part-time Masters of Education program in Counselling, and continued to work as the Placement Officer at Fleming College in Peterborough Ontario. The course work stimulated my thinking and distracted me from my angst and I put the idea of adoption into the back corner of my brain. The year I turned 34, I took a sabbatical leave from my job and completed my degree.

That summer, I was sitting at my desk at work when the phone rang. It was my family doctor. "Lucinda, are you still interested in adopting a baby?" she asked. Caught by surprise, I hesitated for a second before coming to my senses.

"Yes, yes of course."

"I have a young patient who's just given birth to a baby girl that she doesn't want to keep. You can go to the hospital and take a peek if you want. The baby is adorable with the thickest head of black hair."

"That's incredible!" I said, feeling like a space ship had just landed in my office. Immediately, I called John at work and left him a message. As I was hanging up the phone, a thought flashed through my mind, "Black hair, but I'm so fair." Quickly, I put it out of my mind. "Don't be ridiculous, hair colour doesn't matter."

John and I flew into a flurry of activity. We only had ten short days to arrange for a social worker to do the home-study, get a room ready and complete the legal process.

On day nine, the day before the young mother was to sign the adoption papers, I received a call from my lawyer. "I have some bad news," he began. "The birth mother has changed her mind. Her parents have rallied around her and convinced her to keep their grandchild."

Wordlessly, I put the receiver down. John and I could barely speak. With trembling lips, I returned the baby furniture to the store.

That night, I sat alone in the living room trying to make sense of it all. I thought about that little baby with the black hair and how, for a second, I had rejected her. "Was that the reason things didn't work out?" I asked myself, tears flowing down my cheeks.

Then a prayer floated into my head, and my breathing slowed down: "Not my will but Thy will be done." I prayed the phrase over and over again until I was able to say to myself, "This really isn't up to me." I had to accept, once again, that this was something I had no control over.

"Do you really want to do this?" I asked myself. It was a pivotal question. I had a career and every tangible thing I could ever want. Why then did I want to put myself into this emotional minefield? I thought about it and knew the reason came from my heart: I had a lot of love inside me that I wanted to share with my very own child.

—⁓—

I'm not a masochist, just half Norwegian and genetically programmed to be persistent, so I decided to try to adopt, one last time. A year earlier, a friend at work had adopted a baby privately through a local lawyer. It was a long shot, but I decided to give the lawyer a call.

She wasn't encouraging. "A private adoption through me is very unlikely to ever happen again."

Six months later, John got a call from the same lawyer. A baby was to be born in two weeks and she wondered if we were still interested in adopting. I was out of town for the day; when I got home, John met me at the door, hopping from one foot to the other with the news. We held hands and danced around the living room. We were definitely interested.

The first week passed in a blur of preparation. As we entered the second week, I was too excited to eat, and my chest was fluttering so hard I couldn't concentrate at work. All I could think about was this soon-to-be-born baby. During the day, I would briefly close my eyes, my fingers resting on the wrinkles on my forehead, a prayer on my lips.

"God, direct our lives and the life of this little child," I prayed. And then I added a P.S. "Please God, this time can it be our turn?"

John and I talked about nothing else at home, but we were careful not to say anything at work. I couldn't face having to "un-tell" people. I bought just a few sleepers and we borrowed a crib from friends. "Easier to return," I said to myself.

The birth mother's due date came and went. "I'd rather face the pain of childbirth than this emotional agony," I told a close friend. I waited four more days and then called the lawyer. She agreed to call me back. Ten minutes later, the phone rang.

"Mum and her parents are on their way to the hospital."

The following day, she called back to say a baby boy had been born, 12 days late. It was December 20, 1985. The social worker who did our home-study assured us that this birth mother and her parents wanted the child adopted. I was somewhat encouraged, but still haunted by the possibility she would change her mind.

We had to wait another ten days, until the end of December, for the mother to sign the papers. Only then would the baby be released. It was Christmas, a time I normally would be rejoicing in the birth of another baby boy. But not this year. I found it impossible to celebrate and hold my breath at the same time.

Family and friends were praying for us as the end of 1985 slowly ticked forward. On December 30, John and I were sitting in the living room pretending to read when the phone rang. We looked at each other, and neither of us moved.

"Do you want to get it?" he asked. I took a deep breath and picked up the receiver. It was our lawyer.

"I have some good news. Can you meet me in my office at 2:00 today?" "You bet!" "You'd better bring a car seat." "We have one ready. We'll be there." I put down the phone.

"John, she signed the papers; we can pick up the baby today!" I said, skipping across the room into his arms. We hugged each other long and hard, our tears spilling together. It felt so good to finally be able to exhale. Then I remembered the unfinished baby's room. "We'd better get moving; we've got to set up the crib."

John said he was too excited to drive to the lawyer's office. I was too excited not to. We arrived early, our social worker followed, and then the lawyer. We gave each of them a bottle of champagne and a rose. I looked around expectantly, but there was no little bundle anywhere.

"A colleague of mine has gone to the hospital to pick him up," the lawyer explained. I let out an audible sigh. I had waited for this moment for seven years, and anticipation welled up inside me like a helium balloon ready to burst. With my eyes fixated on the door, my fingers stroked the satin border of the soft pink, yellow and blue striped baby blanket on my lap.

"I should tell you," our lawyer Cheryl said, "the baby had a difficult delivery. He's fine, but the forceps caused a skull fracture. The local paediatrician thought it was necessary to have him checked out at Sick Kids in Toronto. He was taken by helicopter and was there for a few days over Christmas."

"That poor wee boy," I murmured. "All the time we were waiting for him, he was by himself in Toronto." Without missing a beat, John said, "He's only ten days old and already he's got his own lawyer, his own social worker and he's had a helicopter ride!" Our laughter released the tension.

Then we heard footsteps coming down the hall. The door opened and a woman with a beaming face walked into the room carrying a tiny baby. She placed him in my arms. He was wearing the soft yellow bunting bag I'd made for him, his little face peering out from under the hood.

Never before had I experienced such a powerful combination of exhilaration and love. I lifted him out of his sleeping bag, removed the knitted white cap from his head and ran my fingers through his fine light brown hair. A joy that knew no bounds filled my heart.

"His head is a bit pointy from the delivery," the lawyer said.

I looked down at his face. "You look like a perfect angel to me," I whispered, touching his cheek ever so gently.

For years, I had held babies that belonged to other women and I'd always had to give them back. But not this time. At long last, I was a mother, and this was my child. All the maternal love that had been bottled up inside me began to flow into this perfect child, my son, lying peacefully against my heart. I felt complete.

There was a flow of baby talk as everyone in the room took turns holding the baby, admiring his captivating blue eyes and button nose. We passed around the gifts that came with him from Toronto: a bright red Christmas stocking big enough for his tiny body to fit into and a soft blue and yellow Donald Duck figure.

Cheryl explained that, initially, our child was to have been adopted by a family from another province. But they were concerned about the lawyer's fees and travel costs if the birth mother changed her mind, so they changed theirs. She told us our son's birth parents were university students and that his grandparents, like us, had a university education. Then she made a statement that was to shape our son's life. "With you, he will achieve his potential."

When we were leaving her office, Cheryl gave me a box of newborn diapers and a six-pack of formula. "This is it," I thought. "Welcome to motherhood."

We drove home with our little boy safely bundled into his car seat. "Can you believe it, John? This baby in the back seat is really ours." I faced backwards the entire 20-minute drive home. I couldn't take my eyes off our son.

We named him Paul after the littlest apostle and Conrad after my Norwegian father. My dad was a humble, gentle man who lived by the principles taught to him by his own mother: honesty, integrity and a concern for others. I had no idea how much Paul's name, with its roots in faith and family values, would come to mean.

—∞—

As soon as we got home, we started taking pictures: John carrying Paul through the door in his bucket seat; me giving him his first tiny bottle; the three of us on the couch with Paul's tiny fingers reaching toward his dad; John's arm around me, the two of us smiling like Cheshire cats.

That first night, we kissed Paul goodnight and I lowered him gently into the white borrowed crib, ten sizes too big. I had babysat throughout high school, mostly to get out of the house on a Saturday night, so I knew a thing or two about babies and was good at changing diapers and giving bottles.

What I wasn't sure about was whether or not I would wake up in the middle of the night. Friends told me that pregnancy and night-time trips to the bathroom had prepared them for being wakened once the baby arrived. That hadn't been my experience, plus I was a really sound sleeper. I went to bed wondering what would happen.

By some mysterious twist of nature, I woke up just before Paul did that first morning. His cry filled me with joy and thoughts of his birth mother.

"Thank you for the sacrifice you made," I said half out loud. I knew my happiness was her sorrow. The social worker had said that women who give their babies up for adoption eventually make the best mothers, because their decisions were based on what was best for their babies. I hoped she would have other children.

I knew in my heart that Paul was ours, but we still had another legal hurdle to overcome. His birth mother had another three weeks from the time he was placed with us to change her mind. The adoption wasn't final until January 20th. That was the law.

My friend, who adopted the year before, had placed her baby with a neighbour for those three weeks in case she had to give him back (which didn't happen). But I knew I couldn't have someone else care for Paul. I wasn't going to hold back my love for him for one day, let alone twenty-one.

It was the beginning of a new year, 1986, and everything seemed possible. It was the year the Challenger lifted into space, and I and millions of others watched the live broadcast of the first Teacher in Space program. We all believed Christa McAuliffe would return to earth and her classroom. No one anticipated that the space shuttle would explode before our eyes in diverging billows of white smoke. I had to believe this would not also happen to my dream.

My journal summed up those early days: "This is the longest three weeks of our lives." I checked off each day on the calendar, and with each advancing tick felt and acted more and more like Paul's mother.

I recorded his firsts in a baby book: when he first turned his head, his first visit to the doctor, his first smile, when he laughed and giggled five days later and, best of all, when he recognized me.

I believed with all my heart that Paul's birth mother wasn't going to change her mind, but I couldn't be certain until it was official. On January 20, with my heart beating like an African drum, I picked up the phone and called the lawyer's office.

The secretary put me on hold, and then said the words I was desperate to hear. The birth mother had signed the final papers. Paul was officially ours.

"I'm taking the day off so we can all be together," John announced. "Group hug," I replied, as we circled our arms with Paul pressed between us.

Later, I dressed our son in a blue velvet suit complete with a miniature bow tie. He slept on the couch while John and I celebrated with champagne and pizza.

Now we could put Paul's birth announcement in the paper. It was traditional except for the ending, which referenced Psalm 117. *Praise the Lord!*

I wasn't the only one who was touched by the arrival of this long-awaited child. To our amazement, friends, family and acquaintances sent gifts from across the country, 81 in all. Paul's arrival into the world and into our lives brought a surge of joy to so many. A friend sent me a poem, which I treasure to this day.

> *Not flesh of my flesh*
> *Or bone of my bone*
> *But still very much my own*
> *Don't forget for a single minute*
> *You didn't grow under my heart*
> *But in it.*
>
> *Anonymous*

The next week, a public health nurse made a mother-and-child visit. "I haven't had nine months to prepare for this," I said hesitantly. "Don't worry," she reassured me. "Just trust your intuition and you'll be fine." It was some of the best advice I've ever had.

All I wanted to do that winter was stay home with my baby boy and wrap him in a blanket of love. I was content to let it snow outside and remove myself from the busyness of the world. I even liked getting up in the middle of the cold winter nights and feeding him. I just loved him so much.

My peacefulness was broken when my employer called after I'd been home for two weeks to inform me that I wasn't eligible for an eight-month maternity leave because "your child is adopted."

I couldn't believe what I was hearing. My son was only three weeks old. It didn't matter where he came from, he and I needed to be together. The unfairness of the decision left me reeling with tears of frustration and anger.

And then a realization struck me: my protective instinct was as strong as if I had actually given birth. From that moment on, I ceased to think of Paul as being adopted. He was my son. Period.

Part of me wanted to quit my job and stay home, but John convinced me that I shouldn't. After some negotiations with my employer, I cobbled together a schedule of working from home with the four months of maternity leave I was granted, along with my vacation time. By the time Paul was eight months old and robust enough to sit by himself, I had found Patty, a vibrant home daycare provider, and returned to work full time.

Because of Paul's skull fracture, at birth, I had to take him to Sick Kids in Toronto for a follow-up visit. A nursing friend accompanied me to the outpatient neurology clinic, and I was grateful for her support. At the registration desk, they couldn't find Paul's name in the hospital records. Panic rose in my chest. Then I remembered that he'd been referred to as "Baby H," the initial of his birth mother's last name.

The cogs of the hospital machine shifted into gear and we were ushered into a tiny examining room. I'd never met a neurologist before and this one was dark and handsome, with long fingers that surrounded Paul's tiny head with tender skill. He pronounced Paul to be in excellent health.

As we were leaving, I looked around the waiting room crammed with parents and distressed children, and turned to my friend and said, "Thank heavens we don't have to come back here!"

"DA DA," ""DA DA," "DA DA." Paul spoke his first words in October, just before his first Thanksgiving. I didn't feel slighted that he chose to acknowledge his dad first; it warmed my heart to see the bond developing between them. They often napped together, father and son asleep, little Paul breathing peacefully on his dad's chest.

Everything was going fine and we all settled into the working-parent routine: dropping Paul off, picking him up, making quick meals, laundry. There was always laundry.

My mother commented that she had never seen such a contented baby. His blue eyes danced whenever someone smiled at him; he ate well, giggled when music played and eagerly looked at picture books. He didn't crawl like the baby books said he should, and sometimes he fell over in his yellow bathtub ring, but that didn't seem to matter. Paul was happy. Our theme song was *No One Else Could Love You More*.

> *More than the greatest love the world has known,*
> *This is the love I give to you alone…*
> *I know I've never lived before and my heart is very sure,*
> *No one else could love you more.*

A first-time parent only sees warning signs in hindsight. For me, it was the time after Paul's six-month booster shot, when he emitted a high-pitched cry, like the cry of a cat, or when he wouldn't stop crying when we were staying with friends over the Thanksgiving weekend. Our friend Brian gave me a "Can't you get him to stop" look, to which I replied, "He's just upset sleeping in a new place."

On a Sunday afternoon in mid-October, when Paul was 10 months old, something happened that I couldn't explain away. He was beside me on our bed for an afternoon nap and had just drifted off when his little body seemed to twitch. It wasn't just one twitch, it was several in a row.

I used the words "seemed to" when talking to the doctor the next day because I didn't want to believe there was anything seriously wrong. There was no doubt in my mind, however, that Paul's body had twitched in small jerking movements.

Our family doctor was reassuring. "It's probably just a leg twitch, which often happens before you fall asleep. To be sure, I'll refer you to a paediatrician. It may take several weeks."

We didn't have to wait that long. The following week, I was out of town at a staff retreat when our meeting was interrupted. I had a phone call from John. "I don't want you to panic," he said, his voice controlled. "Paul is in the hospital. They aren't sure what's wrong with him, but his head was banging against Patty's chest. I'm at the hospital now. Drive slowly and meet me here."

My heart hit my stomach. I couldn't say anything. John repeated, "Just drive slowly and meet me here." All I could say was, "I'll come."

I put the phone back onto the receiver and stood in silence, my hands gripped together pressed against my lips as I tried to take in what I had just heard. There must be a valve in your brain that allows your body and mind to handle life-shattering news a bit at a time. I didn't allow myself to fall apart. I had to get to Paul. I returned to the meeting room and repeated John's words to my colleagues. Some of them walked me to my car. Then, like a robot, I drove slowly, as instructed. In all honesty, I was in no hurry to find out what lay ahead.

At the hospital, I walked toward the red brick building in disbelief, steeling myself with every step. I took the elevator to the paediatric floor and found Paul peacefully asleep in his crib. It was surreal. He looked no different than he had that very morning, when everything was right with the world.

After a couple of minutes, John said, "I'm wiped out and I'm going home." "Won't you stay so we can talk to the doctor together?" "Look, I drove from work, met Patty here and admitted Paul. I told you, I'm tired and I'm going home."

The waiting area was empty. I dropped into one of the hard plastic chairs, closed my eyes and prayed for strength.

"Is the mother the one who's asleep?" I heard a male voice say behind me. "How could I possibly be asleep?" I thought, irritated that I must have appeared unconcerned. The doctor was standing before me, his maroon tie knotted firmly under his chin. "Are you the mother?" I nodded.

"Tests have shown continuous seizure activity in your son's brain. It's more than I can deal with here. You'll have to take him to Sick Kids. Tonight." "But it's almost dark! Can't we wait until the morning?" "They're expecting you," was his curt reply.

There are times in life when your options are seriously limited and this was one of them. I asked one of the nurses if I could use the phone and with shaking fingers, I dialled our home number. After what seemed like an eternity, John answered. "We have to take Paul to Sick Kids tonight. The doctor said he's too sick to be treated here. I'm coming home now for his things."

I must have been crying louder than I realized; a nurse appeared and put her hand on my shoulder. Together, we woke Paul up and got him ready.

I don't remember driving home, but I do remember finding John sitting in the darkened living room, his Molson pain relief in hand. It wasn't his first. Even though I had just talked to him, he seemed surprised to see me. "Why aren't you ready?" I asked. He mumbled something about having fallen asleep. My voice rose. "We have to be in Toronto tonight!"

John got ready and I drove the 128 kilometres to Toronto. Neither of us spoke. Our mood matched the dark, cold October night. As the lights of the city came into view, a thought lifted my heart by a thread.

"Paul is going back to the same hospital where he spent his first Christmas with only strangers to hold him. But this time it's different. This time, he has his mother with him."

—⁓—

The Hospital for Sick Children has always had a wonderful medical reputation, but in 1986 the building was almost 100 years old, and it looked it. Built for adults, not children, it had no facilities for parents to stay overnight, no brightly coloured walls or private rooms. In the dead of night, it was foreboding and sinister.

We took Paul up the elevator to the neurology floor. As we walked down a long, dim corridor, a dry antiseptic smell filled my nostrils. I looked into the large silent rooms lined with metal cribs that looked more like cages.

The neurology resident was waiting for us. He looked as tired as we felt. He signed us in and I placed my baby in one of the cages. It was one o'clock in the morning. I was mute. My heart leaden.

John and I went to a nearby hotel, where we got the hospital room rate. The next morning, he wanted to stay at the hotel for breakfast. Why did I agree? Our son had just been admitted into Sick Kids, and here I was drinking coffee in a comfortable dining room. Were we both in denial? Probably. Nevertheless, guilt rises in me at the memory of the waitress pouring me a second cup of coffee.

"Our baby is at Sick Kids," I said, looking into her face. She responded with a compassionate gaze. "Why isn't she telling me I'm a lousy mother?" I thought. "I've got to get out of here."

When we got to Paul's room, we found him asleep in his crib, his body tucked neatly into the red velour sleeper he'd been given as a baby gift. That was the only thing familiar about him. Electrodes were strapped to his head like the tentacles of an invading octopus.

I stared at my child in disbelief, my heart twisted in anguish. I pressed my body into the cool plastered surface of the wall behind me for support. Its solid permanence couldn't bring me comfort, but at least it held me up.

The diagnosis came a week later. The neurologist called us into a cramped meeting room that smelled of stale air. Paul's doctor was also a mother, and her face gave her away. It wasn't easy for her to say that Paul had a serious genetic condition called Tuberous Sclerosis Complex. She pointed out that the earlier you get a disease, the worse it is. "Like juvenile diabetes?" I asked. "Yes. His development will likely be quite delayed." I stared at her in disbelief.

The neurologist advised us not to read the literature because it was out of date and reported things that were now untrue, such as: "a shortened life expectancy." She explained that the brain of someone with TSC resembled a tuber with calcified areas which prevented normal brain development, and that the benign tumours can also form in the eyes, heart, kidney, skin and lungs.

Then she started talking a new language. It included words like infantile spasms, epilepsy, anti-convulsants, developmental delay, mental retardation, behaviour problems, autism and more. Words that took me into the world of children with serious disabilities.

As I listened, I saw my dreams for Paul fly out the narrow hospital windows. There would be no university for him. The chances of him marrying would be slim, and if he did, he could pass on the TSC gene. My beautiful son, placed with us "so he could achieve his potential," now had a very uncertain future.

The doctors gave us information about a TSC group started by a nurse at Sick Kids. We found out that Tuberous Sclerosis Complex is as common as ALS (Lou Gehrig's disease) or Muscular Dystrophy, but is virtually unknown by the general population.

We were referred to a geneticist and advised to let Paul's birth mother know about the diagnosis, taking small comfort that neither of us had passed on the gene to him. The lawyer told me later that, after hearing the news, his birth mother said, "Does this mean they don't want to keep him?" I wanted to cry out, "No, no, it doesn't mean that at all!" But closed adoption laws silenced my voice.

Meanwhile, our baby looked the picture of health. One morning in the elevator, a doctor with thick white hair and an elfin twinkle greeted us. "What a healthy looking child. I hope you're just visiting?"

When I told him the diagnosis, his smile faded and he lowered his gaze with a murmur of regret. His reaction hit me harder than anything he could have said. Clearly, Tuberous Sclerosis was bad news.

After a few days, I got to know some of the other parents and the staff, and in a bizarre way, the routine of the hospital environment became strangely comforting. It was like being wrapped in a cocoon where nothing mattered except Paul. Within those sturdy brick walls, we were sheltered from the rest of the world. The phrase, "Take one day at a time" took on a whole new meaning. That was all I could do.

Paul was still a cute, blue-eyed baby who drew people to him. One of the older children on the neurology floor sat with him all week, showing him how to crawl. Finally, after eight days of trying, he crawled into her lap. She clapped and shouted with such excitement, a nurse came running. The doctors and nurses loved Paul too. He couldn't talk, but he was good at blowing raspberries through his lips with a *"Brrrr!, Brrrr! Brrrrr!"* whenever the young neurologist appeared.

Paul had been placed on steroid injections to control his seizures, and we couldn't take him home until we could inject the drug into his thigh. The nurse lay Paul on his back and then

removed his chubby legs from his sleeper. Like something out of a
slow motion film, she picked up a long intra-muscular needle and
filled it with the pale yellow liquid. The silver needle looked so
menacing against his tiny leg.

"It has to be this long to go into the muscle," she explained.
"You've seen me do this many times, now it's your turn. Have you
ever done this before?" I shook my head. "You can practice on an
orange if you want, but the sensation isn't the same as on a real
person."

"If this will get Paul home," I said, "I'll do it." I took a long,
deep breath and picked up the needle. As it pierced Paul's skin, my
thumb depressed the plunger, slowly injecting the steroid into his
leg. He didn't cry or squirm. I wanted to cry at how brave he was,
but I was afraid if I started, I wouldn't be able to stop. If Paul could
do this, so could I.

"Most people aren't able to do that the first time," the nurse
said, picking up the spent supplies. I looked at her wanly, resignation
filling my heart. "You can probably leave in a couple of days," she
said.

That night, John informed me that he was returning home
because he "had to get back to work." Nothing would change his
mind and he left. Just like that. After I got Paul to sleep, I went
outside to try and calm down. It was the end of October; high winds
had stripped the leaves from the trees, the flowers had faded and the
grass was dry. That was just how I felt: barren, empty, abandoned.

Two days later, Paul was released. On the way home, I
remembered the conversation John and I had had with the social
worker when she was completing our adoption application

"Are there any restrictions on the type of child you would
accept?" she asked. "Only one," John replied. "I'm open to all
possibilities except a child with mental retardation." I smiled, as I
imagined The Big Guy upstairs saying to one of the angels, "Make
a note of that."

—⁓—

The steroid injections turned Paul into the Michelin Tire baby. His
face doubled in size, and his skin stretched tightly across his bal-
looned body.

"My, he's a chubby one," the bank teller remarked one day. "Yes," I replied weakly, wanting to explain, but realizing it didn't really matter – to her.

Paul had to have his blood level checked regularly, but the steroids made him so puffy, it was hard for the doctor to find his veins. "It's like trying to spear spaghetti in a bowl of Jell-O," he remarked after the fifth failed attempt. So he resorted to another method. He punctured Paul's tiny heel and squeezed the blood out, one droplet at a time. My gut clenched tighter as every red drop slid down the test tube.

Paul's neurologist encouraged us to keep him stimulated. "You don't want him to regress, which is possible with Tuberous Sclerosis," she cautioned.

I think that was the moment I donned a blue and red cape and morphed into Supermom. "I can't let him lose any more ground," I thought. "If most of us use only a fraction of our brain cells, then I'm going to make sure Paul uses all of his." "Keep him stimulated" became my mantra.

One of the best ways to accomplish that was for Paul to interact with other children. Thankfully, his caregiver Patty welcomed him back to her home daycare. He loved being with her, dumping the toys out of the toy box and smooching her homemade spaghetti all over his face at lunchtime.

We arranged for an infant stimulation therapist to come to Patty's once a week to keep his brain active. I went to the sessions and watched as she placed her hands over Paul's to play pat-a-cake, and then we all sang the rhyme with the enthusiasm of Miss Fran on Romper Room.

The therapist encouraged Paul to put the orange, red, green and yellow blocks into a container, but he preferred throwing them across the room. Undeterred, she brought out wooden animals puzzles. Paul tried hard to hold onto the tiny red knobs on the elephant, bear and racoon, but even if he grasped them, he rarely put them in the right place. I watched with an aching heart as he struggled with tasks that came easily to the other kids.

John and I tried to resume a normal life, but it was a façade. Life had changed. The steroid injections no longer controlled Paul's seizures, and his little body started to jerk again. He never lost consciousness, but the episodes left him confused and tired. We tried a number of drug combinations and some experimental ones, but nothing worked, at least not for long.

One day, I pulled into Patty's driveway to pick him up and an ambulance with its siren going and lights flashing pulled in behind me. Patty was afraid Paul had stopped breathing during a long seizure, so she had called 911. By the time the ambulance and I got there, the seizure had stopped. I was grateful I had arrived before they did. I didn't need any more stress. Paul screamed a lot during the day and slept in fits and starts at night.

My faith held me together, and I continued to attend church regularly, even though John had stopped going. It was one more thing we didn't do together.

AS A CHILD, I WENT TO CHURCH EVERY SUNDAY, not always because I wanted to, but because it was required. My parents were older and staunch Presbyterians in every sense of the word: white gloves in church, long sermons, no booze and no Sunday shopping, even though the only store open was the drugstore. My girlfriend and I bought a home-permanent there once on a Sunday; when my mother heard about it, you'd think I'd been caught smoking. That came later.

I was raised to put my trust in God and even as a child, I believed my life had a purpose. I rebelled at times, particularly as a teenager, but my faith remained a constant presence in my life. I started out with a "God is in heaven" Sunday school version, and matured to one rooted in the belief that there is a Divine Presence that, if we open ourselves, can bring wisdom, grace and guidance to our lives. Some refer to this spiritual force as the Creator, Divine Mother, Universal Source, the Great Spirit, or God. Even though naming the Divine is, by definition limiting, I refer to this spiritual presence as God.

When Paul was 15 months old and his seizures had returned with renewed vigor, I went to church in search of inner strength. There were only a few people in the large sanctuary, and I settled into an empty pew with my thoughts. The lighting outside the church illuminated the stained glass window, and the scene of Jesus welcoming the children onto his lap glowed deep red, vibrant blue and dark purple. The richness of the aged oak interior, the glow of candles, and the minister's message of death and rebirth put me in a deep meditative state.

Then, for the first time in my life, I had a vision. Paul was lying in his crib, and two ethereal male figures were looking down on him. They were surrounded by a brilliant white light that shone on Paul with an intensity that astonished me. Then a *knowing* filled my heart. I knew that no matter what happened, Paul was being watched over. I knew, even though he was so sick, that he would be all right.

In the days when we were trying to adopt, I had turned to God, saying, "I am open to any child you place in our lives." Two years later, when we were at Sick Kids with Paul, one of the neurology residents asked me, "Do you ever wonder, "Why me?" I looked her in the eye and answered in all honesty, "No, I don't." She seemed surprised. But I knew from the beginning that Paul and I were meant to be together, even though I didn't understand all the reasons why.

I lived several provinces away from my parents, but kept in regular contact by phone and wrote to them every Sunday afternoon. In one of my mother's replies, she said something I will never forget.

"Lucinda, it's important to treat Paul like a whole child. Remember, his disability is only part of who he is." I knew this advice came from a place deep within my mother's heart and that she had turned to God to find it. She had no idea how much her words of wisdom would come to shape Paul's life, and mine.

During one of our many visits to our local paediatrician, I asked, "If Paul has a developmental delay, does that mean that someday he will catch up?" "No." "Then why use that term?" I replied. I was feeling testy. "Because that's the current terminology for someone who previously would have been described as mentally retarded."

It's not what I wanted to hear. I wanted to hear that I was doing all the right things to keep Paul stimulated and that someday he wouldn't lag so far behind. It was hard to accept that he was a long way from achieving any of his developmental milestones, no matter what terminology you used.

Then on August 9, 1987, when Paul was almost 20 months old, he literally took a step in the right direction. We were in the tiny living room at the cottage, and he pulled himself to his feet and took his first step, from the coffee table to the couch.

"Over here, Paul," I said with out-stretched arms. His little hands met mine. "Paul walked, he walked!" I shouted.

John was asleep, so he didn't see my tears of joy. I scooped all 25 pounds of my "little" guy and we spun around until both of us were dizzy.

Paul might have been slow intellectually, but once he had his feet under him he was fast, often faster than me. One moment he would be happily pounding his pegboard with a wooden mallet and the next, hitting the piano keys or the end table with it. Snow globes were a favourite Christmas gift, but they created a white slimy mess when Paul got a hold of one and dropped it on the floor.

I came to appreciate quality toys from Fisher Price, especially Paul's red and white plastic cassette player. He took it with him everywhere and replayed the songs of Raffi and Sharon, Lois and Bram until they became stuck in everyone's head. The only reprieve from "Skinnamarink-a-dinky-dink" came when his *tape a corder*," as he called it, crashed down the stairs, got clogged with peanut butter or died from overuse. Fisher Price replaced it. Every time.

The balloon-popping, flag-waving feeling I had when Paul began to walk was short-lived. His seizures developed a new intensity and frequency. He would fall down, crumpling like a rag doll, or his arms would start to jerk rhythmically over his head. Absence seizures caused him to stare blankly into space; nocturnal seizures woke him up at night.

Paul was on three different medications, but they didn't control the "brainstorms" in his mind; they just made him irritable, tired and lethargic. His neurologist described him as having "a severe seizure disorder."

I did my best to hold on. I didn't talk about my problems at work, and most of my co-workers didn't ask. For the last two years, I'd put on a mask, one that gave the illusion that everything in my life was fine, and prepared myself for another day of advising students. "After all, who wants to see a fucked-up counsellor?" I'd ask myself.

Every few months, Paul and I would make the trip to Sick Kids in Toronto for a neurology outpatient appointment. The clinic waiting room was the size of a small gym, but instead of basketball hoops, it contained rows of green vinyl chairs, kid-sized tables, plastic doll houses and car garages, and germ-spreading toys.

The room was filled with children you wouldn't see anywhere else: kids with severe facial and physical deformities; children with bandages on their heads; babies screaming in their mother's arms; hyperactive kids like Paul running helter-skelter; and kids in wheelchairs who couldn't run at all. Parents with expressionless faces drank coffee amid the din. Everyone had been put on hold, waiting for their child's name to be called.

"Paul Tiller?" A woman's voice rang out with a lilt that immediately brought us to our feet. We were ushered into a bare cubicle with an examining table, desk and chair, where we saw a neurology resident, a neurology fellow and eventually, the neurologist.

By then, Paul was bouncing off the walls. I had ten minutes, if I was lucky, to have *my* questions answered. To maximize the time I had with Paul's doctor, I showed her the graphs I'd made of the frequency and duration of his seizures. I had a page for every month with the days of the week across the bottom and the numbers 0-20 up the side, which represented the number of seizures each day. At a glance, she had a picture of how he was doing.

"You mean no one else does this?" I asked her in surprise. "Then how do you know what drugs to prescribe?" "Medicine is often more art than science," she told me. "We'll keep trying new drug combinations, and hopefully one of them will work."

Her honesty made me realize that no one had all the answers. In fact, it was beginning to feel like there were no answers at all to Paul's intractable seizure disorder, his epilepsy.

In a last-ditch attempt for control, Paul's neurologist suggested we put him on the ketogenic diet, a high-fat, low-carbohydrate diet that controls epilepsy in some children. At two and a half, Paul was a good candidate. We knew it would be a difficult diet to manage, but John and I were willing to try anything.

Paul had to be admitted to Sick Kids to start the process. Unfortunately, his admittance was delayed twice, once because he had diarrhoea, and then again due to an ear infection.

My mother wrote to me on February 21, 1988 encouraging me to hold on:

> It was disappointing for you not to go to Toronto today, but maybe it's our patience and faith that's being tested. Wee Paul has been on so many antibiotics, another few days at home should be good for him. I felt so good after being at church this morning. The minister cited the plight of Job, how he thought everyone was against him and it was only when he began to think of all the good things God had done for him, and started to put

them into practise, that he finally found peace.
Read Job 42, especially verse 12: *The Lord*
blessed the latter days of Job more than his
beginning.

My mom was sharing the wisdom of a woman in the latter days of her life. She believed that even in difficult times, we can still be thankful, that we must keep the faith, no matter what.

We were back on the same neurology floor, which hadn't changed at all. It still had the same antiseptic smell, long pasty green corridors and metal cribs. Paul's ketogenic diet began with a fast in order to put his body into a state of ketosis. He was only allowed water and sugar-free Kool-Aid. In jugs of neon green, florescent orange and crimson red, they looked like something from a kid's chemistry set.

At meal time, John and I took Paul to a non-medical floor so he wouldn't smell food or see others eating. He'd zoom around noisily on a toy trike, which raised a few eyebrows, but we didn't care. These people had no idea what the three of us were going through.

On the second day of the fast, Paul and I went to his refrigerator for more Kool-Aid. I opened the door and inside was a carton of milk. Paul's eyes opened wide. *"Mommy, milk!!"* he cried. I stared in horror at the white cardboard box and slammed the door. Someone had left milk in Paul's fridge. He struggled in my arms, crying for milk; we were both in tears, as I carried him to his room.

One of the nurses came up to me and said, "Perhaps you should see a social worker." Fortunately, she didn't see my eyes roll. Later, I overhead the doctor say to her, "It's every mother's instinct to feed her child, and Lucinda can't." She had named my torment.

Every few hours, we pressed a litmus stick into Paul's wet diaper to see if his urine had changed to the colour of ketosis. Finally, after 36 hours, it did and Paul's high fat-diet began. We poured four tablespoons of oil made from compounds called medium-chain triglycerides over his food at every meal. Not only did it taste awful, the results exploded into his diaper.

We started the diet at the hospital under the supervision of a dietician and then came home determined to give it our best shot. Paul's diet was high in fat – eggs, cheese, butter, cream – but his carbohydrates were limited to half a slice of bread and half a cup of milk a day. There were no crackers or cereal boxes in the cupboards. We all lost weight.

Paul often woke up crying at 4:30 in the morning; his tummy must have felt so empty. I'd carry him downstairs and look out the kitchen window into the darkness. There were no lights on to illuminate our solitary world. I'd give Paul a few slices of cucumber; the soft pulpy centres and hard shiny green rind kept him quiet until it was time for his oil-soaked eggs. Another day had begun.

Paul took out his frustration on his spring-loaded rocking horse, riding faster and higher until a gaping hole appeared in the horse's backside. Somehow he managed to hang on, and, through it all, so did we. John and I hoped that if we kept at it long enough, Paul's seizures would stop.

But they didn't. He was still taking his anti-convulsant drugs in liquid form, but now there wasn't any sugar syrup to mask the taste. This was the worst part of all. After he finished his oil-soaked breakfast, Paul would look around expectantly for something decent to eat. Instead of food, I filled a syringe filled with his medication, Valproic acid, pried his mouth open, and squeezed the plunger down his throat. Paul would look at me wild-eyed. He screamed, closed his throat and then spat the vile liquid out. If it got into his eyes, his screams escalated to an ungodly level.

We did this three times a day and each time, Paul pushed so hard on the tray of his high chair, it eventually cracked and split into pieces. I called Fisher Price and they were amazed; they had never had a chair tray break before and asked to see it. The arrival of a new high chair coincided with our decision: after five months of this bizarre diet, we'd had enough. John and I packed Paul into the car and we went out for pizza and a beer.

WHEN WE WERE INFORMED that Paul would be in at Sick Kids for two weeks to start the diet, I had arranged to take time off work. John, however, had a different approach. Before we were scheduled to go to Toronto, he said, "I have something to tell you."

"What's that?" I asked with interest. "I've decided to quit my job." "What?" "When Paul comes home, we'll need one of us at home to look after him, so I decided to quit." "When?" "I've already done it."

"What do you mean, you've already done it? We didn't discuss it. We could have worked something out. Paul will be in daycare in the morning. You could have requested a leave of absence. Why would you do this without talking to me first?" "There's no point in you shouting at me. It's done."

I wondered if there was more to his decision than he was telling me and the next day I discovered there was. I was moving his car when I found tiny vodka bottles in the side pocket of the car door. The problems John had coping with his job as a case manager in a federal penitentiary had returned.

We lived outside Peterborough and from our front window, a farmer's field stretched across the horizon and in the back, nothing stood between us and the sky. One evening, as summer was giving way to the cool nights of autumn, Paul and I were in the kitchen together. Before taking him up to bed, I picked him up and showed him the full moon hanging low in the night sky. Paul wrapped his little arm tightly around my neck; his body, so soft and warm, fitted perfectly against my side. Our cheeks touched as we gazed at the moon's radiance. Paul felt like a regular little boy, and I felt like a regular mom. "Remember this moment," I said to him softly. "Remember it forever."

I put Paul to bed and wandered aimlessly around the house before ending up in the kitchen. I could hear John snoring upstairs. I lit a cigarette – an indulgence that was becoming more frequent –

and thought about my life. My elderly parents lived 2,500 miles away, my only brother and his family lived on another continent, and we had lost contact with most of our friends.

"We can do it ourselves," John would say, which meant, "Lucinda will do it." I stood in the middle of my kitchen and realized, unequivocally, that I was alone. There was no one who could "fix" Paul or our fractured family. And then I understood. At critical moments in life, ultimately we are all alone.

I closed my eyes. "It has to come from inside you, Lucinda," a voice within me seemed to say. The realization slowly sunk in. The answers, if there were any, lay within me.

Like drawing water from a well, I pulled on strength from the depths of my being. My chest filled with renewed courage and a prayer: "God, you brought Paul into my life. He is our child. Please help me raise him."

—⁓—

Paul's medical appointments structured our lives. He had speech and occupational therapy at our local Children's Centre and out-of-town appointments with specialists who examined his eyes, heart and kidneys for tumours. Each diagnostic test involved an invasive piece of equipment, E.E.G., M.R.I., Ultrasound, Heart echo, CT scan or specialized eye exam.

Paul developed an irrational fear of medical equipment that continues to this day; something as simple as an ultrasound of his abdomen became an Olympic event. Fortunately, the tumours in other parts of his body hadn't grown, and he didn't develop facial angiofibromas – the small reddish bumps across the cheeks and nose that mark so many kids with TS.

In 1989, when Paul was four, two amazing things happened. The Berlin Wall fell, and Paul's seizures were controlled. The first I barely remember, the second was cause for great celebration. It wasn't until Paul's seizures stopped that I realized how much they affected me. Every time his body began to jerk, jabs of sorrow pierced my heart.

Undoubtedly, there was a relationship between Paul's seizures and his developmental delay. He only had a 50-word vocabulary, while most children his age had over 200. I know because his neurologists asked us to count them, and it didn't take long.

Paul compensated by using the "point and shout" method to communicate: he'd point to what he wanted and shout with a lisp, "*Gracker.*" "*Muuthic.*" "*Juuthe.*" "*TV.*"

This worked for objects, but not feelings. Paul couldn't tell us if he was frustrated, so I'd try and put myself in his place. "Paul, are you throwing your toys because you can't go outside right now?" If I was right, he'd nod his head. If I wasn't, a toy car would fly past my ear. His godmother Diane summed it up best. "It's like Paul is in the 'terrible twos' that never quit!"

Only once was he invited to a neighbourhood birthday party; I was so excited I bought the kid an over-the-top expensive gift but it didn't make a difference to Paul's awkwardness or acceptance. He was rarely invited anywhere. Kids with TSC are known for their rage attacks and screaming episodes. When Paul's circuits got overloaded, he would open his throat and let out a scream that could be heard down the block. I understood why other kids didn't want to play with him, but that didn't make it hurt any less.

In order for Paul to attend a public daycare centre, he had to have a one-to-one support worker, and it was up to me to find someone. Even then, it seemed unfair to ask that of a parent; today it would be outrageous. In spite of the extra staffing, Paul went to the emergency department twice within the first year: once to have his stomach pumped when they *thought* he might have ingested rubbing alcohol that had been left on a counter; and again when he put his arm through a glass door that should have been unbreakable safety glass.

When I took Paul to the paediatrician to have the stitches removed, he told me Paul was a handful enough for two children. "Oh good," I replied. "I always wanted to have more than one child."

We changed daycares, and I found a mature support worker for Paul. She had only been with him for a few months when she announced, "I can't do this anymore. Looking after Paul is having a negative effect on my family." I stared at her in disbelief. How could another mother say this to me? I scooped Paul up, determined that no one would see me cry. When I got home, John was in the living room reading the paper.

"I've just had awful news," I told him. "Paul's support worker is quitting. Will you take him to daycare until I can find a replacement? I don't want to see her." "You're driving into town every day anyway, it's a lot easier for you to do it," he replied, barely looking up. "It's not like you're busy working these days," I shot back. "Thanks a lot!" He glared, got up and left the room.

When Paul was diagnosed with Tuberous Sclerosis Complex, researchers had been exploring the genetic link between TSC and autism. While Paul was never formally diagnosed with autism, he had many behaviours associated with both conditions: aggression, sudden rage, hyperactivity, attention deficit, acting out, obsessions, fixations, slow language development, echolalia (repeating what you've just said) and remaining in his own world – to name a few.

Paul loved to sit on the kitchen floor in front of the glass oven door. He'd position himself cross-legged so he could see himself and then draw his yellow plastic raincoat over his head. Periodically he'd peek out from under his cover and start to laugh.

"What's so funny?" I'd ask. *"Pau raincoa?"* he'd reply as he disappeared with a shriek of laughter. "You're being weird, Paul," I'd say, but he'd just pulled the raincoat even tighter. I knew he was retreating into himself, but he was sitting still for more than 30 seconds, so I let him be.

Paul was barely five when his neurologist recommended that we have him assessed at the Child Development Clinic at Sick Kids. We were welcomed by the therapist into a brightly coloured testing room with a child-size table and chairs. But as soon as John and I tried to leave, Paul began to throw toys and scream. So we stayed and watched as he struggled through each test. I sat on my little chair and tried to "will" him to give the correct response, but it was useless.

The results showed that Paul's thinking skills were "below average to well below average" for his chronological age. The therapist wrote that: "Paul's problems adjusting to novel situations, along with his highly demanding nature," placed considerable stress on John and me. She recommended that Paul stay in daycare for another year, continue to receive regular therapy for his speech, language and motor needs, and that we receive assistance from a behavioural consultant.

When I told a psychologist colleague at work about the test results, she replied, "Paul is pretty young to be formally assessed." I hung onto the shred of hope that he would improve with age, and vowed to keep him stimulated. It was my only option.

—⁂—

John and I didn't relax on the weekends; we just got through them. Paul was happiest when he was moving, either running on his sturdy little legs or riding in the car, so we spent a lot of time driving, just to put in the day. From when he was a baby, we took him to our simple, water-accessible cottage. I'd strap on his miniature life jacket – he looked like an orange Pillsbury-wrapped sausage – and off we'd go down the lake.

From the beginning, Paul loved being on the water. He'd sit quietly in a canoe or rowboat and squeal with delight when he rode in the motor boat. At one time, the seclusion of the cottage, high on a hill surrounded by trees, was our favourite place on earth, but the older and more hyperactive Paul became, the less frequently we went.

My 40th birthday gave us a reason to celebrate and we grabbed it. John gave me a card that took me back to the early days of our relationship. On the front was a picture of a prim woman with greying hair and glasses, her hands clasped in delight, her eyes shining. The caption read: "Today is the first day of the rest of your life." Inside it read: "So don't fuck it up!" It was signed, "To my sweetheart, love John." I loved the humorous twist, but more importantly, I wanted to believe we were still sweethearts.

We decided to take a scenic steamboat cruise on a nearby lake. It was billed as a family cruise, complete with a clown on board. Since Paul loved the water and boats, we thought it would be the ideal place for a celebration. The boat hadn't gone far when Paul started to get restless. I walked him around the boat, we talked to the clown, and I got him a drink, never letting go of his hand.

After a while, he got bored and started to squirm and talk loudly. Other passengers were understanding, but the captain was not. When I asked him if Paul could touch the steering wheel, he shot back, "Why don't I give you some rope so you can tie him up?"

I felt as though he had hit me across the chest with a two-by-four and I returned to my seat in tears. This wasn't the first time, but it was definitely the worst time I had experienced the disdain of a stranger. Paul's thick chestnut head of hair and his clear blue eyes made him look pretty much like any other kid, so when he acted up, some people probably thought it was my fault – that I couldn't discipline him. I considered getting matching t-shirts. Paul's would say: **I'm doing the best I can.** Mine would read: **And so am I!**

MY LIFE WAS LIKE A ROLLER COASTER RIDE. The view from the top was fleeting, and inevitably, was followed by a white-knuckle, heart-stopping descent to the bottom. When Paul's seizures stopped, I wondered what was next, and the following spring I found out.

My dad was 88 years of age and experiencing significant memory loss. My mother didn't know how much longer she could look after him, so I flew home to Alberta to help.

I had only been at my parent's house for a couple of days when John called. "I just got a call from Cheryl the lawyer," he began. "What did she want?"

"She said she knew of another baby who was up for adoption." "What did you say to her?" I held my breath, waiting for his reply. "I told her we could barely handle the one we had."

"What? That's what you told her?" "That's exactly what I told her." "But I would have been interested!"

"Forget it. For-get-it."

"John, I could have made it work. Is it too late?" Click.

This was a week for distressing calls. The next one was for my mother. It was from a nursing home telling her they had a bed for my dad. "I can't do it, Lucinda. I can't take him there," she said. "It's O.K. Mom, I'll do it."

I appeared calm, but my stomach had seized up. I was about to do one of the hardest things ever. I looked at myself squarely in the bathroom mirror, the same mirror I'd looked into countless times as a teenager, and told myself, "Lucinda, if you can leave Paul at Sick Kids, you can do this."

I loaded my dad and a few of his clothes into his old blue Buick and drove him away from the house he had lived in for 44 years. My dad, the independent Viking, didn't want to leave, but after talking with his doctor, he realized he had to do it for "Margie," my mom. She couldn't look after him anymore.

In Dad's new home, a double room, I took my time unpacking

his clothes and placing them in the simple wooden wardrobe. He watched me from the side of his bed. When I was finished, he took my hand. "You've been a good daughter, Lucinda," he said, gazing at me with his pale blue eyes, eyes the colour of the prairie sky. He didn't blame me for uprooting him and putting him in a room with a stranger. He loved me too much to do that. Eight months later, my dad died.

My mom's health had been declining for some time. On one of the many trips I made across the country that year, I helped her move into a seniors' lodge. She wasn't there long before she had a series of strokes; the last one left her paralyzed on one side, with little speech. This once proud and stately woman lay helplessly on her back in the chronic care ward of the hospital, struggling to say the words swirling in her head. I drew a chair to her side, took her frail hand in mine and tried to imagine what she was thinking, just like I did with Paul.

"Home," she murmured, gazing heavenward. "Do you want to go home to God, Mom?" She nodded. Mom stopped eating. She didn't want to be placed in a nursing home.

Paul was in daycare and John wasn't working, but he complained bitterly about the amount of time I was away looking after my parents. I had left home when I was barely 18 years old – 22 years ago – and wanted to be with my parents at the end of their lives. Nevertheless, when I was with them, I felt bad about leaving Paul, and when I was with Paul, I felt I should be with my parents. I was being rent in two. "People only die once," I told John. "I can make it up to the living." Or so I thought.

The last time I saw my mother, she hadn't eaten for six weeks; a pacemaker and ice chips were keeping her alive. She looked up at me and said, "Paul." His name was barely audible on her lips. "Are you concerned about Paul?" I asked. She nodded weakly.

Even though Mom was dying, she was thinking about Paul and how much he needed me. I flew home the next day. I had only been back two days when the phone rang in the middle of the night. I didn't need to answer it to know my mom had died.

One of John's expressions was, "The payback's a bitch." He was going to make me pay for the time I had spent with my parents. When he began to imitate my mother's exasperated tone with my aging dad, he'd stooped to a new low.

Our marriage had been sliding downhill for quite a while, but I knew I couldn't manage Paul on my own. He was so needy I couldn't go to the bathroom without him pounding on the door. Besides, I'd had enough losses and couldn't handle another one just yet. So I pushed my feelings down another notch and hoped our relationship would get better.

There was one thing John and I did agree on: we needed some help looking after Paul. I completed the lengthy application form for respite services, including a section on Paul's behaviour. I handed it in, but nothing happened. Nobody called. The only thing I could think of was Paul's behaviour was so terrible, nobody wanted to work with him. It was only years later that I found out the agency had lost the form.

Paul had trouble falling asleep, so he and I developed a comforting night-time ritual. I'd kneel beside his bed, and we'd give thanks for all the people in his life and then pray for them. I'd always end with the request that Paul "have a good sleep in his own bed and wake up refreshed." Then we'd listen for the train. In the distance, we could hear the sound of the whistle as it floated over the countryside, and through his bedroom window.

"Whooo-hooo." "Listen for the train, Paul." "Whooo-hooo," the train replied.

Sometimes I'd stay kneeling beside his bed, saying my own prayers until he fell asleep. One night something remarkable happened. After my mother died, I'd feel her presence; it wasn't dramatic, she was just there, in a soft, comforting way. I had become used to the feeling of having her near me, and this particular night she felt closer than ever. In a moment of stillness, she seemed to say, "I have to leave you now, Lucinda."

My heart fluttered. Mom had been with me in spirit to help me get through the last six months.

"I know, Mom. It's okay," I said softly. And then she was gone. Sadness filled her place in my heart. I buried my face in Paul's green comforter and, for the first time since returning home after her death, I let myself cry.

—⁓—

The fall Paul turned six, he started public school in a nearby village. Every morning, the two of us and our two cocker spaniels walked to the end of our street to meet the "*thchoo buth*," as Paul called it. Clinging to the silver handrail, he'd hoist himself onto the first step. "Come on, you can do it, Paul!" the driver would say, smiling down on him.

Paul ate his lunch at the daycare centre attached to the school and afterward rested on a tiny cot, lying on his tummy, his hands tucked underneath. Paul and his Educational Assistant Dot played catch in the gym and she helped him with "*compooter*" games in the classroom. Paul loved to hear his teacher "*pray guitar.*" *Old MacDonald Had a Farm* was his favourite. A neighbourhood girl walked him home at the end of the day. John kept him amused until I got home from work; then we took turns.

Paul went to grade one in the morning and kindergarten in the afternoon. I didn't fully appreciate how many kids he had to relate to until I wrote their names on Valentine's Day cards: there were over 40. (And we had thought it would be easier on him to remain in kindergarten for half a day.)

Paul had a hard time keeping up in either class. While the other kids traced shapes and coloured objects, Paul covered *his* pages with green scribbles or red and blue lines. He had a wonderful teacher, who took photos of him at each activity and put them in a scrapbook so he'd know what his day was like. Paul looked like any other kindergarten kid playing at the sand table, with his button nose, toothless grin and eyes the colour of a blue jay's wing – except for the faraway look in his eyes.

Paul liked going to school, but our home life was deteriorating. John was depressed and his mood swings were becoming more frequent. The only thing rising was the stack of empties in the basement. One evening, I was lying on the couch and Paul, imitating his dad, walked up and hit me. "Hit her again," John said. "She deserves it."

John had found a new way to hurt me that exceeded the physical pain and humiliation of him hitting me. The fact that my son was now copying his father made me realize I had to do something.

The next day, I called the Ontario Provincial Police and spoke with a staff sergeant. In 1991, women were still often blamed when things went wrong in the home. "If a woman lays a complaint about domestic abuse, will her name always appear in the newspaper?" I asked. "Yes ma'am, it will." "Oh, I see," I said, my voice dropping. "Does this relate to your situation?" "Yes."

The officer didn't know what to say and there was nothing left for me to say, so I hung up. I felt so ashamed.

"What will other people think?" My mother's words rang in my head. There was no way I was going to have my name and reputation smeared in the local newspaper. I hadn't done anything wrong.

"John isn't horrible all the time," I'd say to myself. "Maybe this episode of emotional and physical abuse will be the last."

I had practically grown up with him, and deep down I didn't want to lose him. We'd met at university when I was 18; he was four years older, even older than my brother, which impressed me immensely. He knew the popular people. We went to dances and parties and, for the first time in my life, I felt like I belonged. I had become whole.

Now, I still had the belief that the kind, intelligent man I married would return "if only." If only he got a job; if only he would stop drinking; if only he went on an anti-depressant; if only I said and did the right thing each and every day.

I must have been delusional when I suggested we take Paul to Disney World. As rational people know, it is full of crowds, lights, fireworks, stimulating rides and novel situations – not a great destination for a kid who's afraid of loud noises, likes routine, and gets upset easily.

Looking back on it, I wanted to fulfill my own childhood dream of going to Disneyland and to live out the fantasy that we were still a family. Paul enjoyed having breakfast with Mickey Mouse and shaking hands with Kermit the Frog, but he got scared on the train ride into the centre of the earth. As in life, once the journey starts, there is no turning back.

"Hey, Paul, let me take your picture!" I said to him on our last day. Dutifully, he stood with his hands at his sides in front of a row of red and white flowers, the towers of the Magic Kingdom in the background. "I wish our life was so picture perfect," I thought, snapping the shutter.

On the plane ride home, Paul had a difficult time sitting still and screamed most of the way. I put my hand over his mouth to try and get him to stop, or at least muffle the sound, but he bit my fingers. When we landed, I took him into the airport washroom and he started yelling again. A woman came in, looked at him and said, "Why don't you just shut up?" I guess she'd been on our flight.

When we got home, we put Paul on Ritalin.

AFTER MY MOM DIED, my brother and I made a donation to the hospital in her memory. I received a thank-you letter that surprised and touched me. It said that a painting would be dedicated with our mother's name on it. We had often wheeled Mom down the corridors to look at the paintings of mountain scenes, grain fields and prairie flowers and I was deeply moved that her name would live on.

It awakened a spark inside me, and I began to think about the goodwill a project like this could create in my own community. I talked it over with my good friend and art lover Joanna, and we received the approval of our local hospital to start a similar initiative. Our timing was perfect; the administrator liked the idea of recognizing sizable financial donations with original paintings that would hang permanently in the hospital.

With his endorsement, we launched Art and Healing to recognize the role that art plays in the healing process. The project lifted me out of the quagmire and allowed me to create something new for the benefit of patients, visitors, staff, artists and the hospital environment.

The experience supported what I had learned from Paul's doctor – that healing is more than medical science; we also need to support a person's soul. The Art Committee took on a life of its own, and 19 years later, the hospital (now a Regional Health Centre), has 400 original, juried paintings in its permanent art collection.

Working on Art and Healing was my respite from the challenges at home. It was an ongoing problem for Paul to keep his voice level down and amuse himself on his own. He had the attention span of a gnat for anything academic, but when he latched onto a computer game, he didn't want to quit. I'd place a timer beside him, hoping that the dinging bell would prevent an outburst when I asked him to stop and do something mundane, like come for dinner. "*Gimme my back my pooter*," he'd shout nonetheless.

Our teenage neighbour Elaine often took Paul to the small playground at the end of our street. "Paul just loved going up and down the slide. He was having so much fun. I think he could have stayed there all afternoon," she'd tell me. Elaine had an intuitive understanding of Paul that continues to this day. When they went swimming, she would pretend to sneeze into the water and Paul would explode in fits of laughter. "When Paul finds something funny, it isn't just funny, it's hilarious," Elaine said. Paul interrupted us excitedly, "*Go thwim, go thlide now Lane.*"

"I want Paul to slide, and swing and swim as much as he can," I said. "I don't want him to grow up to be a sucky kid. That would be like having a second disability."

Sometimes, Paul's eyes would be clear and bright and at other times, they were hooded and dark. His seizures had returned. They were much the same as before: his head and upper body would jerk; he would stare blankly into space or fall down. A black cloud had descended on his brain, setting off uncontrollable fireworks. Fortunately, if there can be a fortunately, Paul would have an aura, a feeling that warned him of an approaching seizure, and he would find someone to hold onto until the storm had passed.

He still participated in a therapeutic horseback riding program in the spring, summer and fall, as well as a therapeutic swim program in the winter. He was involved in Music for Young Children, that is, until the mother of a child with Down syndrome complained that Paul was distracting her daughter. It was bad enough that "regular" kids didn't want to be around Paul, but when a mother whose kid had a disability shunned him, I felt blindsided.

I was doing my best to keep Paul stimulated, but somehow I felt it was never enough. It's a feeling mothers of kids with disabilities have in common. At the end of the year, Paul's teacher told me the truth. "I think it's best if Paul moves to another school and a Learning and Life Skills (LLS) class for children with special needs."

My fingers pressed the corners of my eyes as I tried, unsuccessfully, to stem the flow of tears. In spite of all my efforts, my little guy was to be placed in a segregated class on the other side of the city. "It will be all right, Lucinda, I know the teacher and he's really good," his teacher said, putting her arm around my shoulders.

I was too upset to reply. It was hard to accept what his teacher and neurologist were saying: "Developmentally, Paul is significantly delayed."

That September, when he was almost seven, he got on a mini-school bus for the 40-minute ride to an LLS class that matched his age and developmental level. The seizure medications he was taking slowed him down mentally and physically, and one morning John called me at work in a panic. "The school just called wondering where Paul is."

"What do you mean? I put him on the bus myself!" I replied, my voice rising. "I'll call you back as soon as I hear something." I shut my eyes and prayed, "Please, God, let him be okay." "Remember to breathe," I told myself, running my damp hands against my skirt.

Finally, the phone rang. "They found him asleep on the school bus. The stupid bus driver had gone into a coffee shop and left Paul slumped over in his seat," John said. "Thank God he's all right!" I sighed. "They haven't heard the last of this. I think we should sue them!" He slammed the phone down. Of course, we didn't do that, but I'm sure the head of the transportation department got an earful.

Without complaint, Paul went to his new school, or "*thcoo*," as he called it, on a "*yeyow thcoo buth.*" He liked to "*pray compooter*," but was less enthusiastic when his class went to the gym. It was a boisterous place, and for Paul "*too louw.*"

When Paul wasn't in school, or watching Sesame Street, he would occupy himself with his favourite pastime, running down the street of our quiet subdivision, stealing lawnmowers from the neighbours. It wasn't unusual to find a strange lawnmower sitting in our driveway. When I'd ask Paul where it came from, he'd reply, "*Pau red lawnmore.*" He believed in finders-keepers and was no help in identifying its owner.

"Okay, Paul, let's push on the handle together and see if we can find out where this belongs." Once, on our way down the street, he spotted an expensive weed trimmer lying unattended on a lawn. "*Pau weed eader!*" he exclaimed, his eyes widening. When our neighbour heard Paul's voice, he rushed outside, scooped it up, and put it in his garage.

To make sure Paul wasn't headed for a life of crime, I'd scour the city looking for broken-down gas lawnmowers and drag them home in the trunk of my car. They became our new lawn ornaments.

Paul's other passion was his red and white two-wheeler; he loved riding it up and down the cul-de-sac in front of our house.

"*Pau go fath,*" he'd say. One summer evening, I tucked him into bed and then went into the back yard, where I spent the better part of an hour chatting with our next-door neighbour. The mosquitoes were driving us inside when I spotted a kid in green Ninja Turtle pyjamas riding a bicycle up and down the street.

"Who would let their child out at this hour?" I thought indignantly. Then I recognized that child was mine. Even though it was getting dark, I could still see the gleam in Paul's eyes.

—⁓—

John and I had been married 22 years, and we were together four years before that. Over time, our relationship had had too much wear and not enough care and had unravelled like an old afghan.

John ostensibly quit his job to look after Paul but in reality, he was an alcoholic. Earlier, he'd lost his license for impaired driving, but neither that nor his recently diagnosed diabetes, slowed down his alcohol consumption. He had been to a few AA meetings in the past, but he wasn't interested in going back. We tried marriage counselling, but he walked out of one session shouting, "You blame me for everything, so what's the point of this shit!"

My journal entries helped me see that the time span between John's uncontrolled outbursts and his relative sanity was getting shorter. One night, he went too far. He woke up after drinking and came into the family room, where Paul and I were watching television.

He overturned a small couch, yelling that the TV was too loud. His face was red, his neck bulging, his eyes dark and expressionless. Looking at him in horror, I could tell there was nobody home. He'd worked with federal inmates for two decades, and knew men who had no memory of killing their wives in a fit of rage.

"This is how it happens," I thought. "He is going berserk and could do anything." I waited until John's tirade was over and he'd gone to bed, and then Paul and I left the house. My shame at checking into a motel was matched only by my dread that someone at work would notice I was wearing the same clothes as the day before.

That February, I filed for a legal separation. I drove to the lawyer's office down the same road I had traveled eight years earlier to pick up our newborn son. This time, it was bleak mid-winter. My stomach twisted in a rising knot and my chest was so tight it ached. I felt like I was going to a funeral; my own.

John moved out of the house, thinking it was only temporary, but I knew differently. Over the last seven years, I had tried to keep the light of our relationship alive. By the time we separated, the flicker had been snuffed. When John realized our marriage was over, he looked at me in disbelief and said, "I never thought you'd do it."

"What kind of fool do you take me for? Did you honestly think I'd put up with this treatment for the rest of my life?" I replied.

I realized that John's alcoholism, that seductive mistress he couldn't live without, would have brought an end to our marriage even without the strain of Paul's disability.

"Thank heavens I have Paul to show for all the years I was married," I thought. "At least I have him."

IT WAS THE SUMMER OF 1994 and I had just turned 44. I found it hard to talk to God and harder still to subscribe to a religion that preached "turning the other cheek," not once but "seventy times seven." I had tried that and it hadn't worked. I was angry with everyone and everything, including God.

A psychologist was helping me put the broken pieces of my life back together. "I feel like damaged goods," I said to her one afternoon. "I don't understand why John turned on me. I tried everything to make him happy." "Lucinda, you were raised to believe if you are nice to people, they will be nice back. You need to work through all your emotions regarding John, and it will take time."

Unlike the sadness I experienced when my parents died, and the loss I felt when Paul was diagnosed, the end of my marriage brought waves of emotion that rose relentlessly inside me. The psychologist used an analogy that helped. "The stars shine the brightest when the sky is the darkest. You could use this time to learn more about yourself."

"Do you think I could learn to become less of a pleaser, less of a chameleon, changing my colour to suit everyone else?" I asked. She nodded.

John began coming into the house when I wasn't there, which unnerved me even more. I changed the locks and he was so angry when he tried to get in that he phoned from his own apartment to say he was going to come through my front door with an axe.

He was clearly intoxicated, and I didn't think he would attempt the 20-minute drive to the house. Nonetheless, I notified the police. An OPP officer arrived to take my statement. We sat across from one another at my kitchen table. His black military-style boots with their thick heavy soles were tightly laced, and his upper body was covered with a padded black bullet-proof vest; a gun rested on his hip.

I couldn't believe it had come to this.

But no matter how shaky I felt inside, I had to keep going for Paul. His seizures were getting worse. For the last six months, he'd been waking me up most mornings with a strange, babbling laugh, which indicated a seizure was on the way. They were much the same as before, lasting between one to five minutes, but the effect on his concentration and behaviour lasted the whole day.

John was requesting custody of Paul, which I knew was an act of retaliation. Nevertheless, I had to take his request seriously and asked Paul's paediatrician for a letter outlining his needs. He wrote: "Paul demonstrates impulsivity, short attention span, problems in adapting to change, autistic characteristics, including obsessiveness and poor communication skills, a need for solitary play, and outbursts of anger, which have included screaming, throwing objects, biting, and pinching others. In short, his current medical and behavioural needs are quite demanding." I thought about granting John his request.

The doctor then gazed into Paul's future and continued: "I would anticipate that Paul will live well into his adult life and will likely continue on with the same behavioural and learning difficulties that are currently presenting. I would also anticipate that his medical problems, which include a seizure disorder, will continue for the rest of his life. Behaviour modification and support will be required for this young man, as he requires a long-term commitment for care."

Not surprisingly, John withdrew his request and agreed to give me custody, providing he had regular contact with Paul.

When Paul became upset he would say things like, "*Paul hit. Paul scream. Paul pinch. Paul bite.*" He knew what he was doing but he wasn't able to stop. He had the TSC strike against him, plus he was caught in the emotional maelstrom of our divorce. I knew things were bad when Paul started to scream, and I would look at him and yell, "Stop screaming!" Well, that certainly didn't work.

I asked my next door neighbour Anne to come over if she heard Paul screaming. When things got really bad, I'd pour myself a shot of gin, no mix or ice, and sit at the kitchen table until my heart stopped pounding. I felt like a gunslinger in a Western, steeling myself for a shoot-out.

I had always thought of myself as a patient person, but Paul was driving me to new heights. He was obsessed with the vacuum cleaner, pushing it around the house ad nauseam. Then he'd throw it and start yelling, "*Pau wans Daddy!*" I tried substituting it with a floor mop, with limited success.

One night, Paul came into the kitchen pushing the mop and then, for no apparent reason, started to hit me. As I stooped down to pick up the handle, he butted my head with his, and then tried to bite my wrist. It took all my willpower not to hurt him like he was hurting me.

I turned to a behaviour therapist for help. I told her about this incident and this next one. I was dropping Paul off at school after a doctor's appointment. It was the middle of recess, and a teaching assistant and kids from his class crowded noisily around the car. I turned toward Paul to undo his seatbelt, and as I did, he bit the first thing in front of him – the side of my face." Shock and pain seared through my head. Paul eventually got out of the car, and I went to work in search of a cold cloth and some 'mortal' support.

The therapist told me Paul's behaviour problems were influenced by his developmental delay, his diagnosis of Tuberous Sclerosis and the medications he was taking. She said, quite matter-of-factly, "When he bites you, pinch his nose. This will restrict his breathing and release his teeth."

I didn't think she had ever been bitten because when it happens, all you want is for it to stop. My gut reaction, to get Paul's teeth off me any way I could, felt absolutely primitive.

Thankfully, I had gone back to work when Paul was born and didn't have to worry about money for groceries on top of everything else. Keeping up with Paul was an athletic event: he remained hyperactive, impulsive and had no fear of danger. If I let my guard down, the results could be disastrous.

One summer evening that happened. I was busy getting ready for a potluck supper with friends from my yoga class when I realized my cocker spaniel had disappeared. "Come on, Paul, hop in the car, we have to find Annie," I said. "My friends will be here in ten minutes."

We found her on the street behind us, playing with some kids on their front lawn. I put the car in neutral, pulled on the hand brake, and jumped out to pick Annie up. When I looked up, the car was moving slowly away from me.

"THE CAR!!" I screamed.

My sandals fell off as I ran after it. I watched in horror as the car went slowly down the hill; mercifully there were no kids in sight. Then it started to pick up speed. "Paul, pull the brake, pull the brake!" I yelled at the top of my lungs, my heart pounding like a jackhammer. But the car kept going.

Just then, Ray, a tall, lanky teenager from the neighbourhood, appeared out of nowhere. He ran after the car with the long loping strides of an Olympic sprinter. He was alongside the back door just as it started to veer off the road toward an oak barrel filled with red geraniums. Ray leapt into the air and dove through the open driver's window. The screech of the emergency brake pierced the air. The car stopped dead.

I ran barefoot down the road, the hot asphalt stinging my feet, tears streaming down my face. "Thank you Ray, thank you!" I called out as I went. Ray's t-shirt was dark with sweat, his chest heaving so hard he couldn't speak.

I opened the car door and collapsed onto the front seat. "Paul, what did you do?" He looked at me, wide-eyed with his hands in his lap. I tried to undo his seatbelt, to give him a hug, but my hands were shaking so hard I couldn't manage it. So I gave him hell instead. "Don't ever, ever do that again!"

He watched intently as I pushed the release button and lowered the hand brake. I looked at him looking at me, and wondered if he had done it on purpose. If so, he had taken his love of cause-and-effect to a whole new level.

WHEN MY MARRIAGE ENDED, I lost not only a husband, but also his family. It was just Paul and me, and we weren't a big enough unit to be called a family – families had at least three people.

Then, unexpectedly, I received an invitation to my first-ever family reunion in the remote west coast community of Bella Coola, British Columbia, where my dad was born and my grandparents had lived from 1898-1907. This was a chance to connect with extended family members, some of whom I hadn't seen for over 25 years. Even though it would involve taking Paul across the country by air, train and car, I wanted to go. I wanted to be with people who loved me just because I was one of them.

I booked a flight to Vancouver and a hotel room for one night. It turned out the hotel was on the east side, a seedy part of town. I cranked opened the casement window in our spartan room to let in some air. There was nothing, not even a screen, between me and the pavement four floors below. In horror I realized Paul could easily fall out. The sounds of the street, the sirens, men and women yelling at one another, kept me on high alert throughout the night. The experience mirrored how I felt – it was me and Paul against the world.

Early the next morning, the two of us took a cab to the train station. We walked up and down the platform looking for our train, but the place was deserted. Finally, I approached a taxi driver, who said, "Lady, you're in the wrong station! You want the North Vancouver trains. Get in, I'll drive you there."

My heart hit the sidewalk. If we missed the train, we missed our connection with my brother, our ride to Bella Coola, and the reunion.

We made it onto the train, the Caribou Express, just in time. I dropped onto the red velour seat, Paul pressed his face to the window and we pulled out of the station. The train's deep whistle blew a familiar "Whooo-hooo" as we travelled up the Fraser Canyon alongside spectacular mountain peaks and steep ravines. Instinctively, I leaned to the right, as if I could prevent the train from tumbling into the deep gorge below.

Several hours later, we arrived at our rendezvous location and Bob, his wife Jean and their three daughters were on the platform to meet us. We hugged one another while Paul jumped up and down, excited to be off the train. "*Hi Unca Bob!*" he shouted.

"Come here and give me a hug," his cousin Laura said, opening her arms.

Paul turned side-ways and stiffly put one arm around her, as though affection was rationed. He was happy to see his cousins from Ottawa, but he was only eight, and nervous about being in a strange, new place.

The next morning, we met 20 other family members for breakfast, and then began our seven-hour drive and 6,000-foot descent to the fishing village of Bella Coola, where Alexander Mackenzie first sighted the Pacific Ocean.

We travelled down the "Freedom Road," which wasn't built until 1953. Before then, the village was only accessible by sea or air. The road was a series of sharp hair-pin turns; there were no guardrails and in places, the road was reduced to one lane. When my eyes were open, I noticed that the mountain scenery was stunning. Paul's eyes were closed too; he had fallen asleep against his cousin's shoulder.

The area is rich with our family's history. The first Norwegian settlers, 16 families in all, came to Bella Coola by boat in 1894. My grandfather, Edvard Aslaksen Hage, was called to be the Lutheran pastor and head of the colony in 1898. The area reminded the settlers of Norway, with coastal fjords and steep mountain peaks rising on each side of the valley and beyond that, the sea.

In his journal, my grandfather gave his impressions of the land at the turn of the last century: "Then it was wilderness with heavy timber and no trail. It was a roaming place for wild animals and a hunting ground for the Indians."

We stopped in front of our grandfather's white steeple church, located on the edge of town. Framed by a dark green forest, it looked as if it had stepped out of a painting by Emily Carr.

My first cousins were much older than I and I didn't know them all that well, but inside that church, I knew we belonged together. We celebrated the 65th wedding anniversary of my dad's remaining sister, which reminded me that some marriages last forever.

I thought about my grandmother and how, 96 years earlier, she had left her friends and family in Minnesota and journeyed to this remote settlement, 1,000 kilometres north of Vancouver. She had arrived with a baby in her arms and gave birth to five more, including my father. I gave thanks for the grandmother I never knew, but whose genes I had inherited. Her strength, endurance and faith were the very qualities I needed to parent my son.

Not surprisingly, it was hard for Paul to cope. He couldn't sit still for meals, yelled when he was upset and had trouble complying with my requests. One of my cousins, a retired teacher, took the time to talk to Paul, but others weren't sure how to relate to him. I understood.

The trip wasn't for his benefit – it was for mine. It had given me the chance to forge new ties with my extended family and draw strength from my ancestral roots. My mind was made up. When I got home, I was going to reclaim my surname of origin: Hage.

After five days, Paul and I said goodbye to our relatives and the Bella Coola Valley and boarded a Twin Otter plane for Vancouver. On a cloudless day, we flew above the snow-capped summits of the Coastal Mountain range. The plane soared low over the jagged peaks, the sun turned the drifts of snow to dazzling white and glacier lakes gleamed like emeralds. "If this plane goes down," I thought, "I've seen the face of God."

—∞—

Paul and I now had different last names and I was fine with that: it helped me see him as his own person. I took another step in the name-changing direction, and decided to refer to John as "Paul's father," rather than "my ex." He was still in my life because he was Paul's dad. Full stop. This helped me refer to him respectfully, especially in front of Paul, as well as to put some emotional distance between us, at least in my mind.

That fall, on a crisp, clear day, as the leaves were turning gold, I went outside and planted spring bulbs. With each tulip and daffodil I dug into the ground, I believed that by the time they bloomed, my life would be better. The promise of colourful flowering bulbs was something tangible to see me through the long winter ahead.

Even though it was my decision to divorce John, my heart still ached. It felt as though a colony of bees was living in my chest, and it was hard to eat or concentrate. I reduced my work week to three days and used the other two to try and pull myself together. I had been mad at God as though God was lost, when in fact the lost one was me. Somehow, I needed to find the still small voice of calm within.

A friend lent me a book titled *You Gotta Keep Dancin': In the Midst of Life's Hurts, You Can Choose Joy*. It was written by a man who had dedicated his life to mountain climbing until one day, he suffered a terrible fall and broke his back. His life had been shattered, yet he was able to find joy by rebuilding himself from the inside.

The book talked about the difference between joy and happiness. Happiness, the author said, is a transitory state often influenced by external events, like buying something new, or taking a trip. Joy, on the other hand, is a state of mind; it comes from within. Joy does not simply happen, we have to choose it, and that's possible, even when life is tough. I drew inspiration from the mountain climber's story, and his belief that God's love is greater than any hardship he could face.

Even though I couldn't change the events in my life, perhaps I had more control over how I responded to them than I realized. The most difficult aspect of my life was that John was still in it. He and Paul wanted to maintain a relationship, and we agreed to alternate weekend visits, on the condition that John refrain from drinking when Paul was with him.

That summer, they went to the cottage during their time together. It was the first overnight break I'd had from Paul in nine years. I referred to it as the up-side of divorce.

On the weekends that Paul didn't visit his dad, he'd begin his litany early Saturday morning: "*Pau wantsa boa ride!*" "*Daddy, go coddage.*" "*Pau wanna see Daddy!*" He wasn't interested in big boats, he liked small fishing boats with outboard motors, and even though he couldn't read in school, he could read the names of outboard motors. "*Evinrood, Johnthon* or *Mercree motor,*" he'd lisp through the gap in his front teeth.

To appease him, I'd take him to a small resort nestled on the bank of a river that rented fishing boats by the hour. Paul zipped up his life jacket as soon as we got there." *Mommy get in!*" he'd shout as I untied the boat. "*Choke, pu chord, go fas!*" I'd pull-start the motor and head upstream, the 8 h.p. motor set to FAST.

When he was ready, he'd say "*Pau drive,*" and then carefully reposition himself so his hand was on the throttle under mine. Paul didn't care where we were going; he faced backwards so he could admire the wake foaming behind us in a perfect vee. From this position, he would wave at passing boaters and call out to jet-skiers with a whoop of enthusiasm, "*Jet skiiiii!!*"

When his cousins, or anyone else, visited us in the summer, they were asked the same question, "*Wanna go boa ride?*" No one ever refused. Two local couples made sure they took Paul for a ride in their boats every summer. It was a kindness I've never forgotten.

By the time my divorce was finalized in June of 1995, Paul was going on 10, but he looked like a young eight-year-old. Ritalin had taken away his appetite, his arms were as thin as reeds, and his blue eyes seemed larger than ever in his delicate oval face. His hands, with long, beautifully formed fingers, were the hands of a pianist.

Paul required a lot of extra help inside and outside the classroom. At recess, he wandered around the playground by himself, and when the bell rang, he couldn't remember where to line up. An Educational Assistant guided him into the school, and once there, she put her hand over his to help him hold a pencil; she encouraged him on the computer, prompted him to sound out new words and helped him button his coat. Thanks to Velcro, Paul could fasten his shoes.

His teacher, "*Mither Mith,*" as Paul called him, worked diligently with Paul's "many high needs," once posing a question that no one has ever answered: "Does Paul not understand the request, or is he simply choosing to be passively non-compliant?" As Paul adjusted to his new school, I worked hard to regain my self-confidence. One day, a good friend asked me, "Are you having difficulty not being married?" In place of my wedding band, I was wearing a gold ring I had purchased when my dad died.

"Maybe," I replied, avoiding her gaze. I realized I was ashamed of being seen as someone whose marriage had failed. I didn't want to admit that I had joined the ranks of divorced women. When I finally took the ring off, I was able to say to myself for the first time ever, "I don't need a man to make me feel complete." Shakespeare's phrase, "To thine own self be true," anchored me and helped me hold my head up. It became my new mantra.

That Christmas was difficult for everyone. Paul was scheduled to be with his dad on Christmas Eve. I had never faced the prospect of spending Christmas Eve by myself, and I felt like the last toy on the shelf. I made the best of it by going to church not once but twice that night and visiting elderly friends between services. Fortunately, they weren't shy about offering me a cup of Christmas cheer.

On Christmas morning, Paul and I went back to church. We knelt in silence at the communion rail, Paul raised his cupped hands, lifted his head and looked into the priest's face. His eyes shone. "I wish everyone could come to communion with such pure devotion," Father Michael said to me later.

"MISSER NECK" WAS PAUL'S IMAGINARY FRIEND. I wondered if someone called Paul "a pain in the neck" for him to come up with the name. The thought of "*Misser Neck*" caused Paul to laugh, and laugh.

"Do you see Mr. Neck?" I'd ask him.

"*Yeeessss!*" he'd reply through his giggles.

After ten minutes of uncontrolled hysteria, I'd had enough. "O.K., Paul, it's time to put Mr. Neck away." He usually complied, until the next time.

Keeping Paul busy prevented him from withdrawing into himself, and I was always on the lookout for new activities. The following summer, we were invited to the annual Tuberous Sclerosis picnic, held on the farm of a family whose young daughter had TSC. We had always gone as a family, and I wanted to maintain the connection with other parents.

"We're going to a picnic on Saturday, Paul."

"*Pau doesn wan it.*"

"Come on Paul, it will be fun. We can go for a wagon ride."

"*No, not gooen! Pau stay here!*"

If I'd given in every time Paul said "*No!*" he'd never have left the house. He had as many interpretations for the word "*no*" as the Inuit have for "snow." Sometimes it meant he needed more time, or he wasn't sure. Sometimes he needed more information, or he was too tired to think about it. Occasionally, he really meant "No." I knew he would have a good time once he got there, so on the Saturday I brought up the subject again.

"*No pi-nic. Naw today. Pau wan McDonals.*"

I relented. "We can go to McDonalds after the picnic."

If the skill of manipulating others was on an intelligence test, Paul would have scored 10/10.

When we arrived at the farm, adults and kids of all ages were already gathered on the lawn beside the house. Some of the younger children were jumping in a bouncy castle, while the older ones roamed around.

Conversation between parents was short-lived; someone always needed something. This was no ordinary picnic. The unique signature of Tuberous Sclerosis was evident everywhere. Toddlers, teenagers and young adults were affected cognitively, physically and/or emotionally. Some had raised red bumps in a butterfly pattern across their nose and cheeks, some exhibited the far-off gaze of autism, others looked around shyly, and many drooled. Some had trouble walking, while others had difficulty talking. We were all united in a disjointed kind of way.

Everybody seemed to be there with family members, and after a while I felt alone, out of place. My feeling may not have been rational, but there it was.

"Come on, Paul, let's go for a walk," I said, picking up his soft hand.

Around the corner of the house, a young woman was sitting on the grass with a young boy propped against her. A red kerchief caught the drool from his chin; his long, thin limbs were bent and twisted in the manner of cerebral palsy, and the stigmata of Tuberous Sclerosis lay in a red band across his face. We introduced ourselves.

"Is this your first TS picnic?" I asked.

"Yes, I've just become Adam's mom, so we decided to come," Jen said, "I met Adam at the group home where I work, and I fell in love with him. The adoption was finalized last week."

I smiled pleasantly, but inside I was incredulous. Jen was the first person I'd ever met who chose to parent a child with a disability, and she was doing it on her own. I quickly silenced my "poor me's." Jen got to her feet and pulled Adam to his. As she lowered him into his wheelchair, she said, "It's Adam's turn for a pony ride. I think everyone else is going on the wagon ride."

This was a favourite activity and adults and kids climbed on, or were lifted onto the farm wagon. With Paul at my side, I leaned against a bale of hay and took a deep breath; the air smelled like a basket of fresh laundry. Within minutes, everyone fell into a relaxed silence, lulled by the rhythmic jostling of our bodies and the squeaking wheels on the packed earth.

When we got back to the farm, Paul found a bike to ride, and I found a family to talk to. Their son had just returned from an Easter Seals camp, and they were enthusiastic about the experience. The more we talked, the more I wondered if Paul could do something similar.

First thing Monday morning, I was on the phone to the Easter Seals office, but they told me they only accepted children with physical disabilities. Fortunately, the conversation didn't end there. They knew of an organization called Reach for the Rainbow which, for nine years, had made it possible for hundreds of children with intellectual disabilities to attend regular residential camps in Ontario. The organization was founded by a mother who wanted her daughter, and others like her, to have an integrated summer camp experience.

It was too late for Paul to attend this year, so he and I went on a reconnaissance mission to check out three camps for the following summer. At each camp we visited, Paul watched motorboats zipping up and down the lakes. "*Prease Mom, Pau wanna boa ride!*" he asked repeatedly.

"I know, Paul, but we aren't going to do that today. You'll just have to look."

His frustration was building. At the Presbyterian camp, the one we visited last, the director asked him how he liked it. Paul couldn't hold back any longer. "*Fuck you!*" he yelled.

It wasn't easy walking backwards, mouthing apologies with a semi-straight face and dragging Paul by the arm. I struck that camp off the list as quickly as they eliminated us, and signed Paul up for YMCA Wanakita. I thought I was merely registering Paul for summer camp, when in fact, he was headed for a life-changing experience.

—⁘—

The fall before Paul turned 11, our School Board moved him to a Learning and Life Skills class at a different school. Once again, he had to get used to a new school layout, new teachers and students, and he wasn't travelling there with children from our neighbourhood. He was struggling with the changes in his life, and I was often called at work to pick him up.

On one occasion, I arrived at the school and found Paul standing naked in the staff bathroom with his teacher sitting on the floor in front of him. No one knew why he had taken his clothes off.

"Your mom is here now, Paul, so put your clothes on," his teacher said.

"*No. Pau doesn't wan it.*"

The principal came in and sat on the floor in her tight black skirt. Please put on your clothes," she said in her "I am the principal" voice.

"*No!*"

So, in my "Mother is in charge voice," I took a turn. "It's time to put your clothes on so we can go home."

"*No! Pau wan pennies.*"

The teacher had a jar of pennies they had been counting to pass the time on the washroom floor. "You can't take them home, Paul. They belong in the classroom," she said.

"If that's what it takes, we'll bring the pennies back tomorrow," I replied, as I scooped them up. Paul held up his pants." *Help prease, Mommy. Pau wantsa go home.*"

The following week, he said, "*Pau eat dirt.*" One of his support workers said Paul had dirt in the corners of his mouth when she saw him after school. I thought about the washroom incident and wondered if he was being teased at recess. There was always a reason for his behaviour – if only he could tell us what it was.

He wasn't the only one who was struggling with a range of emotions. One day I'd take a walk in the fresh snow, feel the winter sun warming my face, and God's light filling the road ahead; and the next, after an angry phone call from Paul's father, I'd awaken in the night with a pounding heart. Some weekends their time together went relatively smoothly, but increasingly, Paul's behaviour caused his dad to complain, "Paul has been laughing, drooling and picking his nose for three hours."

Through a mediator, we reduced the length of Paul's visits to a level John could manage. He could still push my buttons, and it was hard to overcome my negative feelings toward him, but that was my goal. I had known a number of divorced people who were so bitter about their "ex," you could almost smell it. I wanted to come through this without bitterness, and to do that, I knew I had to develop positive experiences in my life.

My good friend Lynn was one of the most positive people I knew, even though two of her four children had Tuberous Sclerosis. We thought it would be fun and stimulating to attend a Tuberous Sclerosis Medical Education Conference in Detroit; Lynn's husband looked after their kids, and I hired a babysitter.

The two of us set off early one morning, driving down the highway to Motor City feeling like Thelma and Louise. At the conference, we were introduced to medical experts, new drug therapies and brain-scanning techniques that could pinpoint the exact location of seizure activity. We met a family whose three-year-old daughter with TS was having surgery to remove the tumours in her brain; unfortunately, as it turned out, the operation didn't control her seizures.

The U.S. conference sparked our interest in organizing a similar event in Toronto. One of the leading U.S. neurologists encouraged us, saying, "It's parents who make these things happen." Back home, Lynn secured some funding, and I lined up Dr. Manuel Gomez, the "father" of Tuberous Sclerosis research, to give the keynote address. Paul's new neurologist from Sick Kids agreed to speak, that is, until our next clinical appointment.

It didn't begin well. Paul was bouncing across the room, flicking the light switch on and off and pulling the blood pressure gauge off the wall. "I'm not sure Paul should be on Ritalin," his neurologist began.

"Then maybe you'd like to take him home," I was tempted to say.

"What other medication is he taking?" he asked, peering over his horn-rimmed glasses.

"In addition to his anti-convulsants, he takes a high dose of Vitamin B. The clinic nurse agreed with the reports that it has helped kids with autism," I replied.

"Who is treating him, you or me?" His tone was withering. There were two young neurology residents in the examining room, and I realized that he was showing off. When I mentioned his participation at the conference, his voice became even more condescending. "Oh yes, you're putting on a little meeting. When is it?" He was acting as though he hadn't agreed to speak.

I responded through a clenched jaw, got Paul into the car and began the two-hour drive home. I was about halfway there when my anger bubbled to the surface, and I had to pull off the road. Hot tears streamed down my face.

"You know what, Paul? No one is ever going to talk to me like that again. And I don't care how important they think they are."

There was no response from the back seat, but that didn't

matter. My mind was made up. I wasn't going to be put down anymore, by anyone.

Lynn and I continued to line up doctors and medical researchers from Canada and the United States and, after a year of planning, we held the first Canadian Tuberous Sclerosis Medical Education Conference at the Hospital for Sick Children in Toronto on October 19, 1996. Over 200 parents and medical personnel rubbed shoulders with one another. People came from Newfoundland to British Columbia, as well as from the U.S. A little meeting, indeed!

YOGA AND MY FAITH were two things that kept me stuck together. I had been practicing yoga and meditating regularly since my mom died. It was one of the few things I did just for me. "Your body wants your mind to relax, and your mind wants your body to relax," my yoga teacher said. Through yoga, I released some of the physical tension that accumulated daily, plus it helped slow down my ever racing mind.

I had a better understanding of the relationship between the spirituality of the East and Western Christian beliefs when I met Murray Rogers, a Christian priest and follower of Mahatma Gandhi. "When you go to a deeper love of God, there are not two religions but one truth," he said.

He talked to me and others about how faith rises from within us, emerging out of darkness to bloom like a lotus flower. The lotus is symbolic; its radiant petals are dependent on roots that grow deep in the murky water below. To reinforce the point, Murray quoted Hindu scripture: "Arise! The breath of light has touched us, darkness has fled, the light is fast approaching."

That's what I wanted: to grow deep roots that could withstand times of despair, and eventually be able to radiate God's love.

When Murray visited our home, Paul responded to him as though he was a beloved grandfather. "*Sit bi– sigh me,*" he said, patting the couch, a gesture he normally reserved for those he knew well. As they nestled together, Paul's body relaxed, and contentment filled his face. Paul seemed tuned-in to Murray's approach to life: "Be what you are."

Murray didn't say, "Be *who* you are," but rather "Be *what* you are," and that described Paul. He lived life the only way he knew how – as his true self. "When we are truly living with our humanness, we begin to see heaven," Murray said. How I wish I could sit with him now, but he returned to England the following year, to his final resting place.

—⁓—

My brother Bob and his family had been transferred to Brussels, the capital of Belgium, and they invited Paul and me for New Year's. I had to ask Bob where it was – there was so much going on in my life, I acquired information on a strictly need-to-know basis.

Paul had just turned 11 and was excited to be going on another airplane. He didn't realize just how long the flight would be, but I knew, so I got him a prescription for Valium. I should have requested a dose for me too.

Unfortunately, the sedative didn't calm him down; in fact, it made him more hyper than ever. Then, an hour before we landed, he fell asleep with his head propped crookedly against the airplane window.

"My son is asleep; could I have a wheelchair for him when we land?" I asked the flight attendant.

"Did you book it in advance?"

"No, I didn't think we would need one."

"Then we can't help you."

Paul and I were the last ones to stagger off the plane into the waiting arms of my brother. Paul liked the idea of seeing our family, but he looked sleepily at "*Unca Bob*" and said, "*Pau wantsa go home!*"

"That's too bad, Paul; I think you're staying for a week." That may have been the case, but we had enough luggage for three weeks. Paul couldn't leave home without a few of his favourite things. He had his "*tape a corder*" music tapes and his new fixation, movie videos: *Toy Story, Monsters Inc.* and *Chicken Run* were his current favourites. He had memorized chunks of dialogue and could deliver it in sync with the characters. When it came to action scenes, Paul went into action too. He'd pirouette on one foot, emitting a high-pitched squeal, his arms flapping like a homing pigeon.

"What happened to these covers?" my brother asked, as he loaded a video into the machine. Paul had squeezed each cover flat, as though he was popping bubble wrap, until it became one-dimensional. He carried a video cover with him everywhere, and if he misplaced it, it was a big deal. "*Where Pau's cover?*" he'd cry out, as though he'd been deserted at the mall. A mad scramble to find it would ensue.

Paul also had a favourite toy, Woody, from the movie *Toy Story*

– a skinny boy doll with a spotted vest, brown plastic cowboy boots with spurs and a cowboy hat to match. When you pulled the string on his back, Woody said things like, "Howdy partner, there's a snake in my boot." Paul loved his little friend, but when he called out, "*Pau's woody!*" in a public place, I looked the other way.

In Brussels, the inevitable happened; Woody's hat fell off while we were riding the bus.

"*Where Woody hat?* Paul asked.

"Where is it, Paul?"

"*Lef on a bus, Brushshels,*" he'd reply.

Paul was upset, but it could have been worse. He could have lost his broken down cover of *Chicken Run*.

My brother and his family meant a lot to me. Bob was the only close relative I had, and his daughters were Paul's only cousins. Bob wasn't demonstrative, but his affection for me was evident in his Christmas present: a pair of gold earrings shaped in connecting spheres. "I'll treasure them forever," I said, giving him a hug, believing I would always have his gift.

On the flight home, Paul ventured up the stairs of the Boeing 747 to the first class cabin, and I was close behind. There weren't many people up there, and he sat down in the back row.

"Can we stay?" I asked the stewardess. "It's so much easier for Paul up here."

"I'm sorry; this is for first class passengers only."

"Come on, Paul, we have to go back downstairs."

Paul returned to his place beside the window. I thought he would be happier there, but I was wrong. The man in front of him fully reclined his seat, until it was in front of Paul's nose. With terror in his eyes, he started kicking the back of the seat screaming, "*WAN OUT!!*"

When I leaned over to comfort him, he grabbed a fist-full of my hair and bit me. The overhead map indicated we were directly over Greenland. If there had been an escape hatch, I might have granted Paul his wish. The man in front quickly flipped his chair seat forward, and the flight attendant came running down the aisle.

"Do you want to move to first class now?" she asked.

"No, it's too late," I said. "But I'd appreciate a glass of wine."

Before I had finished it, Paul had fallen asleep.

When we landed, I went to the baggage carousel to wait for

our luggage, and Paul made a bee-line to the pay phones. He loved listening to the dial tone and the beeping sound each button made. Normally, I'd never leave him on his own in a crowded public place, but this time I wasn't worried. I was confident that no one on our flight was the slightest bit interested in kidnapping this kid.

—∞—

My intention to live with a positive outlook helped me seize opportunities when they presented themselves. That June, our Family Resource Centre offered a seminar on neurological disorders, and the head of Neurology at the Hospital for Sick Children was the speaker. After the talk, I said to one of the nurses who had accompanied him, "Do you know anyone who can help me with my son's behaviour?"

"I know of a child psychologist who does play therapy with children who have communication and developmental delays," she said. "The only problem is, her office is a two-hour drive from here." That didn't matter; I would have driven to the moon to get help for Paul.

We were fortunate to get an appointment in two weeks for the initial assessment. The psychologist, a woman in her mid-30s with warm brown eyes and a personality to match, greeted us. "Call me Toni," she said, ushering us into her large office, lined with shelves of books, toys, and educational material.

I sat in one of the armchairs, but Paul wasn't interested in sitting anywhere. He moved systematically around the office, picking up everything he could get his little hands on. I made a move to stop him, but Toni put her hand on my arm and said, "Let him go, it's all right." Paul dumped it all onto the middle of the floor: the computer paper, coloured construction paper, pens, pencils, crayons, books, magazines and toys. They lay in a heap in front of us. The office looked like it had been ransacked by vandals.

"This is the state of Paul's mind," Toni said, looking directly at me. "He is depressed."

It took me a moment to take in what I'd just heard. All I could think of was, "Why has no one thought of this before now?"

"I can help him." Her voice interrupted my thoughts.

"You can? No one has ever said that to me before. No one."

"I have worked with a lot of children with disabilities, and I'm

confident play therapy will help Paul with his emotional needs."
"When can we start?" I replied, rummaging in my purse for a
Kleenex.

"How about next Saturday?"

It had never occurred to me, or anyone else, that Paul might be
depressed. The medical attention had focused on his brain and his
organs; we had forgotten to treat him "like a whole person." Now,
through play therapy, Paul would receive the help he needed, and he
didn't have to talk to get it.

The three of us began the first session together – boxes of
supplies and gym mats were the only objects in the bare treatment
room. I sat cross-legged with my back against the wall and looked at
the dark purple-green bruise on my arm. Paul's teeth had left a
graphic reminder of why we were here. The week before, he had
thrown my coffee mug into the garage yelling, *"Shut up, stupid,"*
banged the kitchen door so hard he put a hole in the wall, spit in my
face and bitten me. "This has to work," I thought. "I can't be
assaulted any more, by anyone."

Toni brought out a variety of toys and materials: dolls, plastic
animals, furry animals, a tea set, a toy house, little plastic people,
white paper, construction paper, pens, crayons and scissors. Paul
poured himself a pretend cup of tea and drank it. Then he picked up
a doll and a bottle and started feeding it, like a baby. "He's filling
himself up," Toni told me later.

Paul selected plastic scissors and started cutting a stack of paper
into little pieces. It seemed like such a waste, but I didn't dare
intervene. After our session, Toni said, "When you're depressed, you
feel empty inside. Paul is filling that space. Make sure Paul has lots
of everything: cereal, paper, crayons, books, whatever he wants."

We saw Toni every two weeks. I knew it was making a
difference when he said, *"Pau wanna see Toni,"* or *"Prease go Toni?"*
After six joint sessions, Toni thought Paul had enough ego strength
to separate from me, and she asked me to leave the room. I walked
down the hall to the sound of Paul yelling and objects being hurled
against the wall. And then it stopped.

When he and Toni emerged, Paul was smiling. This wasn't the
end of Paul's behaviour problems, but rather a new beginning. He
now had an ally who could help him work through scary medical
procedures, loud unexpected noises, problems at school, and his

dad's declining health.

After every session with Toni, I took Paul to McDonalds and the car wash. It had become part of our ritual. One November day, the grey sky was releasing a torrential downpour, but it didn't matter. With the windshield wipers on high, we pulled up to the attendant's booth, and a young man with his raincoat zipped past his chin emerged.

"You want to wash your car?" he asked, with a tone of "are you guys nuts?" in his voice. "It's cheaper than Canada's Wonderland," I replied as he opened the doors to the inner sanctum.

Paul became animated, as the spray covered the windshield with blue, yellow and pink bubbles, encasing us in confetti-coloured foam. "*Brue brushshes!*" he exclaimed, as soft-bristled rollers beat again the car.

"Here comes the rinse," I said when the water whooshed over the car like rain.

The car moved slowly forward on the track under large drying vents. "*Mommy the wind!*" Paul sighed as we drove out the exit and back into nature's car wash.

Feeling pleased that I had satisfied my child, I looked at Paul and said, "So how was that?" He looked at me as though I'd never done a nice thing for him in his life. "*Mommy, Pau wansta car wash!*"

PAUL ACCEPTS PEOPLE FOR WHO THEY ARE, and has always been able to "read" people by the feelings they emanate, not by the colour of their skin, body size, age or gender. His capacity to see beyond external appearances is a spiritual gift. Recently, I found a reference to it in the *Book of Samuel*: "For the Lord does not see as mortals see; they look on the outward appearance, but the Lord looks on the heart."

Paul showed this quality most remarkably in his attitude toward his dad. After years of drinking and smoking, coupled with diabetes and high blood pressure, John's health and appearance had deteriorated. His thinning hair had grown long, spider veins circled his bulbous nose, and his once trim moustache had become a full, untrimmed beard. Paul didn't seem to care: he could see beyond all that – into his dad's heart.

On the Saturdays they were together, Paul would say, "*Go Dad's prace. Get stuff ready.*" I'd help him put his clothes, pills, toys, books, and music into his backpack for his 19 hours of indulgence. He and his dad ate popcorn on the couch, watched the hockey game together and had Paul's favourite food, "*spisgetti.*"

"What did you have for breakfast?" I'd ask. "*Fruit loops!*" Paul said with delight in his eyes. He knew I wasn't a Fruit Loops kind of mom.

Paul's father lived in a seven storey apartment building, with a million-dollar view of the countryside. At the front entrance, Paul had to push the buzzer to his dad's apartment in order to get in. One Saturday, Paul pushed the buzzer repeatedly, but no one answered. It was odd; his father had called the day before to say he was looking forward to seeing him. "Try one more time, Paul."

"*Wanna see Dad.*"

"I know, Paul, but he isn't answering the buzzer."

"*Pau wan Dad's prace. Wheres he?*"

Something felt wrong, so I pressed the buzzer for the superintendent. With some persuasion, she agreed to check on John.

"We'll wait down here," I told her. "If something is wrong, it's better for Paul not to be there." A few minutes later, she returned. "There was no answer when I knocked, so I let myself in. I found him on the floor of his bedroom, unconscious. I've called 911."

My hands were shaking. "Come on, Paul, let's go home. Your dad isn't feeling well today. Someone is coming to help him."

The next day, the phone rang. It was John calling to say he was alright. He had become dehydrated and gone into insulin shock. If Paul hadn't gone to see him, John wouldn't have been found until it was too late. It was the first time, but not the last time, Paul's presence saved his father.

It was a profound moment, and it made me think about the tragedy of John's life. The only person he had any contact with was Paul. He had systematically rejected his mother, sister, brother, his friends and me. It was ironic. The little baby who was "mentally retarded" was the only person in his life he really cared about, the only person who loved him just the way he was. In spite of John's emotional problems, he had been a faithful, loving father to Paul. It was his redeeming feature.

It was time for me to explore the kernel of bitterness I continued to harbour toward him. I thought about the scripture passage, "That you love one another. Just as I have loved you, you also should love one another." God is asking us to not only love those who are loveable, but everyone. I realized I couldn't fully do this as long as I harboured resentment toward John.

I went to my bedroom and asked for God's help; forgiving John was more than I could do on my own. As I prayed, I came to a better understanding of the life-long struggle John had had with his personal demons. His own father died slowly of a brain tumour when John was 11. He broke down in tears when he told me what his aunt said to him at the time. "You're the head of the house now."

I knelt beside my bed and prayed, "Please, God, help me forgive John for how he treated me. I pray that no harm will come to him, and that you will look after him." The words, "I forgive you, John," came into my heart. The burden I had been carrying for so long lifted.

When I forgave John, an amazing thing started to happen; he stopped being angry with me. Like the late winter snow beneath the

March sun, the negative emotions that bound me to the past began to melt away.

—⁂—

As a Community College Counsellor, I led workshops on goal setting and career planning for adult students returning to school. One of the exercises I used was from *The Magic Lamp*, a book on setting and achieving your goals. One of the steps involved a brainstorming activity to tap into the subconscious mind. I asked students to write this question on a blank sheet of paper: *What would I really want from life if I was absolutely, positively certain I would get it?* Then, for the next three minutes, the students and I would write down everything we could think of. Some of the things I recorded seemed far-fetched, others were quite practical: a beautiful garden; a screened-in porch; for Paul to be seizure-free; sharing God's love with others; writing a book; a loving relationship.

I couldn't imagine how Paul's seizures could ever be controlled, but it was what I wished for more than anything.

Something inexplicable occurs when you declare to yourself, and others, what you absolutely, positively want – you begin to tap into the universal energy that surrounds all of us. It's what some refer to as the "collective unconscious," and what Sharon Butala describes as "a manifestation of spirit that flows through the universe behind daily life and is available to all of us." Some may experience it as the power of intuition, an occasional mystical experience, like when you pick up the phone and the person you are calling is already on the line. It helps to explain what was about to happen in my life.

The summer of 1997 was the one I had been waiting for: Paul was going to camp. In preparation, I had planned to take him to their June Strawberry Social.

"Hey, Paul, Camp Wanakita is having a special lunch," I said, perhaps a little too cheerily. "Let's check it out and meet your new counsellor!"

"*No. Pau doesn't wanna a go.*"

So we went.

I knew that camp was going to be good for both of us. At times, Paul clung to me obsessively. Not only did I need to peel him off for my sake, he needed some distance from his goal-directed mother.

Our drive to YMCA Wanakita was a time of transition between

the frenzy of our lives and the peacefulness of rural Ontario. We passed thick groves of sugar maples, white pines and eastern hemlocks; with each turn of the dusty road, I felt the tension in my neck release.

"Paul, we're here. Let's see if we can find some lunch," I said, hoping my enthusiasm would cheer him up.

He gave me a sidelong glance and slowly got out of the car. The dining hall was full of adults and children sitting at long tables, and it was noisy. Camp counsellors, with *Wanakita Staff* on the back of their orange t-shirts, placed colourful bowls of food on the tables. There was lots of everything: salads, cold meat, buns, and strawberry shortcake with real whipped cream.

"Hey buddy, you've got some on your nose." one of the counsellors joked with Paul as he cleared the table. Paul wiped off the cream and then licked his index finger. He even managed a slight grin.

After lunch, I took Paul's supple hand in mine, and we walked to the lake. The air smelled of moist earth, pine needles crunched under our feet, and overhead, chickadees flitted between the branches, emitting their distinctive two-tone call. We eased ourselves onto the warmth of the wooden dock, all around us the lake shimmering silver-blue in the afternoon sun. Paul sat cross-legged and gazed across the water. "*It's a beauty day,*" he said softly.

A tall teenager loped down the path toward us. "Hi, I'm Mike," he said with a ready grin. Paul looked up warily and moved to make room for him to sit down. After we talked about the activities and supports at camp, including access to the camp nurse, I asked Mike one more question. "Do you only work with special needs kids?"

He looked me in the eye and said something I'll never forget. "Oh no, I alternate with the other counsellors – everyone wants a Rainbow kid!"

I couldn't believe what I had just heard. "Are you saying you and the other counsellors want Paul?"

"Absolutely!"

No one had ever said that to me before. The neighbourhood kids didn't have much interest in him, and neither did the Boy Scouts. He was segregated from other students at school and had even been kicked out of Sunday school.

Mike stood up and gave Paul a high five. "Well, Paul, I gotta go. I still have chores to finish up in the kitchen. I'll see you in August."

"*O.K. Mike!*" Paul replied with more enthusiasm than I had seen all day.

Paul and I stayed on the dock a while longer. I wanted to bask in Mike's words, closed my eyes and let them wash over me.

—∞—

That July, my nieces, Laura 15 and Caroline 13, flew from Brussels to Ontario for a visit. "This is my chance for them to have a true Canadian experience," I thought. "I'm going to take the girls and Paul camping."

It was one of those moments when my enthusiasm trumped all reason.

The morning of our departure, I woke up early to pack the car. Into my compact sedan went the dome tent, the Coleman cooler, bags of our food, the dogs' food, four air mattresses, four sleeping bags and pillows, the kids' clothes, and a change of underwear for me. The car was as stuffed as a Christmas turkey.

I was about to close the trunk, when I looked up and saw Laura and Caroline coming across the lawn with their backpacks. "You'll have to sit on them, or put them on the floor," I said, as I closed the lid with a thud. "Okay, everyone pile in. Annie-puppy can sit on someone's lap in the back seat. We'll put Nicky on the floor in the front. Who will sit up here with him?"

The girls looked at one another sceptically. "Caroline will," her older sister volunteered. "She's not afraid of being bitten!" Poor Nicky, the shaggy Lhasa Apso, had a reputation for being a bit nasty.

With seat belts securely fastened, we pulled out of the driveway and headed for the lakes, forests and secluded campgrounds of Algonquin Park. We had been on the road a couple of hours, when the clouds turned dark and ominous.

"It looks like it might rain," I said. "There's a Canadian Tire in the next town; I'll stop and buy some rope and a tarpaulin."

I pulled into the store's parking lot. "I'll just be a minute," I said, and before anyone could say "Can I come too," I had sprinted into the store. When I returned, I proudly showed the girls the bright blue tarp that would keep our picnic table and campfire dry. They glanced at one another and then started to laugh. "We thought you said you wanted to buy some rope to tie Paul in! We were beginning to wonder what kind of a camping trip this was."

We laughed all the way to the park gate.

My latent desire to be a Girl Scout was realized during our three-day adventure. At night, the four of us slept side-by-side in my dome tent, and during the day we paddled our rented canoes, hiked scenic nature trails, and ate camp stove meals under our bright blue canopy.

Paul did a good job of keeping up with his cousins and said with obvious pride, *"Pau did it!"* We all loved sitting around the campfire at night; the kids toasted marshmallows, while I sipped on a glass of red wine. There had been just enough room for a bottle of red inside the spare tire.

Paul revelled in the company of his cousins. *"Oh no Carlin, Pau smarshmellow fell a fire!"*

"Don't worry, Paul, I'll toast you another one," Caroline said, picking up the bag.

On the way home, we pulled into a picnic site beside a gently flowing stream. The girls and I laid out the last of our provisions, the dogs slept under a tree, and Paul stood quietly looking at the water. When we were cleaning up, I realized Paul wasn't with us. "Where's Paul?' I asked my voice rising. The three of us looked around. He was nowhere in sight. "Paul! Paul!! Paaaul!!!" we all shouted.

Then I spotted him. He had crossed the highway and was standing in front of a grey clapboard bungalow. His hands rested on a red lawnmower. He looked up when he heard me. Just then a massive logging truck, loaded with 40-foot logs, barrelled down the highway between us.

"Don't move, Paul!" I screamed, with my arm extended like a crossing guard. "Don't move. I'm coming to get you." Two more cars went by. I flew across the road and threw my arms around him.

"Oh, Paul, never, ever do that again. Never cross the road by yourself."

"Mommy, look, a lawnmower."

"Who cares about the stupid lawnmower, you could have been killed!"

I grasped Paul by the wrist and led him to the side of the highway. "Look both ways, Paul, for heaven sakes look both ways," I repeated as we crossed the road together.

"Auntie Lu, you look pretty shook up, can I get you something?" Laura asked.

"Maybe a glass of water." My mouth was so dry, the words stuck to the roof of my mouth.

"*Sorry, Mommy,*" said Paul, looking sad and small.

"Come here and give me a hug. I was so scared that you would get hurt, Pauli. Don't ever cross the road by yourself again," I said, hoping this time it would sink in.

"*Ooo-kay.*"

We got back in the car, but it wasn't as much fun anymore. After a few miles, I realized we should be grateful, not sad. "You know what, girls?" I asked, laughing. "Perhaps we should have used that rope to tie Paul in, after all."

—*m*—

August arrived, and Paul and I drove back to YMCA Wanakita for his first residential camp experience. The camp director had already told me kids were never sent home because they were homesick. The staff helped children work through their feelings; they wanted camp to be positive experience. I liked the sound of that, having planned a camping trip of my own.

Paul and I arrived at Wanakita along with a hundred other campers, their parents, brothers and sisters, family dogs, and piles of luggage. Some of the duffle bags were so heavy, kids had to drag them. What did they have in there – lawnmowers? If so, they'd better watch out for Paul.

"*There's Mike!*" Paul shouted. Mike wound his way through the throng of people and gear and clapped Paul on the back. "How's it going, buddy? Are you ready for camp?"

Then, in a moment I will never forget, Paul picked up his sleeping bag, looked up at Mike and took his hand. "*Bye Mom,*" he said.

The two of them headed across the recreation area, Mike's big hand surrounding Paul's. I watched him go until he was out of sight. Paul never looked back.

Tears were still spilling down my cheeks when I went into the administration building to use the phone. "Don't worry, he'll be fine," the receptionist assured me.

"Oh, I know," I replied blowing my nose. "Make no mistake,

I'm not sad. These are tears of joy." Paul had done it – all by himself.

The following summer, Paul returned to Wanakita for a two-week session. When I picked him up, I asked his counsellor, "How much did you tell the other kids about Paul's medical and learning problems?"

"Not much," he replied, "basically, we just had fun. The kids in his cabin were great; if Paul was a bit slower, they waited for him to catch up."

Paul had been truly integrated. He had slept in a cabin and under the stars, walked the trails, canoed, roasted s'mores over the campfire, sung camp songs and swum in the lake.

For the first time ever, Paul was treated like a regular kid, not like a kid with a disability. His role models were campers and well-trained counsellors who accepted and valued him for who he was. Trust was built into every aspect of camp life, and it wasn't long before Paul put complete confidence in the counsellors and the camp experience, and so did I. Every summer, and some March breaks in between, Paul continued to go to YMCA Wanakita – a place where he belonged.

―⁓―

Paul's experience at camp helped me to see him differently. If he could handle being away from home for two weeks with typical kids – children without disabilities – then there was a lot more he could do. It deepened my resolve to help Paul achieve his potential, whatever that might be.

In the fall, Paul was moved to his third elementary school. His new teacher tried her best to understand him, and in her mid-term report said, "Paul is a delightful student who always brings an element of surprise and wonder to each day... he is exceptionally well mannered on all outings."

During sharing time in class, however, Paul was reluctant to talk, unless his teacher asked him about lawnmowers. Then he would come to life and talk about "*Pau cutty grass,*" the "*da green lawnmore*" and the sound the engine made when "*Mommy pu da chord.*"

Paul may not have been able to speak clearly, but everyone understood him when he said, "*Preese, Thank you, You're welcon*" or "*Bress you,*" when someone sneezed. Those simple words were a bridge that connected people to Paul and his world. And he was grateful even in the most unlikely situations.

After a blood test, as the technician put a band-aid on his vein, Paul would look up at her and say, "*Thank you laydee*." Inevitably, the technician would turn to him, smile pleasantly and say, "You're most welcome, Paul." He loved this reaction, so he said "*Thank you laydee*" a lot. The 16-year-old girl at the check-out counter, however, was never quite sure how to respond.

Paul wasn't afraid to ask for a hug from someone he knew and often said, "*Hug me prease*." This was sometimes disconcerting. Paul drooled, and there was usually a sodden bandanna around his neck. Nevertheless, this was a sign that he wanted physical contact with others – a positive sign for a young boy with many of the characteristics of autism.

It was 1997, the summer of good things. Paul's neurologist put him on newly approved anti-convulsant medication and the results were amazing. For the first time in a long time, Paul's seizures were controlled. What I had wished for, if I was absolutely certain I would get it, had come true. A soft cloud floated in my chest, and on top of it was a whiff of happiness.

It was time to think about me.

PART TWO

NEW POSSIBILITIES

Paul working at the locks at Young's Point, July 2002

I TOOK AN OBJECTIVE LOOK AT MY LIFE, and it was full – of work. Work consumed my daytime hours and looking after the house and Paul consumed the rest. "Is this all there is?" I began to wonder.

It was the summer of my 47th birthday and before any more time slipped by, I wanted what I'd missed out on as a teenager. I wanted a date. There was just one problem. There wasn't a steady stream of men rushing to my door; in fact, there wasn't even a trickle. Then, by chance, I noticed the "Personals" ads in the newspaper. "Why, I could do that," I thought. So, with the help of a close friend, I did.

In the late 90s, the dating game was played using paper and stamps. My ad appeared in the paper in mid-September, and the first responses arrived in my mailbox a couple of weeks later. Some of the letters were better than others. One sounded like a form letter, one fellow got the name of the newspaper wrong, and another sent his requirements for an ideal mate on graph paper. Never a good idea.

Then a large puffy envelope arrived from a near-by town. The number of handwritten pages impressed me. "Now here's a man with time on his hands," I thought. I found out why. Not only did he *have* time, for the last 25 years he had been *doing* time in a nearby penitentiary. The irony of someone writing me from the penitentiary where John once worked made me laugh out loud. As much as I wanted a date, it didn't include being part of someone's release plan.

I had just about given up hope when a solitary letter arrived at the end of the month. Right away, I knew this one was different. The writer was sincere. He described himself as a carpenter with a small custom home building business, we had many of the same interests, plus he didn't need a day pass. Things were looking up.

His name was Murray, and after a friendly phone conversation, we agreed to meet at a downtown pub. Inside, two wingback chairs were sitting in front of the stone fireplace, as though they were waiting for us. We settled down in front of the open hearth; a low fire was burning, and each time a log popped, red embers showered onto the grate.

The pub was crowded, but the noise didn't seem to reach us. It was as though we were in our own private bubble. Our conversation was light-hearted and natural, almost as though we had met before. I didn't want to mislead Murray, so I told him about Paul and his disability. He leaned forward in his chair, never taking his eyes off me, and said, "It must be hard." (Much later, when I told him his body language impressed me, he said, "Did I do that? My back was really bothering me. I was just shifting in the chair!")

We started seeing one another every weekend, and we talked a couple of times in between. During my lunch hours, I'd go for a walk in the countryside near the College and think about him. My arms swung easily by my side, the deep furrows between my eyebrows began to soften, and my heart soared like black birds flying over the fields.

Murray didn't seem fazed by Paul's disability, and before long the two of them had developed a good rapport. His son was a year younger than Paul, his daughter three years older, and Murray missed living with them. Paul was the beneficiary of Murray's affection; he called Paul "a buckaroo," and pulled him across the kitchen floor by his outstretched foot.

"*No Murree!*" Paul squealed with delight.

Murray enjoyed relaxing with a beer, which would prompt Paul to say, "*No beer, naw for boys, just carprters.*"

At Christmas, we hosted a Solstice Party, inviting friends to celebrate the end of the longest night, and the return of light into the world. It was a fitting metaphor for how we felt.

Ten months earlier, I had been thinking about my dad and how much he loved me. It was around that time I put my ad in the newspaper, and by chance it appeared on September 13th, my dad's birthday. And on that day, Murray, a man my dad would have liked very much, read the ad. Some people would say this was merely a coincidence. I prefer to think of "coincidences" as God's way of remaining anonymous.

That February, Murray asked me to marry him.

"Are you sure you know what you're getting into with Paul?" I asked.

"Yes, and I can handle it."

It was Murray's turn to have his "enthusiasm trumps reason" moment. He was one of the few who make a lifelong commitment to join the world of people with disabilities. Not long ago, I asked him how he came to his decision, and he replied, "I went on faith."

—∭—

I wanted to bottle my joy and pour it over Paul. He was now a frustrated 12-year-old. With the right support, he could enjoy himself and be affectionate; but without it, he was often clingy and obsessive.

One of his supporters was a young university student, Tara, whose personality bubbled like champagne. She took him to a therapeutic swimming program, and he'd exclaim, "*Pau thwim, Tara. Pau jump in!*" She motivated him to swim independently, go down "*da thlide*", and retrieve rings from the bottom of the pool.

At other times, Paul laughed inappropriately and was restless and anxious. One day, he was so tense, he hunched over and walked on his toes, saying, "*Tummy hurts.*" On another, I was asked to pick him up from school. He had his arms and legs wrapped around his teacher and wouldn't let her go. "*Paus head hurt,*" he kept saying. His paediatrician examined him and said he didn't have appendicitis, was not constipated, and the small cysts in his kidneys were not a factor.

Sleeping problems are a common symptom of Tuberous Sclerosis, and Paul didn't miss out on this characteristic. I'd sit on the floor beside his bed and rub his back until he went to sleep. Then, with the skill of a gymnast, I'd lever myself onto my toes and creep out of the room, careful not to step on the squeaking floorboard. If I miscalculated, I'd have to start all over again. Paul rarely slept through the night, and most nights I'd be wakened from a deep sleep by "*Maauumm.*" I thought I'd go bonkers.

I dreaded phone calls at work, in case they were from the school. "Can you come and get him?" were the six words that stopped me dead. I couldn't just drop everything at work to pick him up, plus I didn't want Paul to think if he acted up, he could go home. It made me wonder who was being punished. Fortunately, Elaine, our former teenage neighbour, was still in town. I had her number on speed dial.

"I'll get Paul and have a little talk with the teacher while I'm there," she said. Elaine still had her intuitive understanding of how to relate to Paul.

"God bless you, Elaine." I said that a lot.

Then I got a call from the head of Special Education. The controlled tone in her voice signalled bad news. "Paul is so anxious, he's unable to focus for any length of time, and he clings to his teacher. I think he'd be better off if he stayed at home in the afternoons." With sweaty palms and a pounding heart, I replied, "That just isn't possible." I'd have to figure something out – he wasn't staying home.

I consulted Paul's neurologist and Toni, the psychologist. She did some therapy work with Paul, and the neurologist prescribed an increase in his medication. Paul stayed in school, and we all rode another wave of uncertainty.

No one could figure out what was setting Paul off. He managed to hold himself together during the day, but once he was home, he had laughing episodes that could last for an hour or more. At times, he would laugh hysterically about what he was seeing. "*Mommy, doggies frying!*" or "*Goofy pray a tuba*," while drool poured down his chin.

In desperation, I sent his neurologist a home video of Paul laughing and burping. He thought it was seizure activity and adjusted his medication once more.

I'm not sure I could have kept myself together if it hadn't been for Murray. He brought light into my life – waves of it – and to top it off, he seemed quite oblivious to Paul's behaviour. His friends thought he was amazing, and possibly nuts, to take on Paul as a step-parent, but Murray shrugged it off. "I'm in love with Lucinda, not Paul!"

When I got married the first time, I remember the minister saying, "You are not only making a covenant with one another, but also with God." I had taken those vows seriously; it was one of the reasons I had stayed with John so long. Lawyers had brought closure to the legal aspect of my divorce, counselling had helped me deal with the emotional fallout, faith had led me to forgiveness, but still, something was missing. I needed to set things right with God before I could marry again.

I took the problem to our Anglican minister, and he led

Murray and me through a service called "At the Ending of a Marriage." We prayed for family members who had been hurt, for healing, for the grace to let go of all resentment, and for a new life through God's Spirit. My tears bathed me in the power of forgiveness. The slate had been wiped clean. Murray and I set our wedding date for the Thanksgiving weekend.

—⁓—

In September, Paul was moved to his fourth elementary school and a new Learning and Life Skills class. His teacher asked me for Paul's birth date; when I hesitated, she looked at me askance. In case she thought I had lost my mind, I gave her more information. "He'll be 13 on December 20, but there is so much going on at Christmas, we usually celebrate his birthday on January 10, the day he became ours." Satisfied, she wrote that down.

Paul was able to recognize the names of most of the seven kids in his class, but he still had trouble holding a crayon and would scribble wildly over the shapes on a page. Sometimes he matched the crayon colour to the correct word, sometimes not.

Paul's strength was his memory; it took him awhile to grasp information, but once it was there he could remember events, people and pleasant experiences with surprising accuracy. He was slowly improving his computer skills and speaking in simple sentences, but he had difficulty following two-step instructions. If I asked him to pour a glass of milk and bring it to the table, he'd only remember the pouring part and drink the milk in front of the open fridge door.

He was starting to combine his love of music with his sense of humour. "*Pau wantsa tuba music!*" he'd tell his teacher. This was typical Paul; you couldn't take him literally. He may have been thinking of a local entertainer, Washboard Hank, who played a handcrafted instrument he called the "Fallopian Tuba." Hank would blow on a plastic tube made out of 1½-inch PVC pipe attached to a stainless steel sink. It created deep sonorous sounds, and Paul thought it was hysterical.

Even though Paul couldn't read, he loved books, especially if they were about bugs, insects, reptiles, spiders and snakes. He remained fixated on boats and motors, but it was hard to find books with illustrations unless it was an engine repair manual, and they were pretty boring.

So Paul added magazines about jet skis and boats to his list of obsessions. "*Where Pau magzeenes?*" was now his favourite question. Boat magazines with photos of motors, not yachts, were hard to find and they were expensive. When I discovered a source of pre-owned *Jet Ski* magazines, it was like winning the lottery. Paul would rapidly flip through the pages, barely glancing at the pictures of girls in skimpy bikinis, focusing instead on boats and jet skis tearing through the water. "*Pau jet ski magzeene. Go really fas!*"

Like most kids with an intellectual disability, Paul didn't like change; routine and consistency were his glue. Unfortunately for him, so much in his life was changing. He was in a new school, there was a new man in his life, and soon he would have to leave the only house he knew. Murray had been a custom builder for 25 years and we had found the perfect lot for our new home. When I told my friend Carole, she replied, "It's *beshert* – that's Yiddish for meant to be.'"

That term summed up more than just the building lot. It felt like Murray and I were *beshert*. We spent hours sitting in front of his drafting table designing the house.

"What about a screened-in porch?" I asked. "We can put that off the dining area, right here," Murray said pointing with his pencil. I stared at the drawing in amazement – there was also space to create a beautiful garden. Two more things on my list of things that I had really wanted from life were about to come true.

A YEAR EARLIER, MY GOAL HAD BEEN TO GO ON A DATE, and today, Friday, October 9, 1998, I was preparing for the pinnacle of all dates – my wedding. Joanna was my "best woman" and she and I sat in the backyard, basking in the late fall sun, talking about our friendship and the changes in my life. "I can't believe it, Joanna. I'm actually getting married tonight," I said, closing my eyes and tipping my face into the sun.

"If anybody deserves to be happy, Lucinda, it's you."

Paul arrived home from school. With his chubby cheeks, sweet smile and thick chestnut hair, it was hard to believe he'd be 13 years old in three months.

You have to be a good boy in church tonight, Pauli-wogs. Can you do that?" I asked.

"*Yes Mommy*," Paul replied with conviction.

Joanna and I drove to the church singing "Get Me to the Church on Time" at the top of our lungs. All around us, the evening sky was filled with ever deepening shades of orange and lavender and pink.

Murray's daughter Meghan, accompanied by a young flutist, began the service with music. She was barely 16, but she looked like a fair-haired Audrey Hepburn in her burgundy sleeveless dress and long black gloves. Her fresh soprano voice filled the church with a song of praise and thanksgiving.

The final note lingered in the air. Murray and I were at the back of the church, ready to walk down the aisle together. "Not so fast," Murray whispered, gently pulling on my elbow. "Let's make this last."

It was the story of my life; I was always in such a hurry. I inhaled deeply and savoured the moment. In the front row, firmly planted between Tara and Elaine, was Paul, so handsome in his navy blazer and grey flannels. He didn't speak as we walked past, but his hand darted in a quick wave, then his face lit up. If I'd had buttons on my jacket, they would have burst. We were met by Father Michael, Joanna, and Murray's best man – his 12-year old son Ian – looking grown up, and a little bit nervous, in his black tuxedo.

"Welcome to the marriage of Murray and Lucinda," Fr. Michael's voice boomed. "I always knew this was a marriage made in heaven, and now I know why. We are told in scripture that Jesus was both a wonderful counsellor and a carpenter. You have before you, a counsellor," he nodded to me, "and a carpenter."

Paul was quiet during the readings, hymns, vows and prayers, but when it came time for Communion, he couldn't sit still any longer. He sprang to his feet and made a beeline for me. With the two boys alongside us, we stood together as a new family listening to Meghan's closing song of blessing, "May the road rise up to meet you, may the wind be at your back…"

"That's the best wedding I've ever been to," Murray said at the reception. I had to agree – my face ached from smiling.

A week later, Murray put his work boots on and resumed building our home. Once the walls of the house had been erected and sub-floor laid, we took Paul to see it. "This is where your new bedroom will be," I told him, but he looked confused.

"No, Pau doesn't wan it."

"Let's put on your music. What tape would you like to listen to?"

"No, Pau wantsa go home."

"We could take Molly- puppy for a walk up the street."

"No!"

"If Paul couldn't say 'No,' he'd be speechless," Murray said, shaking his head.

Finally, on the coldest day of the year, the movers arrived. As one house was emptied, another filled up. True to his word, Murray made sure the baseboards were in place, but there was still interior work to be done, plus there were boxes everywhere. If it was confusing for me, it must have been overwhelming for Paul.

We were now within walking distance of *"Dad's prace,"* which was a good thing. Paul was often agitated when I picked him up there, walking ahead of me yelling, *"Pau say no. Stupid. Shut up Mommy!"* People stared, and I smiled sweetly as though Paul was saying, "I love going for walks with you, Mom." I didn't know what was going through his head, but I did know he benefited from 20 minutes of walking and venting between his dad's apartment and his new home.

—⁘—

Before Murray and I were married, his daughter Meghan sang along with Ella Fitzgerald in my living room and his son Ian had his friends over for pool parties. I willingly drove them to camp and to their friends' houses, and we all chatted at mealtime, mostly about the wedding plans and the new house. We seemed to get along fine, but something shifted when I became a stepmother. I now felt responsible. The honeymoon was over.

My parenting style was so different from Murray's. I had been raised with a lot of rules (spoken and unspoken), a prescribed moral code and strong religious values. By contrast, Meghan and Ian were brought up in a free-flowing environment with few, if any, rules and lots of opportunity to figure things out for themselves.

Murray, his children and I were about as far apart in how we experienced family life as we could be. Murray wasn't bothered about what time the kids came home at night or if they came home at all. "They're fine, they're just staying with friends," he'd say.

"What friends, where?" I'd reply. "Don't you think you should call them and find out?"

When Meghan and Ian stayed with us, I felt accountable for them. That's just who I am. Murray wanted to have his kids around him, and I had always wanted more children. We wanted the same thing, but we were trying to satisfy ourselves from two very different perspectives.

That became painfully clear one Sunday afternoon. Meghan, Ian and Murray decided to go out for the afternoon, and they didn't think to include Paul and me. They were smiling and joking with one another as they went down the stairs and out the front door.

I stood at the kitchen window and watched them drive away. My heart dropped hard and fast. "No, this isn't the way it's supposed to be. We're supposed to do things together," I cried. Quite suddenly, I felt abandoned. It was a painfully familiar feeling.

Murray came home a few hours later, after dropping his kids at their mother's house in the country. He'd been in the house less than a minute when I said, "Please don't leave me like that again. I've had lots of experience with Paul and me being left behind, and I hate it. I just hate it."

With Murray's children, I thought I would have the opportunity to build a relationship with "regular" kids whom I could talk to, encourage and support, but Meghan and Ian didn't need that. Like most teenagers, they didn't want more adults in their lives, especially an eager stepmother and a stepbrother with a disability.

They stayed with us when it was convenient for them, and even then, Meghan spent most of the time in her room with the door closed, while Ian remained downstairs talking on the phone. The farther they pulled away, the harder I tried. "Have your friends over," I'd encourage.

"Sure, we could do that," was their reply, but they never came. Everyone knew, including me, that I was trying a little too hard. The three of us awkwardly attempted to fit into our new roles, but being a stepmother to teenagers was like walking into a movie that's almost over. I had missed too many scenes to ever catch up.

Paul was excited every time he saw Meghan and Ian, but they weren't sure how to relate to him. He was loud when he talked, yelled when he watched videos on television, plus he was starting to touch himself inappropriately. The three of them all belonged to the same generation, but they were light-years apart. Paul wanted to be friends with Meghan and Ian, but he didn't know how to make that happen any more than I did.

I'm sure Murray's kids thought there were too many rules at our place, so they started staying with us less and with their friends more. "Why does it matter to me so much?" I'd ask myself. "Why am I looking for approval and acceptance from Murray's children?" I had always wanted more children and a brother or sister for Paul, and now that chance was slipping away. Plus, I still had needs carried over from my own adolescence – to be accepted by everybody, to be liked.

Murray found himself in the middle between Meghan and Ian, and me and Paul. It was a thankless, empty place.

After many months, I came to understand that I had placed unrealistic expectations on Meghan and Ian. I had idealized a blended family as though *The Brady Bunch* really existed. It was time for me to align my expectations with reality and allow for the evolution of a closer relationship with Meghan and Ian, when *they* were ready.

They hadn't had any control over their parents splitting up, and no one had asked them if they wanted Paul and me in their lives. Even though my intentions were good, I had to remind myself, yet again, to accept what I couldn't change. I stopped expecting everyone to show up for Sunday dinners, quit organizing family outings, and put an end to trying so damn hard.

AFTER THE TUBEROUS SCLEROSIS CONFERENCE, I found a paediatric neurologist who appreciated that his young patients belonged to families who were living with their child's disability 24/7. Dr. Munn's manner matched his attire – blue jeans and loafers. He not only asked for my opinion, he valued it. "You're Paul's mom, you know him best," he would often say when it came to a decision about medication.

One day I asked him how he would describe Paul. "He is a great kid. His biggest challenges are his anxiety, and that he's so withdrawn. He is smart enough to know he has a problem, which causes him to be frustrated a lot of the time. There are a lot of unknowns here: the effect of the seizures, the medications he's taking, plus his underlying brain terrain, caused by Tuberous Sclerosis. I see so many parents who keep their children isolated, which further compounds their socials problems. I'm glad you push Paul to get out there and do things."

"It helps that I'm naturally pushy—right, Paul?" I reached over and tousled his hair. Paul gave me a nervous look. He was sceptical around doctors, even friendly ones. Dr. Munn asked Paul to step on the scales. He weighed 90 pounds. Into that slender body went 2,900 mg of seizure medication, a total of 14 pills, each and every day. Paul's seizures were controlled, but at what price?

One of the drugs he was taking was newly approved and in combination with the other two medications, Paul started to put on weight, too much weight. He had so much fat around his stomach, the nephrologist at Sick Kids had trouble reading the ultrasound of his kidneys, so she referred him to a diet clinic at another teaching hospital. I added it to the list of appointments in Toronto – which already included dentistry for people with disabilities, ophthalmology for his eyes, nephrology for his kidneys, neurology and a scheduled MRI scan of his brain.

On top of his medical issues, Paul had to cope with all the changes in his personal life. Not surprisingly, he was having difficulty at school. According to his teacher, he exhibited "inappropriate vocalizations and physical acting-out behaviour." During one episode, Paul overturned his desk and ran screaming out of the classroom into the schoolyard. He needed a firm, steady hand at school, and it didn't help that his teacher was having personal problems of her own.

The head of Special Education set up a meeting to discuss the problem. At the end of it, she looked at me and said, "Lucinda, you have to remember that Paul is a guest in this school."

"In other words, he doesn't really belong in a public school like everyone else, so I should be grateful," I thought. I was too angry to be able to say it out loud.

The situation came to a head when I received a call from the school principal. He'd had enough of Paul's outbursts and had suspended him. I immediately drove to the school and met him in his office. He was holding the suspension letter in his hand. I gave him a look that could have withered dandelions, grabbed the envelope from his fingers and stomped out of his office with Paul in tow.

When I arrived at the Special Education office, the secretary offered me a glass of water and asked me to take a seat. "They're waiting for me to calm down," I thought, "and it could take awhile."

Eventually, I sat across the desk from the woman in charge and said in a shaky voice, "You said Paul would have the supports he needed to remain in his school."

"Well, that's not possible," she replied coolly. "He will have to move to a segregated school to finish his year."

I didn't have the energy to argue. Defeated, I went home, fell onto the couch and pulled a blanket over my head. I was almost asleep when I heard the volume go up on the Paul's favourite movie. Then the screech of "*AIIIYEEE!!*" echoed throughout the house. It went through me like fingernails scraping a blackboard. "Turn it down!" I yelled. "For God's sake turn it down."

—⁓—

Paul was turning 14 and it was time for him to make the transition to high school. I was worried he'd feel overwhelmed in a school with a thousand other students, but the principal assured me that my concerns were typical, and Paul would be fine.

Because of his behaviour problems the previous year, he was

put on the bottom rung of the Learning and Life Skills ladder, into the class for students with "behaviours." Students at this level were called "low functioning," while those who were able to read and/or write were referred to as "high functioning." Paul had been labelled yet again – and being labelled is like a sticker on fruit; it's almost impossible to peel off.

Fortunately for Paul, he had a male teacher with a good sense of humour and a gift for music. "*Mr. Buckler pray guitaaar!*" Paul would say at the end of the day. Hearing his teacher sing and strum his guitar offered Paul a break from the challenges of his day.

He was learning how to follow a visual schedule; recognize his name in print; develop a sight word vocabulary of 10 words; identify coins and their value; and use a proper grip to hold a pencil. The Life and Social skills component of his day involved navigating places like the men's washroom; greeting people appropriately with words rather than a hug; and learning the basics of cooking and cleaning up the kitchen.

I was relieved that Mr. Butler recognized Paul's strengths. On his first report card, he cited, "Paul's friendly personality, his desire to do the right thing and his good receptive skills." He was right, Paul had always been able to understand more than he could express.

Even though he struggled to learn, he enjoyed going to school. "*Paul go Kenner inna taxi! See Mr. Buckler and Kaffy,*" he would say every morning. One afternoon, at the end of the school day, I looked out the window to see the taxi pulling away with Paul still in it. I raced outside. The driver rolled down his window and pointed to Paul. "When I asked him if this was his house, he said '*No!*'"

"Very funny, Paul."

—⁓—

"There's nothing cute about an adult with a disability. Every child with a disability, who tugs at your heart strings, is going to grow up," a man with Cerebral Palsy told me 12 years ago. It made me think about the number of telethons and campaigns that raise money for cute kids with disabilities. Paul's big blue eyes and engaging smile endeared him to people, but someday he was going to enter the adult world, where cute doesn't cut it. And then what?

Even though Paul had just started high school, I began to think about what his life would be like when he left. Most high school students had the opportunity for a work placement or co-op experience, but "low functioning" students weren't considered eligible. My thinking about that changed when I received a newsletter from another school district, with a picture of Paul's friend at his work placement. "So it *is* possible for kids at Paul's level to have a work experience." That was all I needed to know.

I was trying to figure out how to translate Paul's love of motors into a meaningful work placement, when it came to me: Vacuum cleaners. They vibrated and hummed, buzzed and growled – this could be the ideal placement activity for Paul. Mr. Butler and the school agreed that Paul could have the support of an Educational Assistant to vacuum once a week at Applewood Manor, a seniors' residence. Paul loved vacuuming, and the cookies and juice that awaited him when he was done. With pride he'd say, "*Paul vacuum Applewood Manors.*" And he always said Manors with an "s." He knew what manners were.

It became one of those "win-win" situations: the staff and seniors welcomed Paul, he developed valuable skills, and the school had contact with a new employer. It showed, not only was Paul capable of performing work-related skills, but he enjoyed being productive. At the end of the year "*Mr. Buckler*" presented him with a plaque for an <u>Outstanding Enthusiasm, Work Placement Award</u>. Paul's face could have lit up a city block.

—⁂—

Paul had adjusted to our new home, and one of the things he liked best was the sliding door onto the porch. On windy days, he would open the door just a notch and put his ear against it. "What are you doing, Paul?" I'd ask.

"*Paul watch a wind,*" he replied.

He was tuning the pitch of the wind by adjusting the door: not enough air and the hum wasn't quite right; too much and the magic was lost. It wasn't just the sliding door that Paul found fascinating. He loved opening the windows in the living room, his bedroom and the bathroom as well. That was fine in summer, but in December, entering his bedroom was like going to Siberia.

"Paul, you've got to keep the windows closed in the winter," I'd tell him as I cranked the window shut. He was undeterred. "*Paul wan a listen th wind.*"

Perhaps Paul knew something the rest of us didn't. In Hebrew, the wind is called "Ruach," the breath of God.

Our new home brought the added blessing of living next door to Dick and Doreen and their teenaged daughter Sarah. We came to rely on her for after-school support, and to stay with Paul when Murray and I went out. Once Sarah got a car, she would take Paul to the place that was still close to his heart: the car wash.

They had been to the new automated one several times when, one day, things went drastically wrong. They had gone through all the cycles, and the car was inching slowly past the dryers. As it emerged from the car wash exit, the overhead door began to descend. Sarah was 17 and this was her first car. She didn't want a heavy garage door landing on her hood, so she quickly backed up. The door continued its descent and then closed completely. Sarah and Paul were now trapped in a concrete box.

Sarah had a cell phone, so she phoned home. There was no answer, so she got out of the car, looked around and saw a little door on the side wall. "Come on Paul, get out of the car. We need to get some help."

Paul was in his favourite place and he wasn't the least bit interested in moving. Sarah went through the little door herself. She looked around, but there was no one in sight, so she decided to rejoin Paul. Unfortunately, the door had locked behind her. Sarah peered through the small window on the door, and saw Paul sitting where she had left him, looking straight ahead. She banged on the glass, and waved wildly for him to come out. Paul didn't respond.

Panic-stricken, Sarah walked to the front of the building. Fortunately, she still had her cell phone, so she dialled the next best thing to her parents, the police. That produced an immediate response. Not one, but two cruisers arrived on the scene with their red and blue lights flashing.

Two officers sprang from their cars – it looked like a drug bust at the carwash. While the policemen were scratching their heads, a female customer pulled in. She put her toonies in the payment slot, and magically the door opened.

Sarah was so relieved she didn't mind that the pre-wash cycle had already started. She sprinted through the spray and jumped into her car. Paul flashed her one of his best and biggest smiles. "*Sarah, go car wash gen?*"

JANUARY 1, 2000 – THE DAWN OF A NEW MILLENNIUM. The dreaded Y2K bug hadn't destroyed the world, everything digital still worked: my computer, the clocks in the house and, most importantly, my bank card. It was before the War on Terror and the War in Afghanistan, before we knew how to spell the word tsunami. Gas was 65 cents a litre and the world economy hadn't cracked like Humpty Dumpty.

In 2000, technology was more cumbersome, but simpler. I used film in my Olympus camera, Murray's mobile phone was the size of a brick, and we were satisfied with the three television channels we pulled in with "rabbit ears." Paul watched movies using a VCR, listened to music on a tape recorder, and when he went into a bank, he talked to a teller.

A feeling of change was in the air. It was a new century and I was turning 50 – the ideal time to evaluate my life. I had been caught up in Paul's life for the last 15 years, and I didn't want to become swallowed by it. Some soul-searching was in order, and I signed up for a weekend retreat at a nearby Spirituality Centre.

Murray agreed to look after Paul. "We'll hang out together until it's time for him to go to his dad's. Don't worry," he assured me with a laugh, "*everything* is out of control and *nothing* will be alright!"

The Centre, a two-storey mansion with stately white pillars and a deep veranda, looked like it belonged on the set of Gone with the Wind rather than on the shores of Lake Ontario. I walked across the snow-covered grounds toward an ocean of water, inky blue, then dark grey where it touched the horizon. "This is a thin place," I thought, "where the veil between earth and heaven becomes thin." My shoulders dropped.

Free of life's distractions, I went to my room and opened my journal for the first time in two years. I could hardly believe it had been that long since I'd made an entry. I had been too busy with life to write about it and lately, I didn't have as much time for my spiritual life. I realized that I had felt closer to God when I was struggling; in my times of darkness.

At the Spirituality Centre, I fell into the rhythm of silence. As I became quiet on the outside, I entered a place of stillness inside. Thoughts of Paul, his dad, Murray, his kids and my job gradually faded from my mind, and a sense of peacefulness enveloped me.

I picked up a book by Henri Nouwen, a pastor at L'Arche Daybreak, a community for adults with severe disabilities. His writing reminded me that I already had everything I needed to find and maintain a healthy balance in my life. There were no missing bits and pieces out there, and there was no one else I needed to consult other than my true self.

I became still and let this idea tumble around in my head. As I did, I thought about the orchid sitting on my window sill at home. It too had everything it needed stored inside. I had expected it to bloom only once; after all, its roots were crammed into a concoction of dried up bark chips and twigs. How could it continue to support plant life let alone more blooms?

But after a few months of the plant being dormant, I watched in amazement as each new bud swelled with new life, producing one glistening white and purple flower after another. My body eased. The orchid, like me, already had everything deep inside it to flourish. It was time to tap into my own inner storehouse.

I bundled up, walked down to the rocky beach, and thought about the concept of wholeness. I could hear my mother advising me to see Paul as a whole person. An image of him came to mind; complete just the way he is, no matter how others may judge him.

The stones were so slippery, I stretched out my arms for balance and walked penguin-style beside the lapping waves. The northeast wind stung my face with the cold "breath of God." I paused, turned and looked up at the grey winter sky. "Help me remember that you have placed everything within me I need," I prayed out loud.

I retraced my steps, ready to face whatever the new millennium had in store.

—⁂—

The following week, I received a phone call from Paul's teacher, Brent Butler. He was still laughing when he said, "I want to tell you what happened this morning. Paul and I were walking down the hall with another student on the way to the washroom, when Paul stopped in his tracks to look at a couple of girls leaning against their lockers. Come on, Paul, let's keep going," I told him.

He looked at me and said, "*Jeepers a crazy Mr. Buckler!*" "It took me a couple of minutes before I got it – Paul was just like any other guy stopping to admire a pretty girl."

"Well, Brent, Murray and I have often said Paul may be delayed, but he's not stupid!"

Paul was in his second year in Mr. Butler's class, and as he approached his 15th birthday, it was one of his better school experiences. He was having more success controlling his impulses and following routines, plus I hadn't been called to pick him up for weeks. Now, if he could only stop drooling. Reminding him to swallow had no effect, his t-shirts were perpetually soaked.

Mr. Butler understood Paul, and helped manage his behaviour by working with his interests. When Paul started to get loud or unruly, he'd say, "Settle down or I'll remove your *Toy Story* cover or your guitar pick."

Paul had added guitar picks to his list of obsessions, and he wasn't comfortable unless he had one in his possession. They were easy to lose, so I tried to be one step ahead of him and kept a stash on hand. When Paul called out, "*Where's my pick!?*" I was ready. "What colour do you want, black or orange?"

"*Brue!*"

Paul was at an age when typical teenager boys were playing video games at the arcade, or strolling through the mall with their friends. But Paul's world wasn't typical. One of his favourite classroom games was "Duck, Duck Goose," a children's game. After school, he didn't meet up with friends, he came home by himself. There were five Learning and Life Skills classes in his high school, and Paul was smart enough to know he was on the bottom rung of the LLS ladder – the class for students with low skills and challenging behaviours.

Life skills training was a big part of his day, and included picking up the school's recycling and peeling and cutting vegetables in the cafeteria (with hand-over-hand support). With a little encouragement, Mr. Butler took things a step further, and arranged for Paul and another student to have a work placement with our long-time friend Elaine, who had just started a catering business, BE Catering.

"*Paul go BE Cater,*" he'd say with pride.

"What did you do there?" I'd ask him.

"*Paul sweep, peel carrots, do recycle, have a drink!*" he'd say, waving his arms.

You could always tell when Paul liked doing something. He'd get a crooked smile on his face, lift his arms high and rhythmically punch the air. It was a cross between conducting an orchestra and cheering for the Leafs.

On Wednesdays after school, Paul went swimming at the YMCA. Before every class, he insisted that Colleen, his swimming instructor, show him where the pool pump and machinery were kept. Pretty soon, he started calling her "*Colleen Machine!*" at every opportunity. Even when he swam holding a noodle, with Colleen by his side he'd say, "*Paul scared. No drain,*" when he swam in the deep end.

She encouraged him to keep going over the grate that sucked the water out of the pool, the place where a year earlier, a female lifeguard drowned when her hair was caught and no one could free her in time. Paul was unaware of the tragedy, and this was the only pool where he was afraid. It made me wonder if he could sense things at a level that belied his academic intelligence.

—∞—

Paul was the only person I knew who could turn the word "Mom" into three syllables. No matter what I was doing: gardening, hanging out the laundry, making supper, or trying to read a magazine, the sound of "*Maauumm*" interrupted me.

"Just let me finish what I'm doing, Paul."

"*Maauumm, come here!*" he'd insist.

I'd drop what I was doing to fix the current problem – replace the batteries in the Walkman, adjust his computer game, or wash grime off a music CD – and then resume my activities for another 20 minutes, until "*Maauumm*" brought me back once again.

Murray and I were both looking forward to the break that camp offered us, but this summer, Paul decided he didn't want to go. "*No, Paul doesn wan it. Not going a camp. Paul stay here!*"

He must have sensed my stress; I was getting the house, the dogs and him organized for my 50th birthday trip. Murray and I were going to Ireland.

"Look Paul," I reminded him. "It's the only place on the planet where you get to do whatever you want. I'd reconsider if I were you." When Paul and I arrived at Wanakita, he didn't want to get out of the car. Finally, he agreed to sit under a tree with his counsellor Jeff, where he continued his, "*No, no camp*" refrain.

Our plane was leaving that night and my stomach was in knots, but I put on a calm act and reassured him, "You and Jeff are going to have so much fun. Maybe you'll even get to drive the boat." Paul's head lifted slowly when he heard his favourite word. Without expression he muttered, "*Bye.*"

Once Murray and I were airborne, my worries evaporated, and for the next 13 days we hiked, laughed and explored. When it was time to return home, we found out that our flight was delayed by seven hours. We didn't get upset – we were in Ireland after all – so we did the only reasonable thing. We found a pub and ordered a Guinness. I can still taste the dark bittersweet ale through its thick creamy head slipping down my throat like velvet.

At the airport, there was yet another delay; no one knew for how long. As the evening wore on, I became worried that we wouldn't make it back in time to get Paul at camp. I imagined him standing outside the dining hall in the midst of a sea of campers, watching as everyone else was picked up by excited moms and dads, until he was the only one left.

I felt small, helpless, and a million miles from home.

When the plane landed, every bleary-eyed passenger wanted off, but Murray and I made it out the door first.

"Can you drive a little faster?" I asked him, once we were on the highway. "Settle down, I'm already going twenty clicks over the speed limit. The camp knows we're coming."

Wanakita, normally a tangle of activity, was deserted except for two young fellows sitting under a tree. When Paul saw us, he came running with a grin as wide as his open arms.

"I told Paul you guys would be late, so we've been hanging out listening to music," Jeff said. "Paul was fine as soon as you left. He convinced everyone that he should ride in the 'crash boat' to supervise water sports, so he pretty much did that for two weeks."

"Well done, Paul" I said wrapping my arms around him. "You've become a pro at getting people to do things your way."

THE MILLENNIUM YEAR WAS A TIME OF FIRSTS. For the first time, Paul went to the school in his neighbourhood, and he got there on a regular school bus – not a special needs mini-bus or taxi. And when he got home, for the first time ever, I was there. I had retired.

The early retirement door at the College opened for me that summer, and I walked right through it. I'd been working full time since the age of 21; first as an employment counsellor with people on social assistance; then at the Community College as the placement officer and the director of counselling. Over the course of the last 28 years, I'd serendipitously developed the skills needed to help Paul navigate the next phase of his life.

One of those skills was patience, and every morning Paul tested mine. It was an Olympic event to make sure he was ready in time for the school bus that took him to his new school.

I'd start at 6:45. "Paul, it's time to get up," followed at 6:55 with "Okay, Paul, let's get out of bed." By 7:10, my tone had changed to, "Get up NOW Paul!"

He would wander down the hall, yawning and scratching his head and then slump onto a stool at the kitchen counter. He'd pour his cereal into a bowl and twirl and bang the back of the bar stool into the counter top as he ate. Every morning, the notch got deeper, and every morning, as soon as Paul arrived, Murray would leave the room.

"Paul, stop banging the stool. Hurry up and eat your cereal," I'd say, with just a "touch" of edginess in my voice. "The bus is coming in 20 minutes."

"*No!*"

He'd finish his Cheerios and toast, and then scoop all his pills into the palm of his hand and swallow them with a gulp of juice. Our friend Joanna was flabbergasted every time she saw him do it. "Holy crow, some of those pills are huge!"

After breakfast, Paul would wander back to his room and I'd help him get dressed. He needed help. One day he went out the door with his pants on backwards, and most mornings he had to be reminded to turn his underwear around.

"*Where's Paul's guitar?*" he'd call on his way downstairs.

"It's in the case, right beside the front door," I'd call back. He took his guitar to school every morning: it's what got him there.

One morning, Murray went with Paul to wait for the school bus. When he came back into the house, his teeth were clenched. "I told Paul, 'don't stand on the road.' He just looked at me – it was like talking to a brick wall."

"I think he may only be hearing the words, "stay, road," I said. "Why don't you ask him to stay on the driveway, instead? That way you're telling Paul *what* to do, rather than what *not* to do."

The next morning, Murray tried again and this time he came back in the house smiling. "It worked," he said, "I can't believe it." If we were late, the bus driver would stop at the end of the driveway, crank open the door and wait for Paul to make his slow descent. As the door closed, I could hear Paul's cheerful greeting, "*Goood morneen bus driver!*"

You'd think his morning had been a "piece of cake."

At 3:00, the same yellow bus would stop at the corner and the neighbourhood kids would pile out, chatting and joking with one another. The last one off was always Paul. With his head down, and guitar case slung over his shoulder, he'd trudge determinedly up the hill, alone.

I encouraged the neighbourhood boys to play video games with him and they came a few times, but they usually had better things to do. So Paul went downstairs to the family room to watch "*Spisgagit.*" He loved the movie *Inspector Gadget*, especially the scene when Gadget falls out of an airplane. He'd rewind it over and over again, and each time, his screams of excitement would become so piercing you could hear him outside with the windows closed.

I'd ask him to stop, but that didn't work. When I couldn't stand it any longer, I'd run down the stairs, burst into the family room and pull the tape out of the machine. Inevitably, we'd end up in a yelling match.

"*Gimme my back my veeyeo,*" he'd shout.

Even though watching movies was something Paul could do on his own, his obsession with rewinding them disrupted the entire house.

"Why can't you just watch TV like other kids?" I'd ask him on my way back up the stairs, the "veeyo" under my arm.

—⁂—

Paul's new teacher, "*Sheelah*," had a lot of experience with special needs students, and it showed in her compassionate yet firm approach. Paul's Learning and Life Skills class had eight students, six boys with autism, and two girls who were non-verbal. His teacher, and the Educational Assistants, created a safe learning environment. But some days, when Paul was frustrated, he would bite at his arm, imitating one of the girls in his class. The only role models this group of students had were one another.

Paul spent all day in the same classroom, just like in elementary school, often eating his lunch there. He had limited contact with other students in the school; never went to a school dance, belonged to a club or did intramural sports. And it was hard for him to do things with his LLS classmates outside of school because they all had limited communication skills and lived in different parts of the city. At night, Paul was waking up three or four times, often crying from a bad dream, and during the day he couldn't sit still. I was seeing a naturopath for help with my perpetual stomach ache, and thought she might be able to help Paul.

Before I made an appointment, I checked with his neurologist, Dr. Munn. "By all means, give it a try," he said. "I've had patients who reduced their medication after seeing a naturopath." That was good news. One of the three anti-convulsant drugs Paul was taking was reported to affect peripheral vision, and he needed to come off it.

In the naturopath's waiting room, Paul's eyes darted nervously as he flipped through magazines. "*No hospital, no x-rake*," he repeated.

"No, Paul, Dr. Han is just going to talk to you," I replied. "Don't worry, you'll be fine."

She was a slight, youthful woman whose gentle manner put Paul's fears at ease. Looking directly into his eyes, she said, "His pupils are dilated. He seems to be in a daze." I turned to look at him. Drool was sliding down his chin onto his shirt.

"I can cope with Paul's developmental delay," I told her. "But his anxiety is driving me nuts."

Paul was sitting on a straight-back chair, his head and arms moved with sharp jerks and his legs never stopped swinging. When Dr. Han tried to touch his head, he quickly pulled away, "*No, don't touch.*"

She asked him a number of questions and he loudly replied, "*WHY?*" to each one. She turned to the laptop on her desk, paused, clicked, looked at Paul and clicked again.

"I'm going to give Paul a homeopathic treatment for anxiety," she explained. "It's for people who feel dependent, who feel smaller than they are. Sometimes individuals with mental retardation feel inadequate. When you feel this way about yourself, it feeds your anxiety. We need to help Paul change his belief in himself."

Paul must have understood that Dr. Han was on his side because, for the next three days, he willingly put the little round homeopathic pills under his tongue. Each one was the size of plastic pin head – they looked so innocuous it was hard to believe they could have any effect. But within a month, I noticed improvements in Paul's behaviour: He was calmer and more alert.

When we returned for a follow up visit, Dr. Han was equally pleased. After observing Paul and listening to my comments, she said, "Paul, you are definitely more connected, and not drifting in and out as much. And I'm glad you're not as loud." She suggested I give him another dose of the remedy and come back in two months.

Paul's progress continued. He had more energy, was less obsessive and anxious at night, plus his drooling and food cravings for chips and carbohydrates were reduced. Dr. Munn agreed we could begin to cut back on Paul's seizure medication. His eyes started to get brighter, and at our next visit with Dr. Han, he looked quite different. His hands were in his lap, his legs were still and he was smiling.

"His body was stuck," she explained. "From the very beginning of his life, Paul experienced a lot of early trauma that his body absorbed. He had a difficult birth, and was given up by his birth mother. Plus he had uncontrolled seizures and medical procedures that created a fear in him that goes beyond words. Even if Paul could talk, he could not articulate or integrate these very deep, early stages of trauma."

I was speechless: it all made so much sense.

She went on, "A homeopathic remedy is an excellent way to

take care of the subconscious and distorted perceptions of reality. It helps people see life as it is and increases their ability to compensate. We see how it's working through a change in dreams and nightmares. The remedy has helped Paul feel less inadequate.

Dr. Han's face warmed. "Homeopathic treatment can't do everything, however; a person also needs a good support system, positive life experiences, a healthy diet, social connections and spirituality. Paul is getting that through your love, and how you advocate for him. He is also strengthened through experiences like camp and going to church."

I looked at Dr. Han with tears in my eyes. "Thank you for giving me back my son. I knew he was in there, somewhere."

Paul was now better equipped than ever to achieve his potential. And we were about to find out just what that was.

Being retired meant that for the first time in my life, I was home alone all day. The house was so deathly quiet in the morning and fear began to bubble up inside me like water in a percolator. I was used to being busy, and I found it was a whole lot easier than being still. I had the rest of my life ahead of me and I had no idea what I was going to do with it. Some days, I thought about volunteering at a women's shelter, or doing pastoral care, but something always stopped me, and that was my commitment to myself. I wanted to take the time to explore my creativity and discover if I could use my talents to develop a new initiative.

To help me figure things out, I talked, walked and read. A friend told me, "You need to give yourself the space and permission to let your creative juices flow." She gave me a poem by Rumi whose words seemed meant for me:

> *Let your soul take flight like a happy phoenix.*
> *God has created*
> *Your wings not to be dormant*
> *As long as you are alive*
> *You must try more and more*
> *To use your wings to show you are alive.*

It made me think of Joseph Campbell, an American mythologist, writer and lecturer, whose philosophy is often summarized by the phrase "Follow your bliss." Is this what I was searching for – something that would make me feel excited about getting up each morning?

To find out what that "something" was, I began by making a list of the things that energized me: discussing ideas; writing; new experiences; and exploring my spirituality.

"Being small does not serve the world," my friend Brian told me "You need the spark and heat from the sun to ignite you and push you forward." That gave me the impetus to use the hot side of my personality, ignited by the inequities in the social service and school systems, as a way to propel me forward.

I spent a lot of time walking in the country with my dogs, and as I walked, I prayed for guidance. When I got home, I sat quietly, opening myself to the universal energy I knew was there.

After many weeks of listening, reading and quiet reflection, I was able to move from contemplation into action. I had made a decision. I wanted to use my time and talent to create a new program that would benefit young people with intellectual disabilities.

Paul, and others like him, deserved a higher profile in our schools and community; they had been marginalized for so long, it was time someone championed their cause. The more I thought about it, the more passionate I became about being that person.

Perhaps, I thought, this was the reason Paul was placed in my life.

—⁓—

I imagined creating a project which matched regular high school students with their peers in Learning and Life Skills classes. It would help students like Paul participate in the life of their school, increase opportunities for inclusion and transform attitudes toward students who are different.

My idea was reinforced the following week, when I was at Paul's high school for a meeting. I spotted him walking down the hall, but he didn't see me. He was hanging off the arm of a female Educational Assistant, and a girl from his class was hanging off her other arm. Paul looked so dependent – like a kid who couldn't do very much.

I said to myself, "If another student asked him to go to the cafeteria, he'd straighten up and walk down the hall, just like everyone else." It reinforced my belief that Paul was living up to the low expectations that were placed on him.

There was an untapped resource within our high schools: other students. I could see the potential for students in LLS classes to participate in the life of their school with the encouragement and support of their peers. I believed that once typical students appreciated what kids with disabilities had to offer, they could transform attitudes in the school and in the community.

I discussed the idea with two high school Special Education Department heads, who were excited at the prospect of bringing resources into the school to benefit students and teachers alike. But when I applied for government funding, I was turned down. This was a problem. Two high schools wanted to work with me, but I had no financial backing.

The project that I had been so excited about now weighed heavily. I had always worked for an agency or institution; I showed up in the morning, put in a good day's work, and then went home. "This must be how small business owners feel," I thought. "There is no place to hide – the responsibility, the anxiety, falls onto you." I needed to talk to someone who could inspire me, so I called Reach for the Rainbow, the inclusion program that had made it possible for Paul to attend camp Wanakita, and spoke to the founder and CEO, Donna Trella.

She told me the inspiring story of how she created Reach so her daughter, who was disabled, could go to camp with her brother and sister. Donna supported what I was trying to do and suggested that I pursue corporate sponsorship. I said to myself, "If she can do, then so can I."

For the next two weeks, I searched corporate websites online until I was cross-eyed. I couldn't find a fit between their goals and my inclusion project. Discouraged, I slumped into a chair and closed my eyes. "There's nothing more I can do," I thought. "I have to let it go." An overwhelming wave of fatigue came over me, and I fell asleep.

The sound of the phone ringing woke me up.

"How's it going?" my friend Judy asked.

"I just can't seem to get anywhere with funding for my project," I told her.

"Maybe you should talk to my sister-in-law Jane. Her family has a foundation that may be able to help."

I almost tripped over the dog in my haste to find a pen.

Jane referred me to her sister Julie. I reviewed my notes, took a deep breath and dialled Julie's number. I explained my idea and its potential benefits, and Julie replied without hesitation, "I can tell you right now, we will support your project. This is my passion."

I was as excited as the day I found my lost dog.

My first task was to conduct a literature search for articles on relationships between high school students with and without disabilities. The only things I could find were research papers on peer tutoring or peer mentoring, so the project began by giving mainstream students a peer tutoring credit in exchange for their involvement with students in Learning and Life Skills classes.

But this created an imbalance between the students that made the relationships artificial. I didn't want mainstream students to have the attitude, "I'm spending time with you to get a credit." Another problem was the phasing out of grade 13, which meant few students could fit peer tutoring into their timetable. By this time, we had a steering committee, so I took the problem to them. One person offered a solution. "Let's encourage students to participate without giving any incentives or credits."

"It will never work," replied one of the teachers.

"It's worth thinking about," I said. "After all, our goal is for students to develop natural relationships with one another." And then I told the story of a young quadriplegic I'd heard about who died in a recent power failure. "He had all the technology at his fingertips," I said, "but he didn't have any friends. When the power went out, so did his connection with the outside world."

The room fell silent.

"I believe students with true motivation will come forward," the mother of a teenage daughter with a disability said. "Let's give it a try."

The project was on the verge of becoming a new creation. To figure out how to put the pieces together, I went for another walk down the country road near our home. As I walked, I found myself looking into the ditch and thinking about the junk people had thrown out of their car windows: cigarette packages, food wrappers, liquor bottles, cardboard coffee cups.

Then I realized what I was doing. "Lift your head, girl," I said to myself. "Don't let other people's garbage drag you down." At that moment, a hawk soared in the field beside me. I watched as it settled on a tree nearby, and then I understood. When you lift your head, you see the possibilities.

By the time I got home, I had renewed energy and a name for the project – Heads Up for Inclusion.

The name has a threefold meaning: when you raise your head, you see the opportunities around you; individuals with disabilities often need to be reminded to keep their head up; and giving someone a "heads up" lets them know something worthwhile is coming.

I reworked the idea of students with and without disabilities coming together to share their mutual interests, without any external reward. All the students who participated, whether they had a disability or not, would be called "Amigos" – friends. I believed then, as I do now, that there are students who will respond positively to their peers who are different, if they're given the opportunity. And if they don't get that chance in high school, when will they have it?

The president of Student Council affirmed my thinking. "Students are so self-absorbed, you have to put inclusion on their radar screen."

It was challenging to manage a project from outside the school system, and it depended on the goodwill of teachers and administrators. Some were more supportive than others. One day a teacher said to me, "I hope you have a plan for how to manage those LLS kids with behaviour problems. What if they act up when they are with another student?"

Her question and tone illustrated how segregated the school was. The students with disabilities were not only in separate classes, they were in a separate wing of the school. When they were outside their classroom, an educational assistant was usually present, which provided a safety net on the one hand, but a barrier to any student interaction on the other. Typical teenagers didn't want to hang out with someone who had an adult attached to them.

Over the next few months, I worked with teachers, promoted the idea with student leaders, sent letters home to parents and developed an orientation manual.

By 2001, once Heads Up for Inclusion had caught on, Amigos started to spend their lunch hours together doing things that typical teenagers do. For the first time, students with intellectual and often physical disabilities walked down the halls, and ate in the cafeteria, not with an adult but with their peers. The Amigos were sending an important message to the rest of the school: You don't have to be afraid of someone who is different.

—∞—

Even though the project was off to a good start, there were still many unknowns, and so much that was outside of my control. I kept up a good front, but inside I felt vulnerable and scared. I was afraid that the project wouldn't meet my expectations and the expectations of others; that it would run out of money; that something would go embarrassingly wrong.

It was one thing to create a new initiative, and quite another to sustain it. It was an ongoing journey of faith. As students got to know one another, they began to appreciate and value their Amigo, and natural relationships developed. When asked, many students demonstrated that they "got it." Some of their comments displayed their insight:

"I learned so much from my Amigo (with a disability)."

"On the inside we're all the same. We're all human *beans*!"

"Just because someone doesn't talk, it doesn't mean they don't have anything to say."

At a school assembly a couple of years later, two students illustrated what the program meant to them. One girl, her light brown hair framing her soft face, was deaf; the other, slighter taller and equally attractive, was not. The pair walked to the middle of the stage and raised their hands in unison. Using sign language and words, they said, "This is my school." It was a moment that still brings a lump to my throat.

Paul is fortunate that his Amigo Michelle keeps in touch with him when she comes home from university. Her experience was like that of many students: Amigos shaped her life. It all started because I wanted Paul, and others like him, to feel they belonged. According to Jean Vanier, the founder of the worldwide L'Arche communities for people with disabilities, our need to belong is even greater than our need for love.

Heads Up for Inclusion and the Amigos program expanded to other schools, and 12 years later, well over a thousand students have been, and still are, participating in the program. The students rose to the expectations placed on them, and not surprisingly, there was never an incident of an Amigo acting up.

LIKE MOST PARENTS whose son or daughter has a disability, I was concerned about what would happen to Paul when he became an adult, and I was no longer around. He was only 16, but I was 51, and I knew it would take a concerted effort, and possibly many years, for him to become more independent. I was motivated by how quickly time passes, and by my nemesis, fear.

When Paul was a baby and newly diagnosed, I read a newspaper account of a family in Kelowna, B.C. who had an adult son with an intellectual disability. The father, mother and son were found dead in their trailer; it was a murder and double suicide. The parents were aging and in poor health and believed they were the only ones who could care for their son.

I understood how something like that could happen; most parents think no one else can love or understand their child the way they do. I was one of those parents. Nevertheless, I had to face reality. When I died, I didn't want Paul to be left lost, scared and alone.

Our local Community Living Association operated a number of group homes. Because of limited space and long waiting lists, they advised me to put Paul's name on the list early. Our family doctor thought a group home was the only option, so Paul and I visited a couple of residences to see what they were like. The homes were well kept and pleasant, but the residents were men in their 40s and 50s. "This really isn't the best place for a young man," a staff member told me.

"But what are my alternatives?" I asked.

"I'm not sure," he replied.

Not knowing what else to do, I put Paul's name on the waiting list for residential services.

In the meantime, I had a more pressing question on my mind. What was Paul going to do after high school, when he left his social contacts, routines and planned activities behind? If he wasn't prepared for this transition, he could become dependent on me forever.

Murray was also concerned. At dinner, Paul played with his food and with himself, which turned mealtime into an endurance test. One night, Murray looked at me in exasperation and asked, "Are we doing this for the rest of our lives?"

"Let's hope not," I replied. "Even inmates get parole."

I wanted to talk to other parents whose sons and daughters were facing the same dilemma, but I didn't know who they were. Only once, the Special Education department of the School Board arranged a meeting of all the LLS parents, and I became reacquainted with a mother whose son had been in daycare with Paul. The meeting was informative, and she and I asked the department head lots of questions, including, "When are we getting together again?" It never happened.

It became apparent that neither the school system nor the social service system was going to bring parents together. So in the fall of 2001, as part of my role with Heads Up for Inclusion, I organized a Transition Planning Workshop for parents of teenagers with disabilities.

A story about the event appeared in the local newspaper and it included a photo of Paul, soft and chubby, sitting in front of his computer. The reporter described Paul as "mesmerized by a CD ROM game featuring the children's character Arthur," and described his bedroom, "with the stuffed animals and toys on a shelf, and the Franklin poster above his aquarium."

The article was my wake-up call. I still saw Paul as a little boy, instead of a 16-year-old. The time had come to pitch the toys and stuffed animals. This wasn't just Paul's transition, it was mine too.

The workshop, held over three evenings, gave parents the opportunity to think about the future. For many, this was a luxury. Health and disability problems, school issues, finances and the needs of other children were all distractions that kept parents from planning for their child with a disability. We talked about the importance of creating a vision for our children, and then we brainstormed a variation of the question I had used in previous workshops: "What would I really want for my son or daughter if I was absolutely certain to get it?"

I kept my pen moving as my heartfelt desires for Paul filled the page. My wish list was that he could: live independently in the community; have the chance to make a contribution; increase his communication skills; develop more self-confidence and self-esteem; manage his temper and outbursts; be physically fit enough to enjoy an activity; have friends his own age; rely less on me; travel on the bus; know how to walk from place to place; share his spirit for life with others; and be included. And even though it seemed far-fetched, I wished with all my heart that Paul could take fewer drugs and still remain seizure free.

Recently, I came across an explanation for how the universe responds to our requests, in the writing of Francisco Varela, a biologist and co-founder of the Mind and Life Institute, which promotes dialogue between science and Buddhism. He believes that when we acknowledge the lack of substance in the universe and our lives, and stand "in a state of surrender," we become part of the unfolding universe. In this state of being, whatever we need to meet our future will be available to us. Some call this faith.

During the transition workshop, my vision for Paul emerged. I pictured him living, working and being included in activities in our community. A vision is ephemeral without goals and action plans to support it, and my goal was for Paul to have a job that included productive and meaningful activities. I was sure Paul would have been content to live at home for the rest of his life. He wasn't able to imagine an alternative, but I believed in his potential for independence.

In hindsight, the workshop would have been better if Paul and his peers had been present. I wasn't as enlightened then; I hadn't heard the phrase "not about me without me," so I developed Paul's goals on his behalf.

His new teacher was willing to build on his previous work placement at the senior's residence, and she organized a placement for him, vacuuming at a church near the school.

In my goal-directed eagerness, a characteristic that can be annoying, I thought it would be a good idea if Paul also vacuumed the sanctuary of our church on Saturdays. But he wasn't as enthusiastic as I was; the church was empty and, even though someone went with him, he protested. His resistance was telling me that it wasn't just the activity that motivated him; he wanted to be around people, and the more outgoing they were, the better.

Paul had been allocated some government funding for personal growth, so I hired support workers for five hours a week to help him develop new skills. Jamie, a young man with a long beard and a soft smile, took Paul to BE Catering on Thursdays after school, where he washed and peeled vegetables, cleaned dishes and pots and did their recycling. Then the two of them hopped on the bus and walked a kilometre home.

"Paul walks with his head down, and I have to remind him not to run into people, sign posts or tree branches," Jamie said when they got back.

"*Paul doesn wanna walk*," he complained.

There was no physical reason why he couldn't walk, and lots of good reasons why it was a good idea. "Just because you have a disability, it doesn't give you a license to whine," I told him.

Paul could stay in school until he was 21, so we had just less than five years to prepare for the great unknown. I once did career counselling with a young man who had a flat interest profile; he'd never done much of anything, so his interest inventory showed no identifiable likes or dislikes.

To make sure Paul didn't fall into the same trap, he needed to have a range of different experiences. On Saturdays, Christine, a new supporter, took him to the library and to a teen bowling league. If he was having a good day, he would shout, "*Three knock a pins!*" when he got a spare or the odd strike.

Not every day was a good day, however. Paul's behaviour was still challenging, and his young supporters had to learn how to manage and motivate him. Sometimes he wanted to leave bowling before the game was over, or he'd refuse to eat his lunch, or insist on watching *Monsters Inc.* or *Toy Story*, instead of playing a more stimulating computer game.

Paul easily became frustrated, and he could strike out or become non-compliant. His favourite saying was, "*I wanna see Dad!*" In other words, Dad leaves me alone and lets me do what I want.

"Paul is a great training ground if you want hands-on experience in behaviour management," I'd tell his college and university student supporters.

MURRAY WAS ONE OF THE MOST EASY-GOING PEOPLE I'd ever met, but Paul could push his buttons like a pro. The honeymoon between them was over. Sometimes Paul deliberately bugged Murray to see if he could get a reaction; he'd belch loudly at the dinner table, and then stick his chin out at Murray in defiance. If Murray didn't respond, he'd do it again. One night in particular, Murray had had enough, and he ordered Paul to his room.

"*Fuck you Murray!*" Paul replied.

Murray gritted his teeth, looked Paul in the eye, and backed him down the hall. They had gone about 10 feet when Paul tripped, fell backwards and screamed in pain. When I got to him, he was lying on his side holding his arm against his chest.

"*Owww, Mommy,*" he cried out.

"Let's get in the car and have it checked," I said, helping him up, carefully avoiding the word "hospital."

"Do you want me to come?" Murray asked.

"No." It was my turn to clench my teeth.

At the hospital, the doctor carefully questioned Paul about what had happened.

When he replied, "*I trip,*" I breathed a sigh of relief; a Children's Aid worker wasn't going to show up at our door. The x-ray revealed a small fracture, so Paul's left hand and forearm were wrapped in a white plaster cast – just what he needed for his 16th birthday!

When I got home, I could tell by the worried tone in Murray's voice that he felt badly about what had happened. As Paul said, it was an "*accilent,*" no one was at fault or to blame. It was a good lesson in keeping our emotions in control when Paul's demands tested our limits.

Cast or not, it was a milestone birthday and cause for celebration. Paul often got short-changed on his birthday, just five days before Christmas, so we had his party on a night when friends could come, including Paul's buddy Kelly, a high school student who hung out with him once a week to make music. At the party, she played the piano and sang while Paul noisily strummed his guitar to their favourite tune, *Let it Be.*

As the song ended, Paul raised the neck of the guitar, strummed the strings madly with a guitar pick, and then thrust his hand into the air with a flourish. It was his rock star ending.

In adolescents, seizure activity sometimes increases with the onset of puberty, but that wasn't the case for Paul. In the last year, his anti-convulsant medication had been reduced by 1,500 mg. a day, without any breakthrough seizures. Anti-convulsants dampen brain activity, now with fewer drugs he was brighter and more alert, and his attention span had increased. When his aggressive and obsessive behaviour did return, it was usually due to an external event, like an anaesthetic for dental work, a medication change, or deterioration in his dad's health. When that happened, our naturopath Dr. Han would adjust his remedy and inevitably, Paul would get back on track.

Riding the city buses on Saturday became Paul's favourite thing, and bus maps were his new obsession. He always carried one with him: in the car, on the school bus, when he went for a walk, and when he crawled into bed at night. At home, he'd unfurl his map, spread it on his lap and look at all the routes.

"*Read it to me!*" he'd say. After a lot of repetition, Paul memorized the number of each bus and where it went. "*George North number nie go Trent Unersity. Ashburnham pass Dad's prace. Lansdowne Wes number sewen to Lansdowne prace!*" he'd exclaim and then continue, "*Clonsilla number fie go pass hospital. No x-rake!*"

"That's right, Paul. You don't need an x-ray," I replied, shaking my head at how he managed to work his fear of medical procedures into his monologue.

His maps were folded over and over again to fit into his pants pocket, and when he opened them, they were often in tatters. "*Oh no!*" he'd cry. "*Mommy more tape!*" I gave him a laminated copy of the new city bus map for his birthday. You'd think he'd received a brand new X-box.

That fall, the school didn't have the staff to provide Paul with a work placement. They agreed, however, to let him leave school early one day a week for a placement in the building maintenance department at the university with a support worker I hired using his allocation of funds for personal growth.

Paul responded positively to the work environment. He loved the staff and students he met as he vacuumed, swept and mopped. He proudly sorted and collected the recycling from the campus library, including the president's office, and then pushed the large blue recycling bin onto the elevator and down to the loading dock. His support worker prompted him, and the staff gave Paul the words of encouragement he loved to hear: "Good to see you again, Paul." "Nice job!" "Give me a high five!" "See you next week."

When he got home, I'd ask him about his day. "*Paul do recycle Trent Unersity. Crean da froors. Put mop 'n broom away!*" he'd say with a grin, pumping his arms in the air. His placement at the university continued for a year and a half until it conflicted with his school schedule, but the skills he learned and confidence he developed were his to keep.

—※—

"Ian, make sure you lock the door when you leave," I reminded Murray's son, as we walked out the front door together. "We'll be back on Sunday afternoon."

"No problem," he replied. "My ride home should be here soon."

I had taken Paul to his dad's, and Ian happened to drop by just as Murray and I were leaving for an out-of-town anniversary celebration. Ian was now 16 years old and pushing back – hard.

It was the end of May, the perfect time of year for a road trip, plus we needed a break from the tug-of-war we were having with Ian. Murray and I had enrolled in a course, "Living with Difficult Teens," hoping for insights. A recurring theme was ensuring consequences for inappropriate behaviour, but this was almost impossible to do, because Ian could stay at his mother's or with friends when it suited him.

I don't think Ian planned for what happened next; he just couldn't resist the temptation of access to a large home on a Saturday night, sans parents. It probably didn't take long to get the jungle drums ringing. That night, our home became the preferred destination for teenagers from across the city.

When we got back, my first clue that something was amiss was the outdoor Santa lying in the flower bed with its head smashed in.

I slowly opened the front door and greeted Paul and Jamie, his supporter. They were downstairs watching television. "There's been a problem," Jamie said. ".You'll see when you go upstairs."

The carpeting was grey with streaks of black, the railing on the porch was damaged, and there was a phone message to call the police. "I'm surprised you have any plate glass windows left," one of the police officers said when he came to the house. "There must have been over a hundred kids here last night, along with some of the worst people in this city. This was the worst house party I've ever seen."

Ian was slouched against the kitchen counter, his eyes firmly fixed on the floor.

"Do you have anything to say for yourself?" Murray asked, his voice quivering with rage.

"No, everything just … just got out of control," he replied without expression.

"Why didn't you let the police in? Was that too much to ask of you – to protect my house?"

"Is there any way I can get my things back?" I asked. "All my jewellery is gone. I had beautiful things, my mother's things."

"The good jewellery probably isn't even in this town anymore. If you walk down the halls of the high schools on Monday morning, you can probably find girls wearing some of your things," the officer said.

I pictured girls flaunting their new earrings, including the ones my brother had given me, and I wanted to cry. But I couldn't; my heart had turned to stone.

"I can't believe the disrespect people would have for my home," Murray said with more sadness than I had ever heard.

The replacement of the carpets was minor compared to what it took to restore my sense of safety. When I was a kid playing baseball, we'd call "home free," when we touched the base. Your home was supposed to be like that – a safe place, a place of refuge.

I kept hearing the police officer say, "Some of the worst people in town were in your home." Did that mean they would be back? Would they come at night when we were here? Would they wait until we went away again? I drove to pawn shops within an 80-mile radius looking for my jewellery and searched online, but to no avail. On the advice of a Buddhist friend, I practised "non-attachment" – letting go of the desire for material things. It took my intention to "let go of things outside of my control" to a whole new level.

This wasn't the first time I'd felt unsafe in my own home, and I prayed that my heart would find peace. I imagined putting my hand into the hand of God, as Paul did with me when he was a child, and thought about his ability to love and trust – he was much better at it than I was.

Eventually, I was able to journal, "Material things come and go, but nothing can separate me from the love of God." My close girlfriends came over to bless and cleanse the house, and we smudged every room with the smoky fragrance of sage and lemongrass. I felt restored when I knelt beside Paul's bed later that night. "Who do you want to say God bless?" I asked him, as I did every night. It gave me a glimpse into who he was thinking about.

"*My Mom, Murray an' Ian*," he replied without hesitation.

"You're right, Paul. Let's remember to ask God to bless Ian." I kissed him on the forehead and murmured, "Goodnight, my wise little man."

When Murray and I got married, I'd had no idea how hard it would be to be a step-parent. I did know, however, that a leading cause of the break-up of second marriages is the children from previous relationships.

"Remember the advice Father Michael gave us?" Murray said one evening. "The most important relationship is the one between a husband and wife."

"You're right," I replied. "We've been able to do that with Paul, and now we have to do the same with Ian."

After high school, Ian moved to Alberta, where he got a job in construction. A year later, when he had turned 19, he came back for Christmas. "Lucinda, I'd like to talk to you," he said. We sat across from each other at the kitchen counter, and he looked me in the eye. "While I've been away, I've had a lot of time to think about how I behaved, and it's been bothering me. I'd like you to forgive me."

"Oh Ian, I do." I opened my arms. "Let's put this behind us." We embraced with a hug, the kind you get from a loved one you haven't seen for a long time.

Four summers later, when Ian was home for an annual visit, Paul spotted him driving his mother's car. "*There's Brother Ian!*" he said, pointing excitedly. My wish for a sibling for Paul had finally come true.

"O.K, GOD, do you think you could let someone else have a turn?" I didn't believe in the worn phrase, "God only gives us what we can handle," any more than I believed God handed out favours to some and grief to others. I agreed with Rabbi Harold Kushner in his book, *When Bad Things Happen to Good People*, that faith in God doesn't prevent bad things from happening; faith helps you get through them. Still and all, "Enough already!"

The day before, Murray, Paul and I had been at Sick Kids in Toronto for Paul's appointment with the nephrologist. She was monitoring the small cysts on his kidneys. If they grew into a giant cell astrocytoma – which sounds like something from a science fiction horror movie – they would have to be removed. The doctor handed us a requisition form and asked us to return Paul's urine sample to the lab. It sounded simple enough. "Why don't you do it with Paul? It's sort of a guy thing," I said to Murray.

He rolled his eyes. "Come on, Paul, let's go to the washroom together."

"*Why Murree?*"

"Because your mother wants us to."

I watched as the two of them dragged their feet down the hall. They returned 10 minutes later. I knew from the look on Murray's face that it hadn't gone well.

"When we got to the *Men's*" he said, "I took Paul into a cubicle and told him, 'I want you to pee into this cup.' He looked at me as though I was from Mars. I put the cup down and waited for him to have a pee. As soon as he started to go, I picked it up, but when he saw it, he stopped. He pinched off the flow in a millisecond. I tried again, but he did the very same thing. I've never seen anything like it!"

Now it was my turn to roll my eyes. We gave Paul a big glass of juice and waited; then I took a turn. "Come on Paul let's get this done," I said with a mother's confidence, as we walked to the Handicapped washroom.

Once inside, I kept the cup behind my back until Paul produced a thin yellow stream. Then I deftly whipped it out and placed it directly under the flow. Instantly, it stopped. "Come on Paul, you know how important this is," I pleaded. He wasn't going to give me a second chance. Before I could turn around, he was out the door and in the hall. Paul had outfoxed both of us. To this day, he has never produced a urine sample. Fortunately, he hasn't had to; the small cysts on his kidneys eventually disappeared.

The next day, a friend called to remind me about our Homes for Life meeting later in the week. The group was the brainchild of two mothers whose daughters had intellectual and physical disabilities. Once a month, Murray and I looked forward to getting together with the 16 other "Lifers," parents of teenaged sons and daughters who were living with disabilities.

Initially, the group was formed to explore housing options for our kids, but after several months, we realized that if our sons and daughters didn't have meaningful lives, it didn't matter where they lived. So we broadened our vision and committed, "To work together in a spirit of friendship and cooperation, so our sons and daughters will have the supports necessary to lead lives of meaning and purpose in their community." We all hoped that included having our adult children move into their own place someday.

The Zulu word, "Ubuntu" captured our intent: A person is a person through other persons; we are all interdependent, and God made us for companionship, relationship and belonging. In Peterborough, the majority of adults with intellectual disabilities either lived with their parents or in a group home. For many, a group home is the only option, but that isn't what we wanted for our sons and daughters. We wanted them to have a symbol of independence: a key to their own front door.

> *A true home gives*
> *Physical shelter and sustenance*
> *Emotional security and stability*
> *A centre in which to form relationship*
> *A shelter in the time of storm*
> *Roots and belonging*
> *A sense of identity*
> *Memories.*
> *– Anonymous*

As parents, we wanted our children to continue to grow and live as independently as they were able, and we were prepared to work to make that happen. Our Homes for Life group not only educated others, we educated ourselves.

One of our first initiatives was a day-long workshop called "Creative Living Options." We invited people from other communities to share different housing models, including cooperative housing, shared accommodation and semi-independent living. At the end of the day, one mother summed it up best: "We are only limited by our own thinking. If we open our minds and have a vision, the possibilities are endless."

We all need a role model, and Jean Vanier was mine. As the son of a Governor General, he could have led a life of privilege but instead, he chose to live with adults with severe disabilities. In his book, *On Becoming Human*, he wrote, "To be human is to be bonded together, each with our own weaknesses and strengths, because we need each other."

Vanier saw the similarities between young children and many people with intellectual disabilities, in their capacity to accept others as they are. Through his spiritual lens, he saw the gifts people with disabilities have to offer. "Though they are less capable in some ways, many are endowed with simple, loving and trusting hearts. They show a path to love rather than power. They are often filled with a joie de vivre, which attracts and opens hearts and brings joy. Their cry is for a simple faithful relationship."

This described Paul, whose heart shone when he was with people who loved him. "*When Granpa Lloyd, Granma Jo come an visit?*" he would ask. That gave Murray the nudge he needed to invite his parents over.

The moment Paul saw them at the front door, he would call out, "*Hi Granpa Lloyd! Hi Granma Jo!*" By the time they got to the top of the stairs, he would be waving his arms, saying, "*Come sit living room.*" Paul still liked it best when everyone was settled, so he could "*listen to the talking.*"

Paul's acceptance of others fit the description I once heard of a nourishing person: someone whose face lights up when you enter the room, with no ideas for your improvement. Our friend Judy put Paul in that category. When she came to visit, Paul's face would break into a wide grin, and he'd call out her two-syllable name in four, "*Hi Joo- oo-de- ee!!*"

"I love Paul's greetings," she said. "He makes me feel like I'm the most special person in the world."

In my quest to find out how to build an inclusive community, I arranged to visit the L'Arche Daybreak community near Toronto. It's one of more than 100 L'Arche communities around the world, where individuals with disabilities live, work and share their lives with people without disabilities. At L'Arche, the contributions of each person are recognized, valued and celebrated, and real communities develop.

"What happens when we start becoming attentive to the weak?" Jean Vanier asks in *Finding Peace*. "We begin to accept our own weakness. We discover that there are a lot of things we can't do, that we need others! We begin to build community. We can then cry out, I need help – from my friends, my family, my faith, my God, my community and others."

At the time, I thought L'Arche would be the ideal place for Paul to live, but they weren't expanding into new cities, so I borrowed one of their community-building ideas and formed a group called Faith, Fellowship and Food.

One Sunday evening a month, 16 to 20 individuals with intellectual disabilities and family members, gathered in our home for a time of fellowship and celebration with music and a pot luck meal. Murray sang and played the guitar, Paul loudly strummed his, while others jingled tambourines, shook maracas and sang. The volume increased significantly when it came to our favourite tune, *He's Got the Whole World in His Hands*.

As parents, we watched as the young people around us grew in confidence. Jeremy, who didn't talk much, was asked to say the blessing before dinner. Then he started to sit beside Jennifer, a young woman with autism who didn't talk at all. One night, Jeremy became very brave and reached over and held her hand. Kate talked about her upcoming role with Dream Players, and David shared a photo album of his early life. "Where's Jake?" someone asked about Paul's classmate with autism. No one knew, so I did a search of the house and found the six-foot teenager stretched out on our bed in the dark. There was only so much social stimulation he could take.

Our group met for two years before people started to drift away. At the same time, Murray had a serious accident in his workshop. He was cutting a piece of wood on his table-saw when the board kicked back. His hand slipped onto the spinning steel blade. In a fraction of a second, the third and fourth fingers on his left hand were severed above the knuckle.

It was horrific, especially for a carpenter; Murray's fingers could not be re-attached. His first thought was that he had ruined our lives, but by the following week he was able to say, "At least I still have my index finger. It's not too badly cut – I'll be able to hold onto to things." Murray spent the next several months working with occupational and physiotherapists until his recovery was complete, with one exception. He could no longer play one of his favourites, *Keep on the Sunny Side of Life.*

Murray and I had been married four years, and he was becoming used to life in the fast lane. "One thing for sure, it's never dull around here," he said, sipping his coffee one morning. "Come to think of it, I wouldn't mind dull from time to time." Before I met him, he'd enjoyed afternoon naps on the weekend, but those days were long gone.

Paul had been in the bathroom quite a while. I went down the hall to find him buzzing the electric toothbrush over the same four front teeth. I gazed at the reflection of his smooth, round face and soft, dimpled hands in the mirror. Even though he would be 17 in December, he could easily have passed for a 13-year-old. Murray's disposable razor lay on the counter, a reminder that before too long, Paul would have to put a blade against his face. Then it hit me: Paul had just four more years in school. It was time to get serious about planning for his future.

When I heard that our local Community Living Association was offering a workshop on "Supporting People with Disabilities to have a Meaningful Life," I immediately signed up. The female presenter, Darcy Elkes, was a straight-shooter. "Society de-values individuals with disabilities and casts them into menial roles where they will never achieve their potential," she told the group of agency staff and parents. "We all live up to the expectations placed on us, and people with disabilities are no exception. Often, the bar is set too low."

It made me think about Paul when he was 13, sitting at his school desk screwing tops on bottles and jars and then being asked to sort foam blocks by colour. No wonder he overturned his desk and went screaming out of the classroom and into the playground.

My mental flashback was interrupted by Darcy's next comment. "So often meaning in life comes from work, and it's important that individuals with disabilities have visible and valued roles in the community." She asked us to think of a role for an outgoing person with a disability, and someone mentioned a

Walmart greeter. Darcy wasn't impressed. "Just because someone is friendly doesn't mean that's the only thing they can be. Who are the Walmart greeters?" she asked. "They are often the elderly – another marginalized group."

Through photographs and stories, Darcy gave examples of people with severe disabilities who were working in jobs that matched their interests. She told us about one young woman who was obsessed with picking lint off the clothing of anyone she met. Someone turned this socially inappropriate behaviour into a positive role by helping the woman get a job in quality control inspection. A man who was severely disabled loved pizza from Pizza Hut. There were photos of his radiant smile as he worked in the kitchen of his local Pizza Hut. The store owner knew the man would get the job done with the help of his support worker. These jobs were possible because someone listened carefully to what each person wanted, and then provided the opportunity and support they needed.

I realized there were three things keeping Paul, and others like him, from achieving his potential: the attitude of others; lack of opportunities; and funds to hire support workers. As a society we have come to a greater understanding of the accommodation people with physical disabilities require – wheelchair ramps, elevators, sign language interpreters – individuals with intellectual disabilities are accommodated by the support of other people.

As the workshop progressed, we were divided into smaller discussion groups. Fortified by cups of coffee and stale donuts, our task was to think "outside the box" and brainstorm the possibilities for individuals we knew. On the second day, it was my turn to present Paul.

"So what makes him unique?" a woman across the table asked. I told the group about Paul's gifts: his ability to love others unconditionally, his welcoming nature, sense of humour, and a smile that could light up a room.

"What does Paul enjoy doing, does he have any interests?" someone else asked.

I opened the box of Magic Markers, inhaled the fruit-flavoured fumes, and listed the many interests Paul had developed over the years: riding in motor boats; watching jet skis and boats; playing car racing and motorcycle games; riding city buses; bowling; listening to music; playing his guitar and attending live music events; looking at books about insects and spiders; horseback riding; and anything to do with summer – swimming, walking and bicycling, canoeing, fishing.

We talked about Paul's abilities and his challenges, and then someone asked. "What does your son want?"

I thought carefully before responding. "I think the most important thing is for Paul to be accepted for who he is, and to be appreciated. He's really no different from the rest of us."

We started to brainstorm possible roles related to Paul's interests and gifts. We didn't evaluate whether or not he could manage the tasks, we were looking for possibilities, and they flowed: cleaning buses; a landscaping apprenticeship; playing his guitar in a cafe on open-mic nights; looking after maps at the Ministry of Natural Resources; working as a grounds-keeper at a golf course; serving breakfast as a volunteer; cooking breakfast at a neighbourhood coffee shop.

I was writing down all the ideas when a spirited woman piped up, "Why doesn't Paul apply for a summer job at the locks?" I raised my head. "That's a fantastic idea!"

The lakes, rivers and canals surrounding our city are connected by an extensive system of locks managed by Parks Canada, and every summer they hire students to work as Operating Assistants. It's a highly desirable job for any teenager; it pays well, it's by the water, has job status and a cool uniform. Plus, it isn't a stereotypical job for someone with a disability.

Paul had developed some good skills vacuuming in a nursing home, but there weren't many teenagers who would choose that environment. The role of a lock assistant, however, fit Darcy's description of a socially appropriate role for a teenager, plus it matched Paul's interests and his outgoing personality.

"I know I wouldn't have come up with this idea on my own," I told the group. "I needed your input to think outside the box and your encouragement to think big."

I downloaded a Government of Canada application form and put a check mark in the box that stated Paul had a disability. Then I asked three people who knew him well for letters of reference. His teacher commented on his work placements and recommended that, "Paul be given the opportunity to demonstrate his ability and good work ethic." Elaine, from BE Catering, stated, "As an employer, I have found that if supported and guided, Paul can learn a task and then accomplish it independently." Our friend Joanna made the case for hiring people with disabilities, and then said, "Paul's natural curiosity and cheerful personality have the capacity to enrich the experience of others."

When I gave the application package to the woman in Human Resources, she said, "A close friend of mine has a son with an acquired brain injury. I can appreciate what you are facing with Paul. I'll see that his application gets on the Human Resource manager's desk." I wanted to give her a hug.

A few weeks went by, and I hadn't heard anything, so I took a deep breath of courage and called the H.R. manager. He suggested I contact the supervisor for the Trent-Severn Waterway, Roger Stanley. The following week, I drove to his office, pleasantly situated beside a local lock.

"Sit down, sit down," he said, clearing off a chair in front of his desk. I warmed up to him right away; his dark curly hair and effortless grin made it easy. "Why don't you tell me a little bit about Paul?" he began.

I summarized Paul's strengths, mentioned his limitations, and assured Roger that if he hired Paul, a support worker would assist him complete all the required duties.

Then Roger told me a story I'll never forget. "When I was boy living on my father's farm near Orillia, young fellows from the nearby Huronia Centre used to help my dad on the farm. These guys would come with a long list of rules to follow and my dad broke every one of them." He paused, looked down and laughed at the memory. "I realized at an early age that if these guys had more opportunities, they could do a lot more with their lives. They just needed a chance."

The experience obviously shaped Roger's thinking because in the next breath he said, "So when can Paul start?"

I had to close my jaw before responding. "Don't you want to see him first? Paul, can sometimes have, umm, some behaviour issues."

Roger didn't hesitate. "No. I saw a picture of him in a Toronto Maple Leafs sweater and that's good enough for me. We're all hockey fans around here, especially for the Leafs. We need to hire more people with visible differences. You tell me when he can start and how many hours a week he can manage."

We agreed that Paul would work for two or three hours a day spread over four days.

"I'll have Paul start at the locks at Young's Point," Roger replied. "The lockmaster there is a terrific guy. If anyone can make this work, it's Bucky."

I reached my hand across the desk and vigorously pumped Roger's arm. "Thanks so much, this is great, just great!"

I'm pretty sure my feet weren't touching the floor when I left his office. An "*enormon*" – Paul's word for enormous – door had just been opened for him. I wondered how he would respond.

—⁓—

Three weeks later, all the summer students were called to a briefing session in Roger's office. Filled with anticipation, I drove Paul to the meeting. He got out of the car willingly, but when he saw the crowd inside the building he said, "*No, Paul's not going.*"

I tried coaxing him, but this time I knew it was no use. "Don't blow this Paul," I muttered. The swarm of bees returned to my chest.

While he stood beside the canal looking at the water, I kept a forced smile on my face – just in case anyone was looking at us. I wanted to appear that everything was fine, just fine. Once the meeting was over, Roger came outside. "So you didn't like my office, eh, Paul?" he said with a questioning look. "Everyone has gone now so why don't you come inside for a minute and I'll give you your uniform?"

Paul shuffled behind Roger like a kid who'd been called to the principal's office. On the counter were two pairs of dark green shorts, two cream-coloured shirts, two red t-shirts and a green cap with a red beaver and Canada embroidered on the front. For the first time, Paul lifted his eyes. He wasn't sure what a job at the locks meant, but he liked new clothes. This, he could relate to.

Paul was the first person with an intellectual disability to be hired by Parks Canada in this area. For him to be successful, he had to have the right support worker. Paul needed an ambassador who could relate well to the staff and to him. His teacher recommended Wayne, an Educational Assistant in Paul's class. He had an outgoing personality and a demonstrated knack for keeping Paul on track.

Everything was in place when the long-awaited morning came.

Paul put on the forest-green dress shorts with Velcro tabs I'd sewn on, so he could do them up himself, and the golf shirt with an embroidered red and white Canadian flag above the chest pocket and *Canada* on the sleeve. "You look so handsome, Paul," I told him with a catch in my voice. "Why don't you check yourself out in the bathroom mirror?"

He carefully placed the Parks Canada cap on his head and looked at himself in the mirror. A wide smile lit up his face. At that moment, I understood the relationship between a uniform and a person's self-image.

Just then, the doorbell rang. Paul ran down the stairs and flung the front door open. "*Hi, Wayne!*" he shouted.

"Hey, Paul, how's it going? Are you ready to start your new job?"

Paul turned his head sideways and looked at Wayne from the corner of his eye – he wasn't so sure.

"Come on, hop in my car and we'll talk about it on the way there," Wayne said before Paul had time to balk.

In spite of an accepting workplace and a competent support worker, Paul found the job challenging. Some mornings, he didn't want to go to work, and when he got there, he was afraid of the noisy generator in the lunch room and wouldn't put his lunch away. Then he became intimidated by the sound of the lawn tractor. "*Too lowe,*" he'd say.

Persistence was the key. Everyone kept encouraging him, and by the end of the summer, Paul was not only sitting on the lawn mower, he was driving it, with a little help from Wayne. Roger Stanley didn't make any distinction between Paul and the other summer students. He was paid the same as everyone else and expected to perform the same duties. He operated the locks, inspected the grounds, gathered up litter and cleaned the washrooms, toilets and all, by himself.

The local paper picked up the story. Bucky the lockmaster told the reporter he never ceased to be amazed at Paul's capabilities. "He can remember how to shut the pumps off, close the gates, and he's very, very polite to the boaters." Bucky and the other staff became Paul's natural support on the job, and Wayne, while present and responsible for Paul's safety, stepped aside to let that happen.

Paul loved greeting the public as they travelled through the locks. "*Goo-morneen boaters!*" he'd call out, even in the afternoon, waving his arms in an enthusiastic greeting.

When the reporter talked to Roger, he said, "Paul has exceeded all of our expectations. We had some concerns, and I didn't really know what to expect. Paul brings something, and I can't even put it into words, but whatever it is, I like it."

Roger told me he knew when Paul was at the lock without even seeing him. "The atmosphere is different – it's upbeat." Paul brought out the best in everyone and everyone brought out the best in him. He was treated as any other summer student, not as a kid with a disability. Paul began to shine. The next summer Parks Canada invited him back to work at the locks, and the summer after that, and the one after that. It wasn't long before the staff referred to Paul as a "canalie" – one of the guys.

—⁓—

Roger Stanley and Paul Buckner didn't know it, but they are community connectors – people who appreciate the gifts of others and understand how they can be shared. Unwittingly, they were supporting the work of John McKnight, the director of Community Studies at Northwestern University, to build strong, inclusive communities where the focus is on people's gifts and capabilities.

He believed that the biggest enemy of a strong community is naming members by their deficits and emptiness: developmentally disabled, welfare recipient, alcoholic, "identified" student, homeless person, and other pejorative terms. He advocated for the true meaning of hospitality – the welcoming of a stranger into our midst. Most people are wary of people they don't know, but John believed strangers are people who bring gifts from a place we haven't been. He quoted Yeats to illustrate his point. *There are no strangers here, just friends we haven't met.*

Paul was fortunate to be embraced by two authentic communities, the Trent Severn Waterway and Camp Wanakita. He continued at both places each summer, attending Wanakita through Reach for the Rainbow's volunteer work experience program where, in the words of a senior manager, "Paul's contributions and longstanding loyalty are well recognized." It seemed that everybody at camp knew him. A chorus of "Hi, Paul," could be heard from the assembled counsellors and campers when he arrived. "It just wouldn't be camp without Paul," a young counsellor told me one summer.

As soon as the school year was over, Paul would ask, "*When's camp Wannkita? Paul wants a go!*" As the date for his departure got closer, he began to imagine what he would do once he got there. "*Paul drive pontoon boat, do work checks. Drive crash boat. Go really fas!*"

"Aren't you supposed to work too?' I asked him.

Three Camp Wanakita counsellors sent him a birthday card. "Dear Paul," it read. "Thanks for all the smiles and good times you gave us. You were a blast to have in the cabin! We hope to see you next summer!!"

Paul's positive experiences at camp and at the locks became cumulative. Like climbing a ladder, each summer he placed his foot on a new rung and went a little higher. With the support and encouragement of those around him, Paul became more independent; he learned how to behave appropriately and, most importantly, to believe in himself.

He was rising to the expectations that were placed on him, and the view outside the confines of the disability box was starting to look pretty damn good.

PART THREE

PERSISTENCE

Paul and friends at Camp Wanakita, July 2007

THE IDEA OF INCLUSION DIDN'T COME NATURALLY TO ME; I had to learn it. During my childhood, people with differences were not visible in my school or community. I only knew of three people who had a disability. One was the son of an elderly neighbour, who lived in "a home" somewhere in the States. In the way children pick up nuance, I remember the tone in my mother's voice when she told me about him. It was hushed and tinged with "what a shame." The second was a boy who occasionally attended our church with his mother. When I recall his face, he probably had Down syndrome. During the service, he would wave his hands around and make grunting sounds. I envied him. The sermons were so long and boring, that's what I wanted to do too.

When I became a teenager, a friend of mine had a brother, Richie, who had Down syndrome. He couldn't talk very well, but he was kind and gentle, especially toward his sister. She died in a car accident at the age of 19, and when I visited her parents, Richie came over to me and stroked my arm. "You remind him of Sydney," his mother said. She smiled at me with such sadness. Eventually, Richie moved to a L'Arche community, where he surprised everyone by learning how to set the dinner table. Even though he had been well loved growing up, no one thought he could do much.

In 1968, the year I was leaving high school, Roger Stanley's father was welcoming young men from the Huronia Centre – Ontario's oldest institution for people with a developmental disability (originally called the Orillia Asylum for Idiots) – to the family farm. That year, the institution had 2,600 residents. "Put your child in an institution, it's the best thing for them," parents with disabled children were told in an Ontario government film titled *One on Every Street*. It reinforced the message that children with mental retardation "will always remain children and must be cared for as children for the rest of their lives."

In Ontario, the movement toward inclusive communities took

a giant step forward when the last institution for "the mentally retarded" closed its doors in 2009. It takes decades to change attitudes toward people who are different, and that only happens when people rise up in protest, as evidenced by the civil rights movement, the women's liberation movement, followed by the gay rights movement.

The aim of movements, I read recently, is to help the rest of us come to a new understanding of what is acceptable. Even though people with disabilities are not waving placards, increasingly they are claiming their rightful place as citizens in our communities. And that means belonging, inclusion, participation, security, community and being able to vote.

While John McKnight was encouraging communities to recognize and utilize the gifts of all individuals, Al Condeluci, from the University of Pittsburgh, was talking about the importance of relationships. According to him, "relationships are the most important thing we can help people with disabilities achieve." In academic jargon, this is called "social capital;" in layman's terms, it means how many friends do you have?

The "average" person has 150 friends – people they know, do things with and love. For someone with a disability, the average is 25, including family members. Researchers know that the more friends a person has, the better his or her life is going to be in terms of jobs, housing, transportation and opportunities.

They also know that relationships contribute to happiness, healthfulness and longevity. In other words, social capital equals a good, healthy life. As a parent, I wanted Paul to have the same thing every mother wants for her child, to be happy and to have friends. Unlike most mothers, I had to be intentional to ensure he had that, as well as the privileges of citizenship.

When charting new territory, we need role models for inspiration. I found mine in the life of Judith Snow, a woman who was born a quadriplegic and placed in a nursing home at a young age by her aging parents. She probably would have died there, if she hadn't been rescued by a Circle of Support. Judith is adamant that there is no excuse for segregation. She believes in striving for genuine communities, where differences are not only valued and seen to be good, but where we come to *depend* on each other's differences.

Throughout her life, Judith has had to fight just for the right to exist. She won that battle and went on to be the first person in Canada to receive government-mandated Individualized Funding for personal assistance. This allowed her to hire supporters, have her own apartment, earn a Master's degree, and become an artist, workshop leader, playwright and spokesperson for inclusion.

"Today, I have realized that structuring inclusion correctly can lead to world peace," she says. "This is very simply because, as we get better at including the multiple contributions inherent in diversity, we have less to be afraid of, or to resist."

Imagine what would happen to bullying in our schools and communities if we embraced Judith's attitude? If we could truly accept the perspective, insights, and the lessons that individuals with differences have to offer, we'd come to see difference as a source of communal strength.

Too often, we hear people talking about "us" and "them," as though people *without* visible differences get to decide if and when we will let *them* in. The first step to truly seeing each other as human beings is inclusive language. When talking about someone with a disability, the person, not their condition, needs to come first.

In speech or in print, it's better to say, " a boy living with autism" rather than "an autistic boy." It's a subtle distinction, but an important one: Paul is more than his disability – way more. A cartoon I saw illustrates the point. A boy asks a young fellow in a wheelchair, "So what do you prefer to be called? Handicapped? Disabled or physically challenged?"

The fellow in the wheelchair replies, "Joe would be fine."

—⁓—

The year Paul turned 18, I was asked to share his story at a Tuberous Sclerosis Association workshop for parents. I talked about Paul's interests, his experience at camp and his job at the locks, and then drew a Character Wheel and divided it into eight segments. Each one contained a role Paul performed: swimmer, music lover, guitar player, horseback rider, camper, lock operator, video gamer. The last segment contained the words Tuberous Sclerosis. "It's only one slice of the big picture," I told the parents. "Tuberous Sclerosis is what you have, it's not who you are."

In the workshop, I wanted parents to become inspired by Paul's story and think creatively about what their child could do. I wanted them to say to themselves, "If this guy can do it, then maybe my kid can too." The next day, I received a call from a mother who went home and told her daughter about Paul working at the locks. "You mean I could do something like that too?" asked her daughter. For the first time, this girl saw herself as having a future in spite of TS.

I wanted to leap through the phone and swing her in the air. Paul had shown her what is possible.

Students can stay in school until they're 21, but nobody does – unless you have an intellectual disability. Most teenagers can't wait to leave high school and get on with life: to start a job, become an apprentice, travel or head off to college or university. None of these was an option for Paul. What was waiting for him was an ominous black hole. And it was only two and a half years away.

Between camp and the locks, Paul currently had two months in the summer that were fun, stimulating and rewarding. But what would he do with the other 10 once school was over? I asked an LLS teacher what her students did, and she replied, "My job is to teach the students in the classroom." So I turned to the Co-op department, the people who connect students to the world of work, but they didn't deal with kids who were "low functioning."

I imagined Paul sitting at home, obsessively watching videos and driving us both nuts. The image filled me with dread, but it also propelled me into action. With the permission of his teacher, I arranged a work placement for Paul with the contract cleaning company at the Community College. The duties were a good fit, but the environment wasn't. Paul became overwhelmed by the crowds of noisy students as he tried to clean the front doors and main staircase, and the placement ended after one semester. The key to Paul's motivation was a work environment that included friendly people, but not hordes of them.

So I tried again. A new Sport and Wellness Centre had just opened adjacent to the College. It was a modern building with floor-to-ceiling windows; natural light flooded the spacious main floor entrance, fitness area and pool – an ideal location for a work placement.

The Centre was willing to take Paul as a placement student, but his school principal said they didn't have the staff to accompany him. He suggested we take the problem to the school board and the principal of Special Education. At the meeting, my request was simple. I wanted Paul to be given the same opportunity to prepare for life after school as every other high school student.

The principal of Special Ed thought for a moment and came up with a solution. She recommended that Paul and two other LLS students be given the placement opportunity, supervised by one Educational Assistant. It was a win-win situation with an added win: now three students had the chance to learn practical work and life skills outside the classroom.

On work placement days, Paul proudly wore his navy t-shirt with the Wellness Centre's white embossed logo on the chest. Without the large crowds around him, and with the supervision he needed, Paul happily squirted and polished windows, cleaned the gym floor with a three-foot-wide mop similar to the one he'd used at the university, then methodically placed bright orange and blue bottles of Gatorade in the pop machine.

He was guided by the maintenance supervisor, a man he affectionately referred to as "*Dan the man!*" Paul's favourite job was pushing the large industrial vacuum cleaner, which he called "*the Zamboni!*" When Paul talked about the "*Zamboni*" he could hardly contain himself. He'd pirouette on one foot and tilt his head to one side as though he could hear the hum of the motor. As his excitement built, he'd dance across the room, his arms and upper body jerking with glee like a robot doing the boogie-woogie. Paul had found his passion.

OUR HOMES FOR LIFE GROUP, or "Lifers," as we now called ourselves, enjoyed getting together; you could tell by the attendance; there were usually 20 of us gathered around the table. Murray never missed a monthly meeting and neither did most of the other dads. We shared a common purpose. We wanted our kids to become independent, and supported one another on the long, slow journey to get there.

Our group continued to invite guest speakers to explore a variety of topics, from Affordable Housing options, to developing Community Connections, to creating Lifetime Circles of Support. Other parents joined us to hear Gillian Chernets from Toronto talk about how she set up a Support Circle for her adult daughter. Prior to having a Circle, her daughter was like Paul, vulnerable and surrounded by paid people. "No one is paid to be part of a Support Circle," Gillian told us. "Members help a person make decisions about what matters to them and support their quest for a good life." She asked the parents in the room to sit back and think about the most important things in our lives. After reflecting on the question, we came up with a comprehensive list: family, health, security, freedom to make choices, peace, faith, making a meaningful contribution to society, independence and self-reliance.

Gillian congratulated us on our inventory, and then informed us that a good life for our son or daughter included all of these things. The room went silent. Everyone was thinking the same thing, "How on earth is that possible?"

She let us wrestle with this for a minute before acknowledging the task was so huge we couldn't possibly do it alone. We needed to invite others to work with us; we needed to create a Circle of Support for our son or daughter.

She encouraged us to think about who we could invite to become Circle members: friends, family members, neighbours, former teachers. We could include anyone who had created a bond with our sons or daughters and wanted to support their personal vision and goals.

"Their role in the Circle is to listen to what your son or daughter wants, and then help them achieve it," Gillian said. "When Circle members become engaged, they help solve the issues, whether they're big ones, like where does the person live, how can he or she make connections in the community and what advocacy do they need; or day-to-day concerns, such as how to overcome problems at school or on the job, help with developing relationships, or assistance with finances."

"My son spends so much time on his own," a man at the back of the room said, "can a Circle help with that?"

"Absolutely," Gillian replied. "Circle members not only support dreaming and visioning, they also look for occasions to celebrate, or just hang out together."

Then a mother beside me asked the question that was on everyone's mind. "Will anyone want to join my daughter's circle? I feel awkward approaching people."

Gillian was ready for that question too. "From my experience, there are people who want to help a family with a child with a disability, but they don't know how. Sometimes all you have to do is ask."

On the way home I turned to Murray, "So, what did you think of the session?"

"It all sounds fine, but who are you going to get to join a circle for Paul?" he said.

"I'm going to ask Sarah," I replied with more confidence than I felt.

She was looking after Paul that night, and when she asked us about the meeting, I took a deep breath and popped the question. "Would you consider being part of Paul's circle of support?"

Without hesitation she said, "Yes!"

"Really?"

"Of course," Sarah replied, as though the answer was obvious. "I love Paul."

I was taken aback, but I shouldn't have been. Gillian was right. Sometimes people are waiting to be asked, and sometimes those people are right in front of you.

Before I lost the energy Sarah had given me, I made a list of people to call: two friends of ours, a neighbour, two of Paul's young support workers, and a former teacher. Instead of feeling that I was imposing on people, I began the conversation by saying, "We are setting up a circle of support for Paul. Would you like the opportunity to participate?" By the end of the week, I had contacted six people, and to my amazement, no one turned me down.

Gillian had recommended Dave Hasbury as a facilitator for local Circles. He had a wealth of experience working with individuals who had been labelled and marginalized, plus he had a straightforward, unflappable nature. He agreed to steer Paul's transition ship.

Our first meeting was held on a clear winter evening in our living room. Each of us shared something about ourselves and how we knew Paul. The result was a colourful mosaic of "who is Paul" from six different perspectives. Dave then told the group, "Your role as Circle members is to help create spaces for Paul to fit into, because the world isn't designed for people like him. We have to pull together to help remove the barriers that exist for him."

Even though Paul knew everyone except Dave, he retreated to the kitchen to listen to his music. At first, I thought he was being rude, but then realized he was probably overwhelmed and confused about what was going on. His detachment illustrated Dave's next point.

"Relationships are essential for Paul's survival, and that's where you folks come in. Circle members can help him become more comfortable in new situations; you can approach others on Paul's behalf, advocate for him, or help solve problems, so that's it not always Mom doing it." That sounded good to me.

"Paul needs to tell us what he wants his life to look like," Dave said.

"That's going to be pretty difficult," I said. "He relates to things he can see and do. He doesn't think in abstract terms about his life."

"That's not a problem," Dave replied. "We're here to help Paul discover that. As Circle members, we serve as a listening post. We tune in and see Paul differently than the rest of the world does. We see him as a person who has something valuable to give to others."

The group agreed to meet every six weeks. By the third

meeting, Paul had inched his way into the room to take part in the discussion. We were talking about what he could do to expand his interests and relationships with kids his own age.

"Do you want to take the Outdoor Education class at school, where you could learn to canoe, cross-country ski and snowshoe?" I asked him.

He shook his head up and down affirmatively.

Dave then asked the group, "What would it take for Paul to be able to participate in this class?"

"He has to be able to swim eight lengths of the pool," I replied.

"So how can he be encouraged to do this?" Dave asked.

Since Paul was already taking swimming lessons, the group came up with five suggested activities to encourage him to swim farther. I took them to his swimming teacher, who worked on them for several months. But when it came time to put the canoes in the water, Paul wasn't swimming the required eight lengths, so he couldn't go on the field trip.

From the start, the idea of Paul taking a mainstream Outdoor Ed class hadn't worked. I had hoped it would be similar to camp, where he was encouraged by his peers and they benefited from his participation. But the course wasn't set up for kids like Paul. He had knocked on the door asking to be integrated, but no one had opened it and invited him in.

I THOUGHT I HAD LASSOED MY FEARS about Paul's future by making sure he had work placements and a Circle of Support. But fear is insidious. I had stiffness in my upper back and recurring digestive problems and was seeing a physiotherapist for a procedure called Integrated Manual Therapy, a form of body work designed to restore health to the whole body. With warm, healing hands, she gently tapped my heart centre, ribs and torso, "listening" for restrictions or disturbances of the circadian rhythms. When she reached my kidneys, her hands stopped.

"I feel something here," she said.

I felt something too; the area under her palms was pulsing. The sensation travelled up my body to my heart centre, and a wave of sadness flooded my chest. Tears streamed down my face.

"Your kidneys hold your fear," she said, gently picking up my hand. "Breathe deeply and take your time to let it out."

With relief, my tears flowed. Fear and uncertainty about Paul's future had been part of my thoughts for the past 19 years. "Will his seizures ever be controlled? Will they cause even more brain damage? Will Paul have friends? Will his behaviour ever be acceptable? Will he be safe?" And now the one that was twisting inside me: "What will happen to Paul after high school?"

Even though I thought I had that one under control, my body knew differently. The therapist's touch had helped to loosen fear's grip on me, at least for now.

The experience left me emotionally spent, so I decided to go for a walk on a trail near the river. As I walked, I thought about the fears Paul had experienced since infancy and wondered about their cumulative effect.

After his skull fracture at birth, he was airlifted to Sick Kids in what must have been a terrifyingly loud helicopter; unpredictable seizure activity fired electrical impulses through his brain day and night; and frightening medical procedures had been imposed on him since birth. No wonder loud unexpected noises, like the fire bell at school, or the high-pitched wail of an ambulance, frightened him. No wonder he had behaviour problems.

I stopped at a bend in the river and recalled the trip Murray, Paul and I had taken to Skaneateles (pronounced skinny-atlas) in the Finger Lakes district of New York State a few years earlier, an experience that stayed with Paul in a way I could not have predicted. We travelled to meet some friends, and by coincidence, there was an antique boat show at the waterfront. On our first afternoon there, we walked down a long narrow pedestrian wharf to check out the highly polished mahogany and brass boats on display. Without warning, a commanding voice blared over the loudspeaker beside Paul.

"Will all show participants please report to the registration booth?"

Paul froze. I looked at the frightened expression in his eyes and quickly took his arm. "Come on, let's go back." His feet remained welded to the wharf.

"It's OK now. The man's voice is over. We can go," I said, pulling gently on his arm, but he wouldn't budge.

Murray got on the other side of him, and the two of us nudged and half-dragged Paul's body forward until his feet were safely on the grass. He was somewhat mollified, but his eyes kept darting around until we left the area entirely.

Paul couldn't get the experience out of his head. Out of the blue, he'd announce, "*No speaker!*"

"Of course not," I'd reply. "That was months ago."

He wouldn't stop talking about it, so I mentioned it to Toni, the psychologist, during one of our visits.

"Paul is stuck in that experience on the dock," she explained.

"But that was three months ago!"

"I know, but he hasn't been able to process his fear. You need to help him move on by apologizing for taking him there and reassuring him that you'll never do it again."

"Excuse me? I have to apologize? For taking him on a trip?" I could feel my eyes rolling.

"Yes."

"O.K. here goes. Hey, Paul, I'm really sorry I took you to Skaneateles and onto the dock with the speakers. I'll never do it again," I said trying to sound sincere.

"*Pardon Mawmmy?*" He looked at me intently.

When Paul really liked what he heard, he wanted to hear it again. And he really liked that I was apologizing to him.

Toni was wearing her no-nonsense professional look, so I repeated my mea culpa.

"*No more boat dock. No more speaker. Never again, Mawmmy.*" Paul repeated.

"That's right Paul, never, ever again!" And this time I really meant what I said.

Paul sighed and his face broadened into a wide smile. His mother had just apologized to him; life didn't get much better than that. He had processed his fear and never talked about "*Skinny atlas*" again, unless it was with a mischievous grin.

As I left the trail and slowly walked back to my car, I realized that on the inside, Paul and I were the same. Both of us had experienced and suppressed a lot of fear over the years and fortunately, each of us had received the help we needed to release it. I thought about all the people with intellectual disabilities who have unresolved fears and negative emotions; who was helping them?

—∞—

At home, there was a message on the phone from one of Paul's Circle members asking me how I was. I wasn't facing the future alone. Paul's Circle not only supported him, it also supported me.

A meeting was scheduled for later that week to do some serious planning for Paul's final year in school. Our facilitator, Dave, began by saying we were going to identify the things Paul loved to do by using a graphic process called a MAP.

We mounted a large sheet of newsprint on the living room wall, and then Paul handed Dave his box of magic markers. Every time someone came up with an idea, Dave pulled out a coloured marker and captured it graphically. Before long, the sheet was covered with images – a lawnmower, four-wheeler, motor boat, bus, guitar, tuba, car wash, swimmer, and the billowing cheeks of the wind with "Dad's place" written beside it.

Paul was still seeing his dad, but John's declining health meant the visits were unpredictable. He had had prostate cancer surgery the year before, and the radiation treatments left him weak and debilitated. Now he was having problems with his kidneys, never a good sign for someone with diabetes. I looked over at Paul. At the mention of his dad's poor health, he got up and left the room.

"Okay," Dave said, "Now that we're clear on what Paul loves to do, I want you to try and imagine what his day will look like when he is no longer in school."

"What will happen to his life, and to mine," I thought in a moment of panic. It was interrupted by the sound of Dave's magic marker squeaking across the newsprint. Paul had come back into the room and was watching Circle members talk and gesture to one another. Joanna suggested Paul could have two or three little jobs outdoors from May to October, and then others tossed out ideas of things he could do: gardening, raking, mowing lawns or garbage pick-up. I was thinking about all those possibilities when Sarah made a comment that grabbed everyone's attention. "I imagine Paul taking the bus to and from work."

I was incredulous. Paul wouldn't even go into the mall – he'd screech to a halt at the door – and now we were talking about him taking the bus, by himself, to a job. "How could that ever happen?" I asked myself. "Don't these folks know how much trouble Paul has coping in new situations?"

Then I realized that Paul's Circle wasn't limited by having to live with him. They saw him differently than I did, and they were on a roll. They continued to generate ideas about the things Paul could do during the winter months: recycling, vacuuming, working at the bus station, a marina, a music store or a movie theatre. I was so grateful I hadn't interrupted the flow of suggestions with my motherly "yes, buts."

Dave continued to illustrate all the ideas until Paul's MAP was finished. "The first step in all of this is for Paul to learn to be in control of his life, so he can be in the world with greater confidence," he said.

"That's a tall order," I replied, unable to keep quiet any longer. "Paul has developed 'learned helplessness,' which he perfected in school and at home. At times, the expectations on him have been too low, and everyone has done things for him. He bats his big blue eyes and convinces everyone that he is helpless."

Paul gave me one of his sideways looks. He knew exactly what I was talking about.

"Can anyone in the Circle help Paul with that?" Dave asked.

"Sarah, Joel and I can," Pam piped up. "Right, guys?"

Paul was fortunate to have three young people in his life whose role as support workers had morphed into friendship. Dave knew they could influence Paul's behaviour more than any adult. He asked them to encourage Paul to try new things, make his own choices and then stay with his choice.

"Hey, Paul, I have an idea," Pam said as she turned to Paul. "Do you want us to help you organize a cruise boat ride and barbeque with your friends?"

Paul's face lit up. "*Yes Paaam!*"

"Then we'll do it. It will be your first party, and we'll help you plan it."

We had accomplished more than I could have imagined possible. "When do you want to meet again as a group?" Dave asked.

"Let's plan our next get together around Paul's 20th birthday," Catherine said.

"Oh good," Murray piped up, "another excuse to drink champagne!"

YEARS EARLIER, Elaine our young neighbour, had made the comment, "Paul is as strong as his supporters." That was truer now than ever. Paul's independence – his future – depended on good people to support him, and that cost money. The Ministry of Community and Social Services held the purse, and it was up to parents to figure out how to loosen the strings. It wasn't clear how the system worked; some individuals with a disability received a good deal of funding, while others with similar needs received very little.

I had heard about Individualized Funding from Judith Snow and others, and it made sense. When government funds flow directly to individuals, they are able to hire support workers to meet their needs. As a result, they become less reliant on the generic services of agencies, where one program fits all, and they are better equipped to become participating citizens in their communities, with the rights and responsibilities that entails. Paul currently received money to pay for 8 hours of support a week. When he left school, he'd need support for 53 hours a week.

I started applying for Individualized Funding two years before Paul had to leave school. I was hedging my bets. If he got the support money he needed, he could leave the year he turned 20; if not, he could stay in school another year. Throughout Paul's life, I followed my mother's advice and saw him as a whole person, with strengths as well as limitations. Now, in order for him to get the support he needed, I had to emphasize his deficits and describe all the things he couldn't do.

I spent hours preparing a six-page summary of Paul's medical history, his cognitive limitations, communication and behaviour problems, and his need for structure. On the last page, I outlined his goals, which could be attained with adequate support. I included Paul's student profile from the Board of Education which placed him in the "ISA 3 High Cost Needs category" for students with "a severe level of general intellectual disability: those students who had great difficulty with impulse control; severely limited means of communication; extreme difficulty with social interaction, complex multiple needs; intensive support required in out-of-school settings as well as in school."

This was documented evidence which, in a rational world, would justify Paul's support requirements once he left school. But I was dealing with a bureaucracy. My request for funding was turned down.

I appealed the decision, reiterating Paul's complex needs and our desire that he be allowed to move forward with his life. The appeal was denied, and Paul remained in school.

Knowing that Paul could stay in school another year kept me from losing it – I still had some time. A local agency agreed to conduct an in-depth assessment of Paul's independent living skills, which took several months to complete. When it was done, they came up with over 200 things Paul couldn't do. It was so frustrating: I could have told them in 20 minutes what he *couldn't* do. He couldn't read or write, do up buttons or tie shoe laces, let alone screw in a light bulb or operate a fire extinguisher. As a parent, I wanted an objective opinion of what he was *capable* of doing or learning.

It was late November, and the approaching darkness of winter mirrored the panic creeping around the edges of my heart. The church was offering a meditation series for the season of Advent, and there I found the reassurance I was looking for. On the third night, the minister said to us, "What is the deepest desire of your heart?" He gave us a few minutes to write down our answers and then said, "God will come to meet you there."

"I want Paul to have a place in the community and a meaningful life," I wrote. Then I prayed, "May people continue to come into Paul's life to help him become all that he can be." It's a petition that has stayed with me to this day.

I thought about the people in Paul's Circle. Not only did they care deeply for him, they were there to help us solve problems that otherwise would have been overwhelming. We were not alone on any front.

With renewed courage, I faced the fact that in eight months Paul would be out of school. If he was to have a meaningful life, he required support workers. There is nothing more demoralizing than having to beg for your child. And that is exactly what I did. In a strongly worded letter, I made another plea to the Ministry of Social Services:

> Since the age of five, Paul has become dependent on one-on-one Educational Assistants. The current ratio in his class is five staff to eight students. Even though Paul's needs have been acknowledged within the school system, once school ends he is being set adrift with minimal supports. Based on my experience, his boredom and loneliness will lead to frustration and then aggression toward his primary caregiver – me. Paul cannot be left alone and I do not believe that I will be able to cope with Paul's demands and his need for stimulation and activity, twenty-four hours a day, seven days a week.
>
> It does not seem right that Paul is being de-institutionalized but unlike people leaving institutions he does not have funding for his transition into the community. I have contacted local agencies for service and they have told me they have "few vacancies and limited activities." As Paul's mother I am filled with dread about what will happen to him if he doesn't receive the support he needs.

Members of Paul's Circle wrote letters outlining his needs, as did his teacher, and Dr. Robert Munn his neurologist, who said, "In a structured environment, Paul can be delightful. His quality of life is good and his sense of humour pervasive. To see Paul at his best, he cannot have any unstructured time. Certainly the cost of increasing Paul's funding will be far less than placing him in a group home (at a cost of over $60,000 per year) which undoubtedly would be a disaster for both Paul and his family."

The decision came a few weeks later, at the beginning of the New Year. Our request for funding was denied.

My life as I knew it was about to end. "What do I have to do?" I thought. "Chain myself to a government building?"

When I met the director of our Community Living Association at a meeting, he asked me how I was. "I feel like I am standing alone, naked in a large empty field," I replied.

He just looked at me, unable to respond.

—⁂—

Because I was working from home, my days and nights were filled with disability issues. I was either thinking about Paul or working on the Amigos high school program for kids with disabilities. I was beginning to feel like an elastic band that had been over-stretched. Later that spring, the elastic finally snapped.

At the beginning of the school year, I had made a point of mentioning to Paul's new teacher that I wanted him to attend the high school's graduation ceremony. The students in Learning and Life Skills traditionally had a small separate graduation and didn't attend the one for the entire school. This had been going on for years. Paul had been in high school for seven years and he'd done everything that was asked of him. He had earned the right to walk across the stage of his high school along with everyone else. Even though he would be getting a Certificate of Completion and not a diploma, it was his well-deserved rite of passage.

In late May, I hadn't heard anything about the ceremony, so I called the school office for details. "You're too late," the school secretary informed me. "The order for gowns has already gone in."

I felt my head explode.

"You mean to tell me that Paul isn't on the list for graduation?" I said, articulating each word carefully to keep from losing control.

"You'll have to talk to his teacher about that," she replied, as though I had asked her for a bus schedule.

Later that day, I discovered that Paul's new teacher forgot to tell the office he would be going to the graduation. My heart sank. Everyone had assumed that Paul and the kids in his class wouldn't be participating – that they wouldn't want to, or weren't capable.

Just when I thought I could stop being vigilant, I was hit from behind. It was more than a grad ceremony; to me it represented an attitude toward students in the LLS classes, who some people still regarded as "them."

Fortunately, a former teacher of Paul's worked with the committee and came up with a plan. The night of graduation, Paul would be near the front of the line with two other students from another LLS class. Once he walked across the stage and obtained his certificate, he would be led off – there was no way he could sit still for two hours. It was a perfect solution.

The big night finally came. Paul carefully put on his royal blue gown and waited at the beginning of the line. "Paul Tiller," a man's voice filled the auditorium. Paul lifted his head and walked onto the stage, pumping the air with his arms as he went. Halfway across, he turned to the crowd. His eyes were sparkling. There was clapping and cheering. The principal's hand reached out, Paul grasped it and then proudly waved his certificate in the air.

My son had taken his place with justifiable pride. It was one of the happiest moments of my life. It was also the last time the School Board allowed segregated graduation ceremonies. The Principal of Special Education saw to that.

THE FINAL SCHOOL BELL RANG FOR PAUL on June 29, 2006, the day before my 56th birthday. He was thrilled. He didn't dread his future; he took each day as it came and hoped it would be a good one. He had no idea how much effort I had put into making that happen.

In the morning, he announced. "*No more school bus. I gradgiated. I finish.*"

"That's right, Paul. You don't have to get on the school bus again."

"*Never again Mawmmy.*"

There weren't many 20-year-olds who still called their mother "Mawmmy," but most of the time it rolled over me. Sometimes, I confess, I tuned Paul out. Undeterred, when he wanted something, he'd start with "*Mawmmy,*" then turn Mom into three syllables, "*Maaammm.*" If that didn't work, he's resort to "*Lacinda!*" That always got my attention.

One of the things Paul asked me over and over again was, "*When's camp? Paul wantsa go Wanakita.*"

"In July, Paul, you only have to wait three more weeks," I replied. I was looking forward to it as much as he was.

It had been an unusually stressful year. In addition to the strain of Paul leaving school, Murray had suffered a ruptured appendix. Because it had been misdiagnosed, he required extensive surgery, and several months of medical care until he fully recovered.

On the "depletion scale," I scored a 10, and craved some time to stick myself back together. I found out about a remote yoga retreat centre that promised wholesome food, peace and tranquility. Mercifully, Murray agreed to take me there after we dropped Paul off at camp.

The week was sublime, there's no other word for it. I spent my days doing yoga, reading, walking the grounds, swimming and canoeing, with part of each day devoted to meditation and prayer. Eventually, the cobwebs of confusion started to lift.

I started thinking about a solution to Paul's support needs. As the week progressed, one idea kept emerging: we could convert the lower level of our house into an apartment, and a support worker could live there in exchange for reduced rent. Since we couldn't obtain funding to hire someone, perhaps we could barter for Paul's support. I hoped Murray would agree.

When he picked me up at the end of the week, I waited until we got home to present him with the idea. His love for Paul and me was evident; he not only agreed, he said he would do the renovation.

He set to work almost immediately, turning the alcove in the downstairs family room into a small, efficient kitchen with a built-in stove top, cupboards, apartment-sized fridge and tiled floor. Even though the renovations weren't complete, I started showing the apartment in late August. A lot of people liked it and most of them wanted it, with one caveat. They didn't want Paul to be part of the equation.

"Why am I doing this?" Murray asked, obviously frustrated. "I've put in all this time and money and we still don't have anyone to live here!"

"My intuition tells me it's the right thing to do," I replied. Murray trusted my instincts, and the work continued.

In September, we took the problem of how to find a suitable tenant to Paul's Circle. Catherine said she had some contacts at the university, and we began discussing where to place an ad, when Murray turned to Paul, who was sitting on the couch beside him.

"Paul, do you want to live in the apartment?" he asked, matter-of-factly. Without hesitation he said, "*Yes Murree!*"

There was a stunned silence. No one had thought of Paul living there, not yet anyway – maybe in three years, when the tenant could help Paul with the transition, but not now. He had just left school. In a matter of seconds, the idea started to register on people's faces. We had found the missing piece of the puzzle.

Everyone started talking at once. Paul was sitting cross-legged on the couch, with a look on his face that seemed to say, "*Finally, you guys figured this out!*"

Once the commotion subsided, Shelagh, Paul's former teacher asked him, "Do you want to move into the apartment in two weeks or in three weeks?"

"*Three weeks Sheelah!*"

"Then you and your Mom put a mark on the calendar every day until your move."

"*Ohh kay Sheelagh!*"

Paul marked off each day with a big X, but when the moving day came, he had second thoughts. He looked warily at his buddy Joel, who came to help move his furniture. As his mattress was going down the stairs, Paul shouted, "*No Joe, Paul doesn't wanna move!*"

Joel stopped in mid-flight, resting the mattress against his shoulder while Paul continued, "*No, Joe, no!*"

It would have been a disaster if Murray hadn't had his brain-wave. "Hey Paul, you can take your wind chimes to the apartment with you. Do you want to do that?"

He had a dozen wind chimes, mostly from the Dollar Store, across the top of his bedroom window. He raised his head. "*O.K. Murree!*" he said and started running down the hall to his old bedroom. We carried the chimes downstairs and re-mounted the display.

"How does that look?" Murray asked Paul. "*Goood!*"

The things that gave Paul comfort – his sound machine, wind chimes, green plastic fan and clock radio – were still in his bedroom. The only thing that had changed was their location.

It was too early in the day for champagne, so Joel, Murray and I toasted Paul in his new living room with raised glasses of ginger ale, while his favourite video, *Muppets in Space*, played in the background. Paul had just taken his first step toward independence, and it was a big one.

—m—

Paul was going on 21. Typical of people his age, he needed more distance from his mother, especially one like me who was good at telling him what to do. His move to his own living space was a move forward for all of us, but the benefits didn't happen right away; we still had some major hurdles to overcome. Paul no longer had a routine that filled his day, and he and I were starting to collide with regularity.

Over the past couple of years, I had attended many meetings to discuss Paul's transition from school and pulled out his Transition Plan to refresh my memory. I was taken aback: Paul was on no fewer than six waiting lists for daytime activities and service. But being on a list doesn't fill your day. It's like sitting at the bus terminal watching the buses leave and never going anywhere.

By mid-September, Paul was pacing around the house; there was nothing for him to do. Then the situation I had feared and tried so hard to prevent happened. Paul "lost it."

I was outside gardening when he found me. He must have been obsessing over a video that no longer worked because he came out of the door yelling and swearing at the top of his lungs. *"You stupid! Fuck you Mawmmy!"*

Horrified, I got him inside the house where his swearing and screaming continued.

"Stop it Paul, stop it!" I looked into his eyes, my hands on his shoulders.

It was to no avail; he spat in my face, hit me and pulled my hair. Paul was now almost as tall as I, and he was high on adrenalin. I knew a mother whose teenage son with Tuberous Sclerosis had rage attacks so violent, she was forced to call the police. At that moment, I understood why. Paul was out of control.

I went up the stairs, and he followed screaming, *"Shut up! Shhuuut up! Fuck you!"*

Upstairs, he went into the living room and began hitting his head with his right hand and throwing whatever he could get hold of with his left. Papers and magazines flew through the air. This had to stop. I approached Paul with an attempt to restrain him. He lay on the couch, raised his leg and kicked. The hard treads of his shoe hit the side of my face, and a sharp pain shot through my head. I slumped onto the couch and buried my head in my hands.

"Oh, Paul, what is going to become of us?" I cried out.

He stopped. He was physically spent; the rage attack was over. *"Sorry Mawmmy,"* he said weakly.

"Just leave me, alone Paul. For God's sake just leave me alone." I was in no mood to comfort my assailant, even if he was my son.

I wrote a letter to the agencies responsible for providing service to individuals with intellectual disabilities and included the School Board. I wanted to let them know that "the system" had failed us. In frustration, I told them a mother shouldn't have to be assaulted by her child in order to receive help.

"I am a mother. I am not a behaviour therapist, trainer, case manager or a special needs teacher," I wrote. "Those roles belong to you."

I received replies from each agency, a referral to a behavioural consultant, and $1,200 in crisis funding. I requested Non-Violent Crisis Intervention training, but was told that as a parent I wasn't eligible. Perhaps it didn't matter anymore. I had learned the hard way to stay a safe distance from Paul once his behaviour escalated.

I had paid a high personal price for the crisis money and wanted to spend it wisely. Murray and I decided Paul could benefit most from help with his morning routine, and Catherine from his Circle recommended Steve, a man who had experience working with challenging youth. His experience was needed. There were times when we cringed at breakfast as we listened to Paul swearing and throwing things against the walls of his apartment downstairs. Steve enjoyed a challenge; he never raised his voice, and he never gave up on his belief that Paul could learn to be independent. He had only been with us a few weeks when Paul said to him, "*Steve leave.*"

"Why is that, Paul?" he replied, more curious than offended.

In a rare display of insight Paul replied, "*It's too hard.*"

And it was hard. Paul had a list of 18 things he had to do in the morning, from the time he got up until his dishes were done. Steve and I sat down and listened to Paul. Then I photographed him performing the most important steps and put them into a small photo album titled *Paul's Morning Routine*. He could now see what was expected of him, and he started to feel good about completing each task.

Steve had raised his own son, and he treated Paul like a young man. Until now, the people in Paul's life, including Murray and me, had seen Paul as a boy. It was a big challenge for Paul to rise to the expectations a man was putting on him.

Steve would ask Paul matter-of-factly, "Do you want to be a mature adult or a little boy?"

"*Mature aadault.*" Paul replied.

"Then start acting like one!"

"*Yes Steve Lynch!*"

The crisis money we used for Steve's morning hours was running out, so I wrote to our local MPP about Paul's semi-independent living arrangement and his need for personal care. As a result, Paul was approved to have a Red Cross homemaker come in the morning to supervise his personal hygiene and dispense his medication. I was simultaneously grateful and taken aback; I wasn't used to getting a positive response after writing just one letter.

To solve the daytime support problem, we used some of Paul's disability pension, as a temporary measure, to employ Steve for a few hours a week. We also hired Jeff, a young man who took on the difficult task of helping Paul learn how to function without school to structure his life. One afternoon, I watched Paul and Jeff walk up the driveway, and I could tell from the expression on Jeff's face that their trip downtown had not gone well.

"Paul decided to run ahead of me down the street," he told me. "I asked him repeatedly to slow down and he replied 'no' and just ran further ahead. When he got to the intersection, he didn't stop or look, but instead ran across the street. When I caught up with him, he was at the bus stop laughing, thinking it was a funny game."

I turned to Paul with the look that only a mother can give. "You could have been hurt! You have to listen to Jeff!"

"*Sorry.*"

Paul wasn't really sorry, because the following week, Jeff had problems with him again. "We had a snack at Tim Horton's, and when we were walking down the street, Paul began having a major laughing outburst. He was laughing and banging on signs, poles and mailboxes on our way to the grocery store. He ran into the store and right behind the checkout, where he continued to laugh hysterically. Fortunately, the cashier knew him and asked him to settle down." Jeff was understandably frustrated.

Paul was testing the limits and it reminded me of the game Red Rover; his supporters and I had to hold firm to keep him from breaking through, for his sake.

I told Jeff that Paul had been in an equally defiant mood the day he and I went into the drugstore for his pills. As soon as he got inside, he dashed behind the dispensing counter, laughing and waving his arms around, refusing to come out. The pharmacist didn't think it was the least bit funny. "Get out!" he said sternly, pointing to the door.

"You have to be strong to work with Paul," I said to Jeff. "And able to withstand embarrassment," I said to myself.

For his entire life, Paul had been in a structured environment that looked after his needs, and he was struggling with the demands that were being placed on him. All of us wanted to help him make the transition to adulthood, but ultimately, Paul had to do it himself.

THEN SOMETHING SERENDIPITOUS HAPPENED that would enhance
Paul's life in a way I couldn't have planned, organized or charted.
And of all places, it happened at the mall. Paul and I were at the
food court ordering some Manhattan Fries, when I spotted John
Perkins, a man I hadn't seen for years. He was sitting by himself, so
I asked if Paul and I could join him. He was pleased and started
showing us photos of his daughter, who was teaching overseas. This
was the first time John had met Paul, and I was impressed by his
ability to draw my son into the conversation.

"John, have you ever thought of working with people with
special needs?" I asked him after we had talked for some time.

"No, I haven't," he replied. "It's never really occurred to me."

"Well, you're a natural. Your ability to relate to Paul is
amazing."

We parted company that day and our paths might not have
crossed again, if I hadn't had my "bright idea."

Since the beginning of time, I had taken Paul to weekly
swimming lessons, and I was sick of it. I was tired of the struggle in
the family change room, a cramped, awkward space with metal
cubicles that reverberated at the slightest touch. The space was so
small that Paul's vocalizations bounced off the walls and ceiling. It
was like being in an echo chamber with a monkey.

As I drove home one afternoon, with my ears still ringing, my
bright idea hit me. I'd ask John if he would be interested in taking
Paul to his swimming lessons. The worst thing he could say was,
"No," and I could handle that.

His reply was heart-warming. "Well, Lucinda, it's interesting
you should ask. My daughter Amy was a member of the Trent Swim
Club, and I spent a lot of time at that pool. I'd be pleased to take
Paul to his lessons."

"Thanks very much," I replied, trying not to sound desperately
relieved.

For two years, John took Paul swimming, but his involvement

didn't end when the lessons did. The two of them became good friends, and seven years later, they continue to see each other every Thursday afternoon, to do errands and indulge Paul with *"an ice cap anna Boston creeem!"* at Tim Hortons.

"We're always running into people who know Paul," John said. Then he started to laugh. "He knows so many people in this town, he could run for mayor!"

Not only did John become an integral part of the Circle of Support, he became a close male friend when Paul needed it most. And to think, it all began with a chance encounter at the mall. Or was it?

Each positive experience in Paul's life built on the one before. He no longer complained about his morning routine; in fact, we found out he liked his apartment more than he could verbalize. Because Paul's living room used to be our family room, our television was still there, and occasionally Murray and I would go downstairs and watch it after Paul was in bed. He never complained or came out of his bedroom, so we thought he didn't mind. Then he refused to sleep in his bedroom, saying *"Paul sleep on a couch."*

"Why do you want to sleep out here when you have a nice, comfortable bed," I'd ask him.

He would just look at me.

This went on for several weeks. The only time Paul would sleep in his own bed was when Sarah looked after him. "That's odd," I thought. "If he can go to bed for her, then there isn't anything in his bedroom that's bothering him." Then it finally dawned on me. Paul's bedroom wasn't the problem, Murray and I were. As soon as we bought our own television and put it upstairs, Paul never slept on the couch again.

Around this time, the provincial government introduced a new program designed to give young people with disabilities a "Passport" into life in their community. The parents of teenagers and young adults with disabilities were encouraged to apply for funding and there was a buzz of excitement in our community: the government had finally listened to the concerns of families and was responding. This program would provide Paul with the funding he needed to lead a meaningful and independent life. I spent hours preparing the application, outlining his goals, the activities that would flow from them, and the impact it would make in his life. I explained what he had accomplished and expanded on what adequate funding would mean to him. It was tight, clear and the best I could do.

I took a breath and waited.

Paul had been out of school for five months when the letter from the Ministry arrived. I inhaled deeply and slit it open. It read, "I regret to inform you that we cannot provide you with support from Passport at this time. However, your application will be kept on file and considered once additional funding becomes available." "Shit!" It was the first and only word that came to mind.

My consolation was that most families who applied from our area were turned down. A pall descended on our disability community. I wanted to stand in the legislature and scream, "Don't you realize how hard it is to raise a child with a disability? How dare you cast us and our kids aside?"

The government had encouraged all of us to apply to a program that wasn't adequately funded. Why did they do that? Did they want to measure the need that existed in communities across the province so they could budget for the future? Or did they want to raise the hopes of struggling parents so they could smash them to smithereens?

Members of Paul's Circle signed a collective letter of appeal to our local MPP, the Minister responsible for Developmental Services, and Members of the Opposition. We weren't sure if our letters would make a difference, but it was better than doing nothing.

I re-submitted my annual request for Individualized Funding. I knew there was money in the system, and I believed Paul deserved it as much as anyone. Six weeks after we had been rejected by the Passports program, another government letter came in the mail. In a rush, I opened the envelope with my index finger, giving myself a paper cut. I pressed my finger against my lips and tentatively withdrew the letter. It was from the Ministry that provided Paul with funding for eight hours of support a week. They had just increased Paul's weekly allotment to sixteen hours.

"Hallelujah!" I cried out, waving the letter above my head. It wasn't all I had asked for, but it was a step in the right direction. Finally.

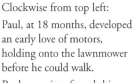

Clockwise from top left:

Paul, at 18 months, developed an early love of motors, holding onto the lawnmower before he could walk.

Paul, age nine, found this "green lawmore" in a friend's garage.

At 2½ Paul "drives" an ATV. It sparked a passion that continues to this day.

Paul, in 2009, graduated to the John Deere. Here he rides with fellow Parks Canada employee, Tim.

No matter what the season Paul, age six, is in our backyard "cutty grass."

Clockwise from top:

Paul and Luncinda taking a ride on the Otonabee River in the summer of 1995.

Paul's first canoe ride at the cottage when he was six months old.

At four years of age Paul was happiest when he was in a fishing boat so he could see the motor.

Top to bottom:

Fall cleanup at Camp Wanakita, October 2012. Paul is taking the Johnson for a final spin.

"I did it!" On Paul's first winter holiday in March 2013, he was brave enough to ride on a much-loved Ski-jet with a friend.

Left page clockwise from top left:
Steroid injections turned Paul into the "Michelin Tire baby".

Paul's godmother "Dee-Dee" with Paul aged three. Diane died of cancer in May 1998.

Paul enjoys his second birthday with his grandparents Conrad and Margaret Hage.

Paul, his dad and "Annie" in 1992; the summer of our 20th wedding anniversary.

Elaine, Paul's first babysitter and good friend, now has two daughters of her own.

This page top to bottom:
Paul loved the "puter" in senior kindergarten.

Paul, 19, with his video cover and our dear friend Joanna.

Paul, 23, enjoys being with was with all three of his cousins: Claire, Caroline and Laura.

Sarah helped Paul organize a party when he was 19; a boat cruise followed by an Hawaiian BBQ. His friend David loves karaoke.

From top to bottom:

On Paul's 20th birthday Murray helps him pop the cork.

Paul, aged 21, is at the city bus terminal. He is waiting for the 9:20 bus, map in hand.

From an early age Paul loved music. He plays his own guitar with open tuning.

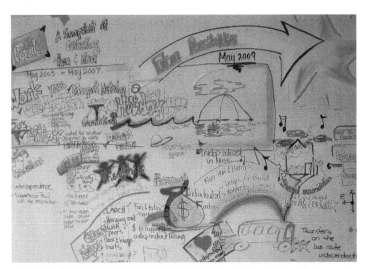

Clockwise from the top:

Paul's MAP and PATH graphically illustrates what he had been doing in 2005 – 2007 as well as where he wanted to be in May 2009. He accomplished it all.

Paul cleaned the washrooms for ten summers as part of his job with Parks Canada.

Paul proudly vacuums the hallways of the Holiday Inn in the fall of 2013.

Paul loved his work placement at the Sport and Wellness Center with "Dan the Man."

Clockwise from top left:

Paul was four and a half in June 1990, the summer his grandfather died.

A hot day on the dock at Camp Wanakita in 2011 – where Paul is one of the guys.

Paul moves into his own apartment on March 5, 2010. Independence Day!

Paul celebrates his 28th birthday in Toronto with his cousin Laura and her husband Laurence.

Our Homes for Life group had gathered on many occasions to look at how our sons and daughters could be more connected and contribute to our community. It was a new way of thinking for many. Traditionally, people with disabilities were grouped together into "day programs" or group activities, as though everyone was the same. Now that Paul had some funding, we had a chance to put the plan we had been working on into action.

Murray and I had examined ways to increase relationships for Paul and enhance his participation in the community. We had made a list of the significant people in his life, along with his gifts, strengths, what motivated him, and when he was happiest; and then we identified organizations that might welcome him.

One of those places was the breakfast program at the Salvation Army. Now that we had some funding for a supporter, the connection was made and Steve started taking Paul to the community breakfast at 7:00 every Friday morning, where Paul set tables, served breakfast and did the dishes. Steve played an important role in helping Paul relate to the other volunteers, and before long, one of the men, who wouldn't even look at Paul at first, started talking and joking with him, just like everyone else did.

Paul's world was starting to expand. Jeff supported him doing volunteer work at the YMCA, where he cleaned the men's lockers and wiped down the exercise machines. Afterward, they had lunch at a neighbourhood *"Coshsee Shop"* with the hope that, in time, "everyone there would know Paul's name."

He continued to operate the "Zamboni" at the Wellness Centre, and with Steve's assistance, he started to help his friend Matt lift weights. Matt uses a wheelchair, and this was the first time Paul was able to give a helping hand, rather than receive one. On Wednesdays, he connected with friends at a communal kitchen, where they learned how to share the tasks of cooking and cleaning up. *"Look I show you,"* he would say when he opened the packet of food he had prepared.

At home, we started to reap the benefits of Paul having his own space. Now his support workers worked with him in his apartment, instead of in my kitchen, and Murray and I finally had more privacy. Paul's life was coming together, and as a result, his aggressive outbursts began to disappear, and so did my disturbing dreams.

Paul was not only connecting to his community, he was also learning how to live more independently. For a few hours each week, agency staff helped him buy groceries for his breakfasts and lunches, do his banking and learn to clean his apartment. Paul knew how to clean bathrooms from his job at the locks, and he had experience vacuuming at work placements, so with the help of pictures and some prompting, he cleaned, vacuumed, dusted and did his dishes.

I was learning too. I observed that one young woman never told Paul what to do; instead she asked Paul to think for himself. If he said, "*Kimberly whats next?*" she would reply, "Look at your pictures and tell me."

"*What are we doing after?*" was his favourite question.

"What do you want to do when you're finished, Paul?"

"*Go to Tim's!*" You could put money on that response.

Paul was volunteering for three different organizations, where he learned valuable skills and developed good work habits; nevertheless, I held onto my dream that he would have a job. If Parks Canada saw Paul as a valuable employee, then there must be someone else who would hire him. In his book *Synchronicity: The Inner Path of Leadership*, Joseph Jaworski makes the point that we don't have to be bound by conventional ways of seeing the world; we can literally choose the kind of community and world we want to live in. "Our world, our communities, our organizations will change, only if we change," he wrote. One way to make that happen was to have individuals like Paul in valued and visible roles.

In my "leave no stone unturned" approach, I arranged for us to meet with a career counsellor at a government-sponsored vocational program. At our first meeting, I gave her a fact sheet titled: "What others have said about Paul Tiller." It included colour photos of Paul performing a variety of tasks and comments from his supervisor at Parks Canada, a former teacher, and staff at the Wellness Centre. They noted his positive attitude toward work, his contribution to the workplace, and the impact of his engaging personality. This was evidence of what Paul could do.

Sharon, the vocational counsellor had a positive attitude and she saw Paul, not as a young man with limiting disabilities, but as someone who wanted to be included in his community. She looked over the fact sheet carefully, asked about his experience and then said with confidence, "I think Paul deserves a chance to be employed." She "got it." And so much faster than most.

Sharon recorded Paul's work history, his strengths, the barriers he faced and his needs, and put all the information into an application for a federal government youth employment program. If his application was approved, a wage subsidy would provide him "with an equal opportunity to transition into paid employment in an appropriate work environment." Since the approval process would take some time, she suggested that Paul find a volunteer position that had the potential to become a job.

This was a topic at Paul's next Circle meeting, and members came up with a list of possible work locations: Parks Canada; a long-term care facility; cleaning city buses; groundskeeper at a golf course; an animal shelter; Alumni House at the university; a delivery business; the performing arts centre; taking orders and delivering sandwiches for BE Catering; a grocery store; contract cleaning in malls, apartments or institutions; the Wellness Centre; the YMCA. I thought it would be fairly straightforward for Paul to move from being a volunteer to a potential employee, but I should have learned by now that nothing in the disability field is straightforward. We ran into union issues, lack of available positions and unanswered phone calls. I was under the misguided impression that doors would fly open for Paul when, in reality, we couldn't even pry them open. By December, we decided to suspend the pursuit of work-related activities and focus instead on Paul's 21st birthday.

"Do you want to have champagne at your birthday party?" I asked him rhetorically.

"*Yes prease Lacinda!!*" Paul associated popping a cork with a good time and he wasn't disappointed. His young friends came and played their guitars; Judy gave him a painting she did of a city bus; there was chocolate cake and glasses raised to a chorus of "Happy Birthday, Paul."

The event gave rise to my new motto: Misery comes unbidden, celebrate whenever possible!

"WHAT TIME IS THE 9:20 BUS?" Paul had been asking this question
for years. What I think he really wanted to know is: what am I doing
today, who is supporting me, how am I getting to the bus, and what
do I need to do to get ready? "What time is the 9:20 bus?"
represented these questions and so much more. Life began when he
got on that bus.

Paul loves everything about city buses, the rumbling sound the
motor makes and the feeling of independence when he rides the bus
all by himself. He had been doing it for two months and nothing
went wrong – until one wet day in March.

I'd driven him to the bus terminal, and waited out of sight as
he took his place in line under the sign for the # 6 Kawartha bus. It
would take him to the Wellness Center where he was meeting his
friends for a swim. It began to rain and Paul clutched his bus map
close to keep it dry. He was still carrying it with him everywhere.
He had folded it over so many times it looked like a beat-up piece
of paper. You'd never know by looking at it, how important Paul's
bus map is to him; that it helps him feel connected to his
community.

I watched as he jiggled impatiently from one foot to the next
until the driver came and opened the doors. Paul pulled his wallet
out of his pocket, showed the driver his bus pass, then made his way
to the back of the bus where he slid onto a backward facing seat. I've
asked him repeatedly to sit at the front so he doesn't miss his stop,
but he pays no attention. For years he had to sit at the front of the
school bus so kids wouldn't tease him, and now he's going to sit
where he wants.

Satisfied that Paul was on his way, I left for a meeting at one of
the high schools. When I returned home there was a message from
Kim, Paul's supporter, asking me to call. She told me Paul didn't
arrive at the Wellness Center on the 9:20 bus after all. She waited for
the second bus to appear 40 minutes later, and when Paul wasn't on
it, she had the driver radio the bus terminal to find out if anyone had
seen him.

"Tell them to look for a young guy holding a bus map. His name is Paul," she'd said. Within minutes Kim got the good news. Paul was standing patiently under the sign for the # 6 Kawartha, bus map in hand. He must have forgotten to get off at the Wellness Center and not knowing what else to do, stayed on the bus for the return trip to the terminal. One of the drivers knew Paul by name and told him that his friends were still waiting for him. With that, he climbed back on board.

This time, as the bus got closer to the Wellness Center, Kim could see Paul lift his arm and then pull it down. He'd remembered to ding the bell.

Paul and I had both learned a lesson in safety and survival that day. I realized how important it is for him to be known in our community, and he learned to stay in one place. And that place he chose was one he loved – "the bus terminaw."

Later that fall, Paul had a unique opportunity to mentor high school students with disabilities and inspire them by his example. As part of a new government program, he was asked to deliver a presentation about his job at the locks. This was a big stretch for him. He couldn't read, the only word Paul could write was his first name, and his verbal skills were limited, but Linda, a coach with the program, was convinced he could do it. She met with him once a week in his apartment, and they developed a Power Point presentation. It illustrated how Paul's interest in motors, boats and people related to his job with Parks Canada.

His former teacher, Mr. Butler, arranged for Paul to visit his first high school to give his presentation. Paul stood at the front of the class facing a room full of Learning and Life Skills students and teachers. He was wearing his dark green and cream Parks Canada uniform, which usually filled him with confidence, but not today. He kept gazing out the window with a grim expression on his face. Paul had done his presentation several times before, but when asked to do it in front of people he knew, he wasn't able to say very much. Even so, I wished the school principal had been there. It had been six short years since he wrote: "Paul requires continual monitoring to travel throughout the school, to eat, go to the washroom and to facilitate his program at school."

He had come such a long way, and he wasn't done yet.

In the New Year, we heard from Sharon at Vocational Services that the wage subsidy program could change at any time. "If you find an employer for Paul, let me know right away," she told me

Even though the Wellness Centre enjoyed having Paul there, they were unionized and could not hire anyone whose wages were subsided. Things looked promising at the YMCA when Paul was offered a volunteer position preparing snacks for the kids in daycare, but he wasn't comfortable travelling through the dark, narrow corridors of the building, so the opportunity was put on hold until the new Y was built in the spring. In the meantime, Paul vacuumed carpets in one of the office buildings owned by Community Living. It occupied him for a couple of hours a week, but it wouldn't lead to employment.

Paul's Circle and I believed in him and we continued to hold the goal that he would have a job beyond the summer months, and eventually take the bus to and from work. The question remained, who would hire him? I gave it a lot of thought and wondered what would give him the best chance for a job. Then it came to me. There were hundreds of miles of carpets in apartment buildings, offices, and businesses in the city. Perhaps vacuuming could become a job for Paul. What we needed was a community connector to open some doors – someone who knew a lot of people and was well regarded. And I knew just the person.

John McNutt, a former Rotarian, community fundraiser and businessman was on a first-name basis with hundreds of people in town, from the mayor to the owner of a popular pub. He met with Paul and Catherine from Paul's Circle, Sharon the vocational counsellor and me, and we brainstormed employment possibilities. Then John came up with an idea. "The Holiday Inn is a good employer; they've been in town a long time and have a reputation of treating their employees well. I have worked on a couple of committees with their personnel manager. Do you want me to give her a call?"

In my enthusiasm, I sounded just like Paul. "Yes, please!"

With one phone call to the hotel, John set up an appointment for Paul and Steve. They would ask if Paul, with Steve's support, could vacuum the carpets as a voluntary work placement. The personnel manager said she would call us back.

—◊—

It was the spring of '07, and Paul had been out of school for almost a year. He had some social contact with people his own age through Special Olympics bowling and softball, but his friends group had lost their facilitator and they weren't getting together as often. Relationships rely on communication and this was one of Paul's biggest challenges. He had difficulty expressing himself and sometimes he had trouble understanding people, especially if they spoke too quickly or mumbled. He was most comfortable when he had a support person to bridge the communication gap.

I was always on the lookout for new social experiences for him and one day came across a brochure for a supported six-day houseboat vacation for people with disabilities. When I showed it to Paul, his eyes lit up at the photos of people cruising the lakes and canals, under the blue skies of summer.

"Would you like to go on a houseboat vacation without your parents?" I asked him.

"*Yes prease!!*"

"Look, Paul," I said, showing him the route on the map, "the boat goes through the locks at Young's Point where you work."

Murray and I drove Paul to the boat launch site in early June. The other passengers were already there: a woman in a wheelchair and two men who had taken the trip every year for the past five. The captain and young male staff member welcomed Paul and without hesitation, he climbed onboard carrying his pillow, sleeping bag and duffle bag stuffed with clothes, magazines, his Walkman, a week's supply of batteries and his bag of medication. As the boat pulled away from the dock, a look of panic crossed Paul's face. "*Where's a bus map?*"

"Good grief, Paul, you don't need your bus map on a house boat!" I called back.

"*Where's it?*"

"Look in your back pack," I said, giving him a farewell wave. He disappeared and returned a minute later waving the tattered map in his hand.

The houseboat stopped at five locks, and at each one the Parks Canada staff recognized and greeted Paul by name. I don't know which part of his holiday Paul enjoyed most: having a Parks Canada employee operate the locks for *him*; driving the houseboat "*all by myself*," or the thrill of his first independent vacation.

While Paul was away, we got the call we had been waiting for. "I've talked to the manager of the hotel," the personnel manager from the Holiday Inn said, "and we're willing to give Paul a try. He can vacuum the hallways two mornings a week, provided he comes with a support worker."

I was jubilant. A prominent business in town was giving Paul a chance.

On his first day, he was given a royal blue shirt with the hotel's name embroidered above the pocket and his own name tag. It signalled to Paul, and everyone else, that he belonged.

His enduring love of motors was paying off. When he flipped the switch on the dark red industrial vacuum cleaner, it came to life with a deep roar. Paul placed his hands firmly on the handle and set off down the long hallway. He kept going until either the tension on the chord told him to stop, or he pulled it out of the wall socket. Then he'd walk back, unplug it and carry the heavy loops to the next outlet. Paul repeated the process for all four floors, cheerfully greeting the housekeeping staff along the way.

"*Good morneen Vicky!*" he would call out, as though she was a long-lost friend.

"Good morning, Paul. How's it going?"

"*Pretty good,*" he'd reply, manoeuvring the big machine around her housekeeping cart.

We'd hit on the right combination – a welcoming workplace and duties that matched Paul's interests. He shone.

Seeing the pride in Paul's face when he put on his Holiday Inn shirt gave me a feeling of true satisfaction, and I wished that I could relax into it. Managing Paul's life had become a part-time job, and the pay was lousy. If there had been someone else to do it, a facilitator for instance, I would have welcomed them with outstretched arms.

People kept telling me how lucky Paul was to have me for his mother. The compliments were well intentioned, but sometimes they made me feel uncomfortable. I was fortunate to have the skill set, the connections and the time to push for Paul's integration, but what about the young person with a disability whose mother has three other children and a full-time job? Doesn't he or she deserve to have a meaningful life too?

For inclusion to work, the system needs to change. We provide post-secondary education and employment opportunities for people to work in schools, hospitals, daycare centres, jails, agencies and institutions. We also need to be training and employing people to be life coaches and facilitators for individuals with intellectual disabilities.

According to a recent article in the *Globe and Mail* (April 11, 2012), "Ontario invested $1.7 billion in developmental and residential services in the 2011-2012 fiscal year." As parents, caregivers and concerned citizens, we should be asking the question: how much of that money is going directly to individuals, and how much is feeding the bureaucratic machine?

According to stats from the Ministry of Community and Social Services (March 31, 2012), the individuals/families who get direct funding through programs like Passports and Special Services at Home receive only 9.25% of the total budget. In addition, there are almost 13,000 people with intellectual disabilities who are wait-listed for these services.

Just imagine how lives could be transformed if a portion of the remaining $1.5 BILLION went directly to individuals and to the training and salaries of their support workers. Then everyone would have a chance to have a good life, no matter who their parents are.

—⁂—

In September, Paul's Circle met to hear about the things he'd been doing since the last get-together in May. Paul was wearing his bright green Wanakita T-shirt with *Staff* printed on the back. When someone asked him about his summer, he became excited. "*Paul went a camp, drove pontoon boat, go really fast!*"

He passed around pictures of his houseboat vacation and an overnight camping trip with his friends.

"Did you go on your own, without Mom and Murray?" Catherine asked.

"*Yes!*" Paul said, raising his arms into a vee for victory.

I had his Performance Appraisal from Parks Canada and read it out loud: "Paul did an excellent job this year. His interactions with the staff and public are superior, and everyone enjoys being around him. Keep up the good work, Paul!"

We had invited a graphic facilitator to record the meeting. Linda taped a six-foot-long piece of paper to the wall and then, in pictures and big fat letters, she illustrated some of Paul's accomplishments over the last two years. When Joel mentioned that the two of them had gone to the local bar on St. Patrick's Day, Paul started to laugh. Linda responded by drawing an overflowing beer stein, beside it listing things young guys can typically do at a bar – play darts, hang out with friends, order a plate of wings, or shoot pool – all ways Paul could expand his leisure activities with friends. Alongside *Accomplishments*, Linda placed *Future Possibilities* inside a yellow arrow pointing to a bright orange and yellow star. "What do you imagine Paul's future will look like two years from now, when he's 24?" she asked the group.

After some discussion, a picture began to emerge. It incorporated Paul having paid employment either at the Holiday Inn or somewhere similar, and continuing with Parks Canada every summer. It included a bag of money symbolizing Individualized Funding, which would allow Paul to hire support workers to assist him with work, volunteer, recreation and leisure activities, and the tasks of daily living. A red heart and caring hands symbolized Paul's increasing independence from "Mom and Murray," and a green bus carried Paul to new experiences.

"Paul, would you like to live in your very own apartment in the community?" Linda asked him.

Paul nodded his head "*Yes!*" he replied.

I was surprised by how clear he was, when presented with that idea. He didn't have any friends with disabilities who were living on their own, but he had visited his cousins Laura and Carrie, who lived in their own apartments in Toronto.

"Then perhaps you could explore different living options with your mom or a friend from your Circle," Linda suggested. "This could include living in a house with your friends, having an apartment with just one friend or living on your own."

Whatever option Paul chose, the group felt it should include three things: it should be near a bus route; afford him both companionship and privacy; and allow him to have his own key to the front door.

Linda advised us that an important first step was to list the skills Paul needed to learn: using a cell phone, developing personal safety in public, learning more bus routes. And then work on them. The evening had been exhilarating. We not only put our goals for

Paul on paper, we developed specific ways he could achieve them. Paul might actually be able to have a life of his own. And it was becoming increasingly clear that's what he wanted.

TO PARAPHRASE THE SPIRITUAL TEACHER AND AUTHOR Eckhart Tolle, spirituality is about finding our true self, our inner light, and recognizing the light within others. It's a lifelong process of learning, developing, changing and accepting, made easier with the help of a Spiritual Director.

I was fortunate to meet Jennifer, a Spiritual Director who could help me find the answer to a question I had been wrestling with for many months: how can I reconcile my desire to serve God by helping others, and still have time for me? (As if raising Paul wasn't enough!)

She began by saying, "I will say a silent prayer and we will remain in silence until you are ready to speak. Listen to what God is saying to you. It could be the issue you thought you wanted to talk about when you came; it could be something else. You might want to talk about what you see or feel, or even what you are preparing for supper. It's all good – it's all food for God's grist mill."

I nodded and closed my eyes. Then panic seized me: what if I can't come up with anything? What if I draw a blank? "Relax and slow down," I told myself. "You can do this."

Once I became still, an issue emerged I wasn't expecting. I thought about it for a few minutes, opened my eyes, and began. "I'm very concerned about the father of my son Paul. He is in poor health and I don't know what to do. If I try and help him, he will likely push me away, but I feel I should do something. After all, he's Paul's father."

Jennifer and I discussed my dilemma, and then she advised me to return to silence. The depth of my emotion surprised me, and then an insight emerged. I would respond to John with compassion. It was really all I could do and it would be enough.

John's deteriorating health meant his visits with Paul had become sporadic. In the past, he would call each week to say whether or not he could see him, but lately his calls were infrequent. One morning, I was surprised to hear John's shaky voice on the other end of the phone. He told me he had received his third diagnosis of cancer. "I'm not up to taking Paul, besides, I have no food."

"I'll bring you something. What would you like?"

"Don't bother."

"It's not a bother; the grocery store is at the bottom of the hill. All you would have to do is come down in the elevator and pick it up."

"No."

"Look, John, you're diabetic. If you don't eat, some morning you're just not going to wake up." Silence. Then a dial tone.

The exchange weighed heavily on me, but there was nothing I could do. I remembered my conversation with Jennifer and how I had asked God to show me how to relate to John. I had reached out to him in a spirit of kindness, and I believe he knew that. I called him a few days later, but he didn't answer. I wasn't surprised. He used call display to keep people at bay.

The following week, I was driving home past John's seven-storey apartment building and noticed two police cars in front of it. I had a gut feeling they were there because of him.

My neighbour Doreen came over to say the police were looking for me. I returned their call, and within minutes there were two police cars in my driveway. The officers told me they had found Paul's father dead in his apartment. They had tracked me through the phone message I'd left. They were looking for John's next of kin and that was Paul. It was November 2007.

How was I going to tell Paul that his father had died? And what would that mean to him? Would he be able to understand? A lot of people without a disability have trouble with the concept of death; how was I going to explain it to Paul?

John's brother said there would be cremation without a service, so there was no rush to tell Paul. The next day, I went to our independent bookstore, and they suggested a children's book that illustrated the life cycle of living things, including people. That afternoon, I asked Paul to sit down beside me on the coach so we could read it together. At the end, I told him gently, "Your dad has been sick for a long time, Paul, and the other day he died."

He didn't say anything.

"I'm so sorry, Pauli. I know you and your dad loved one another. Can I get you anything?"

"*No answer*," he said and looked the other way.

When John was young, he had been an altar boy, and at one time he went to church regularly. Even though he had severed his relationship with the church, and ties with his mother and sister, I felt it was appropriate to have a service in the church for Paul's sake. His friends and Circle members came to support him; we said some prayers; the minister spoke in simple terms about death and faith, and we all sang, "He's Got the Whole World in His Hands" accompanied by Steve on the guitar.

"I'm sorry about your dad," his friend David said as he wrapped his big arms around him.

"*Dad died*," Paul said the following week. He was sitting on the couch, looking sad and vulnerable.

"Your dad loved you very much, Paul," I told him as I held him tight. "You'll be all right. I promise. Do you want to put your dad's picture on your dresser so you can remember him?" He nodded, expressionless.

When we drove by his dad's apartment building, Paul would look up with yearning and say, "*Dad's prace. I wanna see dad.*" John had left him without saying goodbye. I would have given anything in the world for Paul to be able to see his father one last time.

My eyes brimmed with tears, but crying would have upset Paul even more, so I breathed deeply instead. "You had a good time there with your dad, Paul. I know it's really hard that you can't see him anymore."

Paul's grief was palpable, but it knew no words. He went through the motions of his day, but when he got home, he'd sit by himself on the couch upstairs, staring listlessly out the window. I supported him the best way I knew how, by telling him how much I loved him, and by baking his favourite chocolate chip cookies.

Paul's loss gave me new insight into the power of forgiveness. I was grateful I had let go of any bitterness toward John. It allowed me to tell Paul, in all honesty, how much his dad cared about him. It took him about six months to grieve. Then, as the robins began their song of spring, his spirits lifted. Paul got off the couch. He was back.

—m—

As the coordinator of Heads Up for Inclusion, I was continually looking for ways to promote the Amigos program within high schools, so students could experience what the physicist David Bohm believed: that we are all connected to one another by "living fields of thought and perception." According to Bohm, when we dissolve the barriers that separate us from one another, we realize we are really "one mind, one unit, with individual awareness."

I contacted a marketing teacher at the college for advice on how to increase the awareness of the Amigos program. "Let's bring your students and mine together," Brian said. "This is a great way for college students to get hands-on marketing experience."

We arranged for half a dozen Amigos to meet the business students in the college's spacious boardroom. Standing at the far end of the board table, Brian said, "Why don't you guys tell me about this Amigos program?"

He wrote everything down on the white board behind him, and then he and his students brainstormed promotional strategies. They were in the midst of a lively exchange when a small voice from the other end of the table called out, "That's impossible."

Brian whipped around, his marker still poised in the air. "What did you say?" he asked.

"What you are asking us to do is impossible," Amanda, a high school student in Learning and Life Skills repeated.

Brian became animated. "Let's look at that word more closely," he said, writing it on the board in capital letters. "If you take the word IMPOSSIBLE and put an apostrophe after the 'I' what have you got?"

Amanda thought about the question, and then responded, "I'm possible."

"Exactly!" Brian said with the enthusiasm of someone shouting Bingo. "When you believe YOU are POSSIBLE, then nothing, and I mean nothing, is IMPOSSIBLE! I want all of you to remember that." He looked at Amanda. "Will you tell yourself, I'm possible?"

"Yes, I will," Amanda replied, with conviction.

Brian's remark was much more than a play on words. To cite Joseph Jaworski again, "We create possibilities through our declarations, our way of being and our actions." In other words, we have to change how we see *ourselves* if we want others to change how they see *us*.

Too often society devalues people with intellectual disabilities, seeing them as a drain on resources or a burden. I wanted others to appreciate what researchers like John McKnight knew: strong communities recognize the capacity of all people, even those who are traditionally marginalized; and in strong communities everyone is included in the life of the community.

Paul was trying his best to do just that. He'd been vacuuming at the Holiday Inn for seven months, with the same enthusiasm as the day he started. Co-workers acknowledged his commitment on Employee Recognition cards commenting on "the great job Paul is doing," and "for always smiling and making our hallways sparkling clean." His name tag now had four gold stars pinned onto it; each one represented a positive comment from a fellow employee.

It was time to ask the Holiday Inn the question we held onto from the beginning: would they actually *hire* Paul? His supporters, Steve and Kim, made an appointment with the personnel manager to make the request on Paul's behalf. Paul was at the meeting, but he didn't have the vocabulary to say, "I've been working my heart out for the last nine months. Would you consider hiring me?"

Once again, the personnel manager said she would have to check with the hotel's general manager. Collectively, we held our breath.

The next day, the phone rang. I was in a different kitchen than the one 22 years earlier, when I waiting for the call from the adoption lawyer, but the butterflies in my stomach felt the same.

"Is Lucinda there?" the female caller asked.

"Yes, speaking."

"It's Joanne from the Holiday Inn. I'm pleased to offer Paul employment at our hotel."

I exhaled. "That's wonderful Joanne! Paul will be thrilled! I'm thrilled!"

This was my moment to savour. It had been so long in coming, and I didn't want to share it with anyone, not yet. Paul had just been hired by a well-respected company for four hours a week. Not only that, he would be paid at the same rate as everyone else in housekeeping. The years of nudging, encouraging, and advocating had come to fruition.

When Paul got home, I told him the good news. "You're an employee now, Paul."

"*An emproyee,*" he repeated. "*I vacuum all four floors. I show you.*" Paul pointed to the out-stretched fingers on his left hand. "*One, two, three, four.*"

The next day, when Kim and Paul returned from the Holiday Inn, she called up the stairs, "Lucinda, you've got to hear this. When the staff in housekeeping heard that Paul had been hired, they all cheered. They knew how hard he worked and how much he deserved it."

It's hard to talk when all you want to do is cry.

That fall, the Holiday Inn wrote a short piece about Paul for the Employment Equity page of their national newsletter. The picture of him in his blue shirt brought out the colour of his eyes, and the story brought out his character.

"Paul Tiller is a young man who loves many things, including motor boats, lawn mowers and vacuum cleaners. When Paul graduated from high school, he was looking for a job that would relate to his interests. Paul has an intellectual disability which presented challenges to him entering the labour market. The Holiday Inn Peterborough-Waterfront worked with Paul's job coach to coordinate a work placement vacuuming hallways. Paul's job coach helped him learn the skills required for the job, including positive guest relations. After seven months of training, Paul's performance was evaluated and he was hired part-time as a member of the hotel team. He is so proud to be recognized for his efforts."

—⁓—

Paul's outgoing personality came naturally. He would wave at passing cars and greet strangers on the street with, "*Good morning sir,*" or "*Hey there, haare you?*" There was a fine line between being friendly and risky behaviour, but Kari, his Saturday supporter, reassured me. "Paul's greeting puts a smile on people's faces, which is nice in a world where people are normally too busy to share a friendly 'hello' on the street."

Kari worked with Paul while she attended university, and over those years, both of them grew. "Not only have I learned a lot from Paul about how to treat a neighbour and how to inspire others, but by watching him achieve many of his goals, I learned how an individual can thrive with proper support, encouragement and guidance," Kari wrote. She is now in Ottawa working as a behaviour therapist with children with autism.

The relationships Paul has with Kari, Michelle, Sarah and Joel are like a wheel that keeps turning, evolving, enriching the lives it touches. Joel was in our home every Saturday for two years while he was studying to be a police officer. "I think we see more of you than your parents do," I said to him one afternoon. Even though he moved to Australia, he still keeps in touch. In a recent email, he said, "I am now in a management position. I have you and Paul to thank for giving me the foundation and opening my eyes to the possibilities for people. Without you guys, I would not be the person I am today."

Supporters and Amigos often enter the disability field thinking they are spending time with someone who, at first glance, appears to be needy. Once the relationship develops, however, they realize how much the person with a disability has to teach them. In the words of one of the high school Amigos, "It (Amigos) has changed me as a person – it's made me a leader. One of the biggest problems with society is we are scared of people who are different from us. Just being with Amigos makes you feel like differences are okay."

Helping people with disabilities develop relationships is one of the most important things we can do. Because of the time and commitment it takes to connect individuals with one another and to their community, people with disabilities often become isolated, disconnected from others.

"Loneliness is the only real disability, and for people with disabilities, loneliness is epidemic," says David Pitonyak. I attended his workshop on "The Importance of Belonging," where he advocates for schools and agencies to focus on relationship-building for people with disabilities. He doesn't pull any punches: "If what we are doing doesn't help people connect into meaningful relationships, it's a waste of time."

When asked who their friends are, all too often individuals with a disability will list their support workers. "A friend is someone who isn't paid to spend time with you," I'd remind Paul's supporters. Some of Paul's support workers eventually did become his friends; unfortunately, most of these young people have moved away to pursue their careers. It's hard for guys like Paul to make friends, and it's even harder to lose sight of them. Facebook doesn't come close to sharing a bus ride or going to a movie with a friend.

When Paul was younger, it would take him several weeks to get over a friend or supporter leaving, but he's become resilient. He's learned to stay grounded in the midst of change and loss, even when it hurts. It's a survival skill we all need.

PART FOUR

LETTING GO

Going to the Reach for the Rainbow ball, November 2009

It was the summer of 2008, and I turned my attention to the goal of Paul living in his own place with a friend and supporter in two years. The date was not arbitrary: in 2010, I would turn 60.

"By then, I want to be out of the business of full- time parenting," I told Paul's Circle.

"Me too!" Murray said, thrusting his arms in the air, Paul-style. I embraced the concept, but had no idea how hard it would be for me to let Paul go.

In spite of, or maybe because of, the time and attention Paul required, Murray and I had become adept at carving out time for ourselves. Every year, when Paul was at camp, we went on a holiday together. It was the right time to take a longer vacation, and we made plans to be out of the country for four weeks in the fall.

Catherine made it possible by agreeing to stay in the house and look after Paul and the dogs. Three weeks before our departure, I began to panic. I'd never been away from Paul for longer than the 13 days he spent at camp; 28 days seemed like an eternity. I had a dream that he was a small boy and I had left him alone in a house to rest. When I went back for him, he was gone. The river was nearby and I ran frantically from person to person asking if they had seen my boy, but no one had. My heart was pounding so hard, it woke me up.

I was about to take the first step in actually letting Paul go, and it scared the hell out of me. I asked God for help, and in silence my answer came. God's presence has been with Paul and me throughout his life. It has given me strength and helped me overcome adversity. No matter where I am, and no matter what happens, that isn't going to change.

When Murray and I returned home, I expected Paul to throw his arms around me. Instead, he greeted us from his apartment as though we'd been away for a weekend. It was a turning point for both of us. He'd not only proved he could live with someone else for an extended period of time, but he had fun doing it. Murray and I too relished our taste of freedom – and we wanted more.

My travel euphoria began to dissipate when I returned to the reality of daily life and a month's worth of email. I was hitting the delete button with a steady rhythm when I came across a writing contest sponsored by Imagine Canada. They were inviting individuals to write about their favourite Canadian charity and the reason it had made an impact on your life. The incentive was a chance to win $5,000 for your charity and the deadline was a few short days away.

"Maybe I can write about Paul's camping experience with Reach for the Rainbow," I said to Murray. "He'll be away at Wanakita for fall clean-up this weekend, so I'll have a block of time to myself."

"Go for it!" he replied.

Paul was driving to camp with his "*best buddy Alex*," who had been a counsellor with Reach for the Rainbow; their relationship blossomed when Alex moved to Peterborough to attend university. The two of them were going to Wanakita for the weekend to drive the Ranger through the forest, clean up the waterfront, and bring the pontoon boat in for winter storage. It was the sort of thing that young males do without a second thought, but for a guy like Paul, going away with a buddy was a big deal. I don't know who was more ecstatic, him or me.

His departure put me in the mood to express my gratitude to Reach, and their role in helping Paul grow in confidence and self-acceptance. My fingers flew over the keyboard as I recounted how camp had contributed to Paul's skills and abilities, helped him land a job with Parks Canada, embark on his first independent vacation, and secure a job at the Holiday Inn.

With a light, carefree stride, I walked into town to mail the story. Halfway there, I imagined winning the writing contest, and in gratitude, Reach for the Rainbow would invite Murray and me to their spectacular Crystal Ball. It was a million dollar fundraiser; the dress code was black tie, and the ticket price was $750 per person, just a tad out of our league. As the mailbox clanged shut, the image took hold. I pictured Murray and me dancing at the Ball, my turquoise wedding dress – the one I yearned to wear again – swishing against his legs.

It must have been my upbeat mood that caught the judges' attention, because two weeks later, Imagine Canada called to say I won the contest. Then David Neal, the program director for Reach for the Rainbow, phoned to say how pleased they were, not only for the $5,000 donation, but also for the recognition. My story would be featured in an upcoming *Maclean's* magazine. I was delighted. But he didn't mention anything about the Ball.

"I guess I'll have to wait until they figure that part out," I told Murray, truly believing they would.

Two days later, the phone rang again. It was Donna Trella, the CEO of Reach. She expressed her appreciation, and then said, "As a thank you, we want to invite you and your partner to be our guests at the Crystal Ball. Perhaps you could think it over and let me know."

"We'd love to come!" I replied – perhaps a little too quickly.

Walking into the ballroom was like stepping into a fairyland: the expansive dining area was dimly lit, with twinkling lights and flickering candles on each of the 200 tables. Men in tuxedos and women in shimmering floor-length gowns sipped champagne and moved gracefully throughout the room. All around us was the sound of 1,500 popping balloons, some with amazing prizes inside.

At our dinner table, I sat beside a woman who had just flown in from a private resort in the Caribbean. She said, "I told the owner his resort would be a great auction item for this gala. He was interested, but I didn't have any information on Reach for the Rainbow. Then I remembered a story in the latest *Maclean's* magazine about what Reach had meant to one young boy. Fortunately, I had the magazine to give him."

I replied, "That boy was our son Paul, and I wrote the story." Murray was listening to the conversation. "Do you happen to believe in coincidences?" he asked her, before whisking me away to the dance floor.

The next year, we weren't invited to the Ball, but Paul was. He and Alex were asked to sell Reach for the Rainbow memberships to the guests. I wasn't sure how Paul would manage in the midst of a thousand people, not to mention the popping balloons, but once he knew Alex was going, he raised two thumbs and replied "*Yes!*"

This was one of those "once in a lifetime" opportunities for Paul – his chance to wear a tuxedo. He tried it on at home to make sure everything fit: first, the white shirt with the tiny buttons, next the black pants with the shiny stripe, then the bow tie, matching vest and jacket, and finally he slipped on the black patent leather shoes.

"Let me take your picture, Paul," I said picking up my camera. He struck a pose leaning against the back of the living room couch with his hands and long delicate fingers resting comfortably on his knee. He turned his head and looked into the distance. Perhaps he too was imagining what it would be like to go to the ball.

The shutter clicked.

The moment was mine forever.

—ɯɯ—

It was time to return to the reality of everyday life and the challenges of working on behalf of Heads Up for Inclusion and Paul. There was no escaping the disability world, even in sleep. My dreams reflected my feelings of vulnerability and insecurity, with the recurring theme of protecting Paul.

I needed to find a way to resolve my anxiety, and remembered my father's advice when I was 23 (the same age as Paul), to turn to the 23rd Psalm in times of trouble. When I came to the phrase "he makes me lie down in green pastures," I realized the psalmist was not passively suggesting rest; he was giving explicit direction to "lie down."

If I wanted greater peace within, once again I had to try and do less, to slow my pace. When Paul was a pre-schooler, my mother-in-law had said to me, "Lucinda, I've never seen anyone do things as fast as you." I took it as a compliment, instead of recognizing it as a caution. Because of Paul's darting movements and penchant for trouble, I had developed the habit of doing everything with speed, buzzing from place to place, never lighting in one spot for long – I was a human house fly.

Over the years, Paul had slowed down, but I hadn't. It was time to break the multi-tasking habit and put away the stop watch. In keeping with the wisdom in the Serenity Prayer, I had tried to accept the things I couldn't change, and now I needed to ask for the courage to change the things I could.

One way to do that was to limit my involvement with Heads Up for Inclusion and the Amigos program. I decided to hand over the reins to a new coordinator while remaining on the Board. It was easier to change that, than to let go of my concern for Paul.

Most people didn't realize the angst I felt about Paul's future. It was rare for me to share my inner turmoil. I was the product of a stoic upbringing where emotions were rarely discussed, which was hard because I had lots of them, plus I wanted people to see Paul in the most favourable light. Most of all, I didn't want to admit to others, and myself, that I was scared. Fear is a universal feeling among parents, but we seldom talk about it. For those who have a son or daughter with a disability, most of our friends and family members have no idea what is going on inside our hearts.

"My family was absolutely not there for me," a friend whose daughter is now an adult said. "When I talked to them about that, they thought they had supported me, but they never called and asked how they could help."

"I have so much trouble asking for help," a young mother told me. "I want people to think that everything in my family is okay."

"Do you also have trouble letting go?" I asked, knowing her answer would be the same as mine.

"I want to have a say about what happens in my daughter's life," she replied.

When parents of kids with disabilities get together, we rarely talk about ourselves – the movies we've seen, where we've been, or current affairs. The focus is always on our kids.

"We worry about the health of our children, but we don't always take care of our own," a mother from our Homes for Life group said. "I'm disappointed at not taking the time for myself." She was recovering from surgery and, as was the case for many women I knew who'd raised a child with a disability, her health had suffered.

I knew I was susceptible to health problems too, and tried to maintain a balance between my body, mind and spirit by being active outdoors, and through yoga, journaling, reading and learning, meditation and prayer. There were times I envied Murray, who was able to accept and roll with each day as it came. He didn't worry about the future – like Albert Einstein he lived knowing that "it comes soon enough."

As 2009 BEGAN, I resolved to be more joyful, dance a little and be less intense. I rediscovered joy in ordinary moments, and took the time to pause. One morning I looked out the kitchen window and saw the young boy next door jumping on his snow-covered trampoline. He scooped snow into his small shovel then bounced into the air, releasing the white crystals as he went. On the way back down, he tried with all his might to catch the falling snow in his outstretched shovel. Joy filled every part of his small body causing me to laugh out loud.

Paul loved shovelling snow too, not in the air, but on the driveway. He'd never make a living at it, though; he shovelled the same four-foot path over and over again. He loved being outside, no matter how cold it was, and had become interested in snowshoeing, tramping through the woods at his grandfather's cottage. The last time we were there, he spotted the snowmobile sitting in the yard and said, "*Paul wantsa go for a ride!*"

"But you're afraid of snowmobiles," Murray reminded him. As much as Paul loved motors, he had always recoiled at the idea of riding on a snowmobile, until now.

"*Paul wantsa go fas!*" he replied, undeterred.

Murray's brother Eric was an avid snowmobiler, and he agreed to take Paul for a ride on the lake. We found him some old clothes in the basement, piled on several layers, and then placed a worn helmet on his head. "You look like a spaceman on a moon walk," I told him as he went out the door.

Eric was already on the machine with the engine running, and Paul climbed on as though he had been doing it for years.

"Hang on," Eric yelled as he gunned the engine.

"*AIIIYEEE*," Paul squealed over the roar. They took off, leaving the smell of gas fumes in their wake, and soon were out of sight. Murray and I followed their path to the shore, and within minutes heard the drone of the motor. We watched in amazement as the machine sped by in a trail of flying snow. Paul raised his hand in a wave but, for safety's sake, Eric grabbed it in one swift movement and reattached it to his own waist. This was more than a snowmobile ride for Paul. It was a turning point.

"*I did it!*" he exclaimed when he got back. "*I did it by myself!*"

Along with appreciating moments of joy, I resolved to be more attentive to the blessings that surrounded us. I was grateful for our friends and their loving acceptance of Paul; for his ability to stay on his own for longer periods of time; for his faithful supporters; and for Murray's unconditional love, which allows me to be fully who I am.

Blessings are fascinating; they can be readily apparent, or they can arrive in disguise. Sometimes it takes time, hindsight, and often the grace of God for a blessing to be revealed. Paul's life was like that.

During the difficult days of his childhood, getting through each day was a challenge, and I would have recoiled if someone had told me that Paul's life was a blessing. It was only hindsight that provided me with that understanding. I heard someone say, "We live our life forward, but only truly understand it backwards." It's true. For the past 23 years, I'd been under the misguided impression that I had control over the good things in Paul's life. Then something happened that proved me wrong. Later that spring, he came bursting through the front door shouting, "*Mom, take a look at this!*"

"What is it?" I asked as I went downstairs to meet him.

"*Mom, I got a new watch!*" He unzipped his backpack and pulled out a watch box, opened the lid and handed me a silver watch with *Holiday Inn* on its face.

"*Look.*" He pointed. On the back, was the inscription: Employee of the Month.

"Oh Paul," was all I could say.

"He also got a gold star for his name-tag and a certificate," Kim said, closing the front door.

"*Read it to me*," Paul said, pulling the certificate out of his backpack.

"Okay, listen to this. The general manager of the Holiday Inn said that you are 'a bright spot in the day of all your co-workers. You have a great attitude toward your work, consistently displaying exceptional enthusiasm, motivation and drive.' "

"His picture will be in the main hallway for the month of June," Kim added.

I looked at Paul, with his man-sized watch sliding off his slender wrist.

"Do you think I could have a hug?" I asked, extending my arms.

"*Sure, Mom,*" he said, wrapping both arms around my shoulders.

I had been looking for joy and found it, along with something else. Humility. Paul had earned his award without any help from me. He had done it all by himself.

—∞—

We didn't live on a bus route, and most supporters came by car, with one exception: one woman rode her bicycle to our place, even in the pouring rain. The sky was still low with dark clouds as Paul and I watched her hop on her bike and coast down our driveway. With her black raincoat flapping behind her, she reminded me of Nanny McPhee.

"*I wanna go my bike,*" Paul said after she disappeared up the road.

"The rain has stopped, so go ahead," I replied. "Don't forget your helmet."

We live on a hill facing a busy street and Paul always walked his bike down the driveway to the side street, so without a second thought I went to my bedroom to change my clothes. Within minutes, I heard the front door bang open, and Paul yelling. A man's voice called, "Is anyone here?"

I ran down the hall zipping up my jeans as I went. At the front door stood two of my neighbours and a young man I didn't know. Paul was in his apartment crying.

"What's happened?" I asked as I raced down the stairs.

"I didn't even see him," the young man exclaimed. "He came out of nowhere and ran right into my truck!"

"What?"

"We just happened to be driving by," my neighbour explained, "and we got a glimpse of Paul flying down the driveway on his bike. Then he hit the side of this man's truck." It was a one ton diesel pick- up.

In disbelief, I went over to Paul, who was jumping up and down. "Are you hurt? Let me see."

"*No Mom. Paul's scared.*"

I helped him take off his jacket. There was a small tear on the sleeve, his pants were muddy and there was a red patch on his cheek, but that was all. I ran my hands over his upper body, but he didn't react. "Where are his shoes?" I asked.

"They must've come off in the ditch after he took the side mirror off my truck," the driver said, his voice shaking. "If he hadda been a second earlier, I would've hit him head on and he'd be dead."

"Oh my God," my hands flew to my mouth, and my eyes squeezed shut.

"His bike is still in the ditch. Do you want me to bring it up?"

"I'll come with you. Will you be all right for a minute, Paul?"

Wide-eyed he nodded. The rest of us walked down the driveway.

"If you need anything, let us know," my neighbour said. I gave him a weak wave and then turned to look at the ditch. The long grass was bent over where Paul's body had landed. Beside it, a menacing rock emerged from the ground. I stared at it with a mixture of horror and relief.

I dragged his bike onto the lawn – the front wheel and the handle bars were twisted into a pretzel – and went inside to take a closer look at Paul. His right arm was red and starting to bruise, but he could move it over his head. Taking him to the hospital would only add to his trauma. I took a deep breath and then another one, as the familiar feelings of terror, relief and gratitude merged. The talk about bike safety would come later; right now I wanted to feel him close.

"Paul, do you want to have a cup of tea and sit beside me on the couch?"

"*Yes Mommy, with milk.*"

We sat side by side looking out the window, our bodies pressed together, just like old times. We were still there when Murray came home. "What happened to Paul's bike? Was it hit by a train?"

The following week, Sarah, who was now training to be a nurse, said, "Maybe you should take him to the hospital for an x-ray, just in case."

I knew it had to be done before Paul went to camp, and I girded myself for the trip to the emergency department. The attending doctor recommended an x-ray, and Paul vehemently replied, "*No x-rake, no x-rake,*" all the way to the x-ray room.

He wouldn't hold his arm still, making it impossible for the technician to get a clear image. We had been at the hospital for six hours. It was time to pull out my trump card. "Paul, if you want to go to Camp Wanakita next week, you have to have your arm x-rayed."

Without hesitation, he placed his arm on the plate. Within seconds, we were done. The results showed a tiny hairline fracture. Paul was given a flimsy gauze sling and told to wear it for a few days. Fat chance.

Thirteen days later, we picked Paul up at camp, and I blinked in disbelief. He was wearing a blue Velcro cast on the *other* arm.

"Paul was so excited to get to the water, he tripped backwards over a tree root," his counsellor said. "We went to the emergency department at the local hospital, and Paul was just great. We waited a long time and then he had an x-ray with no problem. The doctor said he should leave the cast on for another week and then get it checked."

I was incredulous. Not only had Paul lightly fractured both arms in the last month, he had just gone to the hospital and had a dreaded "*x-rake*" without complaint. It gave me a rare glimpse at another side of Paul – a guy who, at times, can hide his ability under a disability barrel.

"So, Paul, have you got any more tricks up your sleeve?" Murray asked him on the way home.

"*No Murr-eee!*"

Our life was still a roller coaster. There were fewer high-speed descents, but I was still clutching the safety bar. I was concerned that Paul hadn't fully recovered from his run-in with the truck. Even though he wasn't complaining, he was irritable and touching himself inappropriately. His latest habit was gulping a large glass of water when he was listening to his favourite song or watching a movie. He'd simultaneously gulp, gag, and laugh, spraying water and spit everywhere. I thought I'd go mad.

It was time for him to see Wei Wei, our naturopath, for a tune-up. He sat expressionless in her office, his hands moving deeply in his pockets, as she gently ran her long slender fingers across his neck and clavicle.

"I can feel the muscles knotted on the right side of Paul's neck and collar bone. I think he would benefit from a Bowen treatment," she said. "It helps relieve muscle tension and pain, and brings the body back into balance."

Paul agreed to the treatment, as long as he could leave his shirt on and remain seated. Wei Wei moved her thumbs and fingers on the muscles and tissues around his collar bone. "I use a very light touch," she explained," so the body will relax. If you press too hard, the body resists and tightens up." After a few minutes, she said, "I'm going to pause now and give Paul's body time to make its own adjustments. I'll be back in a few minutes."

When she returned, she repeated the treatment. Paul's body started to visibly relax. He had come into her office mute, with his head down. He was now making eye contact as he talked, and his hands had left his pockets. I knew that Bowen treatments often work quickly, but I never expected results this fast.

"What would you want to do now?" I asked Paul on our way out the door.

"*Go to Tim's*," he replied with the assertiveness of someone who knows he has the upper hand.

UNLIKE MANY OF MY FRIENDS, whose children had married and were now producing grandchildren, I was still in the midst of full-time parenting. The last thing I wanted was to become a grandmother; what I wanted was an end to the daily grind of being Paul's case manager, caregiver, advocate and financial planner. There wasn't much time left for just being Mom.

Six months earlier, I had submitted my annual request to the government for Individualized Funding. I took full advantage of being "an older parent," making the point that I was approaching 59. Paul would need to live on his own someday, why not now, when he was a motivated 23-year-old. Of course, I heard nothing back.

A few weeks earlier, Paul and I had been at Pizza Hut and we ran into a man who is on the committee that decides who gets "support dollars" in our community. He and I knew one another, and he greeted me and Paul, who mumbled a half-hearted "*Hi*," keeping his head down. Over the years, this man had read many pages about Paul's needs, but to my knowledge, he had never met him, until now.

I had often wondered if my ability to make things happen for Paul was actually preventing him from getting adequate funding. "On paper, does he appear more capable than he really is?" I asked myself. It was a Catch 22: Paul needed me to advocate for him but maybe, unwittingly, I was standing in his way. I had carefully used government funds to help him move forward; I hoped we weren't being penalized by his success.

Some weeks later, when Paul returned from his 14th summer at Camp Wanakita, a letter-size government envelope arrived in the mail. I left it on the kitchen counter for a couple of days along with the bills. Letters from the government seldom brought good news. When I finally did open it, I cried out in disbelief. "It is my pleasure to inform you that, on behalf of the Intake Review Team, Paul is approved for Day Support." I sat down and reread the letter three times.

It had finally happened. Paul could now be supported for 30 hours a week and, if we planned carefully, he could have the independent life he wanted (at 40% of the cost of a group home). The money came from the provincial government, and it would come to Paul every year – it was Individualized Funding with a different name.

"Thank you," I whispered again and again.

I waited impatiently for Murray to come home; I wanted to see the expression on his face when I told him and Paul the good news. "This calls for champagne!" he said heading for his wine cellar. Ever the optimist, he always had a bottle on hand, just in case something good happened.

"Would you like some too, Paul?" I asked.

"*Yes prease Mom, Paul wantsa ginerale.*"

I thought about our encounter in the pizza shop with the man who had been part of this funding decision and wondered if meeting Paul face-to-face had made a difference. Maybe it was just a coincidence. I'll never know.

Each person on Paul's support team was more motivated than ever to help him develop his independent living skills. Steve suggested that on the days Paul was going to work, he take a taxi from our house to the bus station rather than have me drive him. "It's another step in Paul being independent, and one less thing he relies on 'Mom' for," he said.

I was trying to back off whenever I could. If I forgot, Steve was there to remind me. He was still supporting Paul two days a week: Thursdays at the Holiday Inn, and Fridays when Paul and his friend Jeremy swam and worked out at a local gym before coming back to Paul's apartment for lunch. Jeremy, a few years older than Paul, has some reading ability, but his global intellectual disability dictated a comparable level of support.

Phyllis, a "Team Paul" member from Community Living, suggested that Paul become more skilled at using his cell phone. "It's an important safety tool for Paul to be able to call people, tell them where he is, as well as receive calls."

The next day, the phone rang. It was Paul practising his phone skills downtown after work.

"*Hi Mom.*"

"Hi, Paul. Where are you?" I asked.

"I'm right here."

—⁓—

A friend and I were looking for ways our adult children could increase their independent living skills, and I came across a project in Ottawa where young adults with disabilities lived in a college residence for one month in the summer.

The participants were enthusiastic about the experience, so I borrowed the idea and submitted a proposal for Paul to live in our local college residence with a friend with a disability, and a supporter. An occupational therapist would do an Independent Living Skills Assessment. Paul and his roommate would then practise the identified skills, learn how to be good room-mates, as well as have the experience of living on their own in a safe environment. I included a budget and outlined the long- term benefits for everyone. It was a good idea but it was not approved for funding.

Persistence has been found to be an important character trait for parents of a child with a disability. Another request I made was in response to the government's "Innovative Residential Model Initiative," which was designed to "... help an adult with a developmental disability live more independently in the community." My friend Linda and I put together a creative housing request on behalf of her daughter, Paul and two other young people; all costs would be shared and reduced over time. We were optimistic that our plan would be accepted, but our hopes were soon dashed. The government housing initiative had sounded too good to be true, and it was.

It was becoming increasingly obvious that we had to make things happen on our own. Then, out of the blue, Steve told us he had been working with Jeremy's parents, Terry and Shannon Booth, on a plan for Jeremy to move into his own place and wondered if we were interested. Murray and I knew the family through our Homes for Life group, and we were receptive to the idea of Paul and Jeremy becoming room-mates and sharing the cost of support workers. When we asked Paul if he wanted to live in his own apartment with Jeremy, he replied with an emphatic *"Yes."*

It was the fall of 2009; Murray and I had just celebrated our 11th wedding anniversary and were as keen as ever to become "empty nesters." We met with the Booths and Steve around our kitchen table, and had an animated discussion about where the guys would live, who would support them, and how much it would cost. But after three hours, we had more questions than answers.

"There has to be someone out there who can help us," I said. "Paul and Jeremy aren't the first to be doing this."

"Let's arrange a meeting with Community Living and find out what resources they have to offer," Terry suggested.

"You set that up and I'll search the Internet to see what I can find," I replied.

After clicking on link after link, I found the Family Support Institute in British Columbia, and they put me in contact with two families who had an independent living arrangement for their adult children. One father told me via email that his 21-year-old son had been living in an apartment for a year with a peer caregiver.

The problem with that arrangement was he and his wife were "worn out from all the micro-managing that's required when you hire a younger peer to be your support worker. If our caregiver leaves, then we will have to do the training all over again."

He was looking into a model where a cluster of three or four individuals would own their own condo in the same building, and a caregiver would come in from 5:00-10:00 pm to help prepare a meal and organize social or recreational activities.

The mother I contacted wrote to say that she and her husband were planning to move out of their accessible home and have their daughter remain there with a friend. I didn't tell Murray about that idea; there was no way we were moving.

I kept searching and eventually made contact with a Community Living Association in St. Mary's Ontario. They had years of experience helping individuals move from institutions into their own homes. In an act of grace, they referred me to Marilyn Haywood, a woman whose depth of experience was matched by her generosity. She suggested that we all meet in Toronto to share our ideas over lunch. We told her that our current plan was for Paul and Jeremy to live in a three-bedroom apartment with a live-in student who would provide evening and overnight support in exchange for rent.

Marilyn listened carefully and then said, "If you are looking for a three-bedroom unit the guys can afford, it will probably mean a townhouse in a complex geared to low-income families. Is that where you want them to live?"

Terry, Shannon and I looked at one another and shook our heads.

"Where the guys live is important. You want them to be able to develop friendships with their neighbours. Perhaps you don't need a third roommate. Instead you could have someone stay overnight, even on a pull-out couch, until the guys are comfortable on their own and have built relationships within the building."

Marilyn encouraged us to look at the big picture and to be creative when looking at all the possibilities. "Don't just think about affordable housing; consider regular apartment buildings and 'Rent to Own' options too."

Paul and Jeremy were eating slowly and without comment, but their gaze travelled to each person as the conversation about their future circled around them.

"What do you think about the idea of living on your own?" Marilyn asked Jeremy.

He lifted his head and quietly said, "I like it."

"How about you, Paul, what do you think about having your own place?

"*Good*," he replied. He was still the master of one-word utterances that expressed volumes.

At the end of our time together, Marilyn emphasized the importance of carefully planning each step of the move so we didn't have to back-track. From my work with college students, I knew how important it is to experience success when learning a new task; failure can destroy a person's motivation to try again. The five words I never wanted to hear were: "*Paul wantsa move back home.*"

We were embarking on the most important journey of Paul's life, and it would require time and effort to make it work. I'd finally come to realize that my energy is a finite resource. It was time to completely let go of my role with Heads Up for Inclusion and the Amigos program and let others take over.

I had wanted to stay connected by remaining on the Board, but I'm lousy at sitting in the back seat. It wasn't an easy decision to make – Heads Up had become a big chunk of my identity. People would say to me, "It was your baby," as a way of explaining why it was hard for me to let it go. It was more than that. I was removing myself from working in the disability field and preparing to let Paul go at the same time. And it was hard.

At night my dreams were so wild, it's a wonder I got any sleep at all. I dreamt about being shot at, exposed without my clothes on, riding on a steno chair in traffic, being robbed of my wallet, and trapped in a cage. I didn't need Sigmund Freud to tell me I was approaching burn-out, if I wasn't there already there.

Cheaper than psychoanalysis was the chance to participate in a 10-day pilgrimage on Celtic spirituality in Ireland, where I could attend to my inner life and hopefully regain my footing. With 15 other men and women, I explored the nature of God, the wisdom of the Celts, and the significance of three early Irish goddesses – the Maid, Mother and Crone.

I was drawn to the symbolism of the Crone, who has special meaning for women my age, whose bodies have cycled through child-bearing years to a place where deeper spirituality and wisdom reside. It was reassuring to appreciate this stage of my life. As my hair becomes greyer, my inner life has become richer: as one phase of my life ends, another is being reborn.

One afternoon, walking alone in the Irish mist, I composed my first ten word Haiku poem.

> Creator God
> the less I try
> the closer you are.

The prospect of letting go was starting to take root. I didn't have to do battle with anyone anymore: not Paul's behaviour, his father, the school system, the legal system, the social system, or the medical system. It wasn't too late. There was still time to embrace the next phase of my life and discover myself anew.

WE TOOK MARILYN'S ADVICE regarding where Paul and Jeremy lived and embraced the idea of a two-bedroom apartment with temporary overnight support (made possible with support from Community Living Peterborough). We also followed her recommendation to hire a facilitator to help us with the planning phase. "The planning you do now will become the basis of a long-term strategy for these guys," she told us.

The stakes were high, and we needed someone with experience to guide us forward. There was no one in our area with the expertise, so we arranged for Judith McGill, a life-planning consultant from Toronto, to spend the day with us. It was a grey, mid-November day, but our spirits were high as the Booths and I gathered with Steve to begin the first of many planning sessions. Murray was at work but the guys were there. Paul would pull up a chair and listen, while Jeremy preferred to watch TV downstairs.

Judith began by asking us for two things: the vision we had for our sons, and our greatest concerns. My vision for Paul remained much the same: that he would have a life of his own, a home of his own, and the opportunity to assume his rightful place in the community. My concerns were mostly about how the move would be handled. Would it happen all at once or be phased in? I was concerned about knife safety and accident procedures and whether Paul's loud vocalizing, especially when he listened to music, would affect his neighbours. And then, as if there weren't enough to think about, I wondered how and when the topic of sexuality would be addressed.

Judith took note of our responses and then asked, "What are the roles of the parents and the coordinator?" We identified what needed to be done for Paul and Jeremy – all the things we did as parents and never wrote down, and all the areas covered by supporters. Our list covered four pages of flip-chart paper and included 14 key roles – from household chores to meal planning, personal care, safety, staffing, finances – and 74 activities to accomplish them.

"I'm surprised at how much goes into making sure these guys have a life," Terry said. "And you don't realize how much we've been doing until you see it on paper," I added. "Now that things are clearly laid out, it's time to assign responsibility for each activity," Judith said. "This builds accountability and ensures that everyone is clear on who is doing what."

This was the easy part. We handed over the day-to-day operations to Steve, who would assign tasks to the supporters, while Terry, Shannon and I maintained responsibility for our sons' health needs, the final hiring decision, and funding.

"The coordinator and staff will now play a major role in Paul and Jeremy's lives, but ultimately it's the parents who are the last man standing," Judith said, putting quotation marks in the air with her fingers around the word "man." It would be three years before I fully appreciated the significance of her remark.

"How did it go?" Murray said, coming into the kitchen, his jeans covered in a fine layer of drywall dust.

"We've just solved the problems of the world," Terry said, looking at his watch. "I don't know about anyone else, but I'm ready for a glass of wine."

"Just a minute," Murray replied. "I have that very thing downstairs, just let me change my pants."

Each of us had our role to play.

—✺—

The next step was to find an apartment for Paul and Jeremy, and our preferred option was for them to live in one of the city's new Affordable Housing complexes. The apartments were for individuals living on a fixed income and not specifically for people with a disability; if Paul got in, he would be integrated into his community. There was an application process and a waiting period and for the first time, I didn't mind. It gave me time to prepare to say good-bye to my boy.

So many times over the years, I had looked out the kitchen window and watched Paul come up or go down the driveway. My mother told me she had done the same thing when I was a little girl. One late fall morning, as the sun played hide-and-seek with the clouds, I watched Paul saunter down the drive, holding Molly's leash in his left hand. He paused and sat on the stone wall to adjust his shoes. He was wearing the black patent leather ones he had worn to the Crystal Ball.

"Hold onto this moment," I told myself. "You won't be seeing this much longer." He turned at the bottom of the driveway and slipped from view. I thought my heart would break with missing him. And he hadn't even gone.

I moved throughout the house, not able to stay in one place for long. I felt so tired, stretched out on the couch and closed my eyes. A weight descended on my chest. For so many years, I had pushed to make things happen in Paul's life, and I was weary. "Could I do this one more time?" I asked myself.

Then a melody floated into my head from the Irish Blessing my stepdaughter Meghan had sung at our wedding: "May God hold you in the palm of his hand." My whole body softened into the cushions. I didn't have to do this alone.

A couple of weeks later, a woman from Affordable Housing called to say she and a colleague wanted to meet Paul and take his application to the next level. When they arrived at his apartment, clipboards and briefcases in hand, everyone sat down, everyone, that is, except Paul.

"Pull up a chair," I encouraged him.

"*No, Paul wantsa stand,*" he replied, remaining close to the door.

The woman in charge explained that they were selecting people for the apartments who were open-minded about differences. "We want to create a feeling of community in this new building."

She asked Paul a number of questions; some he could answer, others I answered for him. Then she turned to him and said, "So Paul, do you want to live in your own apartment?"

"*NO!*"

The room fell silent.

She didn't know about Paul's many interpretations for the word "no." He likely meant "Not today," or "Not right now," or "Let me get to know you better." She didn't know about the time, years earlier, when Paul and I were going through Customs at the airport. The Customs Officer looked at my passport, saw that we have different last names, looked at Paul and asked, "Is this your mother?"

"*NO!*" he said with the same conviction. "Then why don't you go home with this nice young man," I replied.

The woman from Affordable Housing didn't know how Paul's mind worked, and I watched in horror as she wrote the "No" word on his application. I tried to explain, but I think she wanted to make sure I wasn't pushing Paul out the door. Two days later, I got a call from the director of the Housing Corp. She had made some inquiries and confirmed that Paul *did* want to move; the CEO of Community Living had heard him say so. There were no two-bedroom apartments available, however, so Paul and Jeremy's names went on the list for a one-bedroom apartment each.

A month went by, we hadn't heard anything about the apartments, and I started to have second thoughts. Paul was getting mixed up with his pills at night, it was winter and he'd forget to wear his hat and gloves, and every night he needed prompting to get ready for bed. How would he ever manage on his own? Would he feel lost and scared? Would his early hospital experiences, plus being given up at birth, create feelings of abandonment that would surface when he moved? I had to find out.

I made an appointment for him to see a local psychologist who specialized in cognitive impairment. At the end of the session, she reassured me that Paul's move to independence was absolutely the right thing to do. "The first couple of months may be tough; Paul is no different than anyone else who is living on their own for the first time. The important thing to do is persevere."

"I can do that," I replied. She had no idea that "Perseverance" was my middle name.

She suggested that Paul develop a mantra to repeat if he got upset, for instance, "I am okay, I am strong." "If he calls, don't rush over to the apartment; let Paul work it out with his supporters. If they aren't there, ask Paul to repeat the mantra and add, 'I'll see you Sunday' or 'Take a deep breath and make yourself a cup of tea.'"

"My husband and I decided that once Paul moves, he will only come home on Sundays for the day, rather than for the weekend," I said.

"That's good. Paul needs to establish in his mind that the apartment is his home," she said. "When you're planning his move, I'd also recommend that you put a lot of support at the front end, and then withdraw it as needed."

We had been talking for about 40 minutes. Paul was getting

restless and wanted to leave. "I know it must be hard listening to all of this, Paul," she said. "Does it make you feel anxious?"

Paul nodded his head and inhaled deeply.

"Would you like something to drink?"

"*Coffee with milk,*" he said, looking at me out of the corner of his eye, knowing I couldn't or wouldn't say, "Wouldn't you rather have juice?"

The coffee was gone in two gulps, and the psychologist asked, "Are you going to buy some furniture for your new apartment?"

"*Paul's goeen a buy new T.V.!*" he replied, pumping his arms in the air.

That's all he talked about all the way home, and all he talked about for the next four weeks.

JANUARY 2010. We toasted the New Year with a wish that Paul's goal for independent living would be realized. In the second week of January, I received a call from the director of Affordable Housing inviting us to a meeting at her office.

She began by saying, "I want everyone to understand that we rent apartments for people on fixed incomes. We do not offer any form of support for tenants who have Paul and Jeremy's needs."

"We understood that from the start," Terry replied. "We have all the support arranged should Paul and Jeremy move into one of your units."

"Well, I'm pleased to tell you that Paul and Jeremy have been approved for a one bedroom apartment each."

"Hurray!" Terry, Shannon and I shouted. Our team had just scored a winning goal.

"Paul, give me a high-five!" I said reaching across the table to him.

"*Here Mom*," he said as our hands smacked together.

"We have 30 units at Saunders Court, and at the present time we have 70% occupancy," the director continued. "It will take a couple of weeks before the guys can select their apartments. We're working on getting them side-by-side units so they can share support, as you requested. They should be able to move in by early March."

"Paul loves looking out the window; will he have a unit where he can do that?" I asked, trying not to sound too pushy.

"All the units are lovely, you'll see," she replied. "Even the ones on the lower level have sliding doors with a view. Now, if you're ready, it's time for Paul and Jeremy to sign their lease agreements."

She passed the long white legal documents to each of them along with a pen. I slid next to Paul to explain what he was signing. With the pen in his left hand, he carved his first name in large capital letters on each page.

"I want to get a picture of this moment," I said pulling out my camera.

"We are witnessing the signing of the Declaration of Independence," Terry added. "Be sure to send me a copy!"

This was a momentous occasion, and how I longed to have one clear emotion. The Irish understand the duality of life, and I took comfort from the words of Daniel O'Leary: "Every joy has its sorrow. We have to learn to hold ambiguity in our lives. This is always the way it will be: it is the way it is."

The following week, on Friday, January 22, I received a call from Affordable Housing. The apartments were ready.

"Paul, we're going to see your new apartment today," I told him.

"*Lacinda,*" he replied with some hesitation. "*What are we doing after?*"

"We'll probably come back home."

This had become Paul's standard response to an activity; he always wanted to know what was coming next. Lately, he had added a new twist which made his question impossible to answer: "*What are we doing before-after?*"

Murray rescheduled his working day, rounded up his tape measure and notebook, and we drove to Paul's new apartment building. The Booths and Steve were already in the lobby and we all waited for the director to arrive with the keys. Everyone was excited except Paul. He stood apart from the group with a bewildered look in his eyes. His dark blue parka was zipped up to his chin; his toque was pulled over his eyebrows and ears, and his hands were jammed in his pockets.

When the director arrived, we all squeezed into the elevator and rode one floor down to the terrace level. "You guys are at this end, close to the elevator. This is your apartment, Paul," she said, unlocking the door. "Flick on the lights."

"This is really and truly your new apartment," I said, admiring the open space that contained a galley kitchen, eating area and small living room.

"Where shall we put your new couch and your TV?" I asked enthusiastically.

Paul didn't reply. He took his hands out of his pockets and went to the only thing that looked familiar, the sliding patio doors, and tuned them to the wind. Satisfied that they worked, he began to walk around the apartment as though it was a mine field. Slowly, and silently he made his way into the bedroom, through the walk-through closet to the bathroom. When he opened the door to the walk-in storage closet, he lifted his head. "You could put your vacuum cleaner in there," I told him, "your new black one."

With that, his face brightened. "*Paul's vacuum!*" He went inside and inspected the space carefully. At last, he could picture something concrete, his vacuum cleaner in his closet, ready for action. Satisfied, he closed the door and announced, "*Paul wantsa go.*"

We drove home, but I could easily have run there and back again. This time, there were no mixed emotions, and I revelled in the feeling of unbridled joy. It was my turn. It was Paul's turn.

I emailed photos of the apartment to Paul's Circle and to friends, and my girlfriend Joanna wrote back, "I'm actually sitting here in tears thinking about Paul's accomplishments; how much he has matured and now he's ready for the next step in his life's adventure. You must be so very, very proud of your son. I hope you never forget to remind yourself of how you reached for the stars and kept the faith."

I sat back in my desk chair and thought about all the challenges Paul and I had been through. He was taking his rightful place in the community with all the rights and responsibility that entailed. "You bet I'm proud of you, Paul Tiller!" I called out.

"*Pardon Mom?*" came a reply from downstairs.

The following Saturday, we took Paul shopping so he could select his own living room furniture. For so many years, he sat cross-legged on the floor in front of his television, but now he liked stretching out on the reclining chair in the living room, so he chose a recliner and a tan-coloured couch to match. "How about a colourful rug?" I asked.

"*Paul wantsa orange one,*" he said choosing a burnt-orange area rug.

The saleswoman understood the significance of Paul's purchases, and suggested we put everything together in the show room so he could see how his new living room would look. Paul immediately jumped into the chair, yanked on the lever to raise the foot rest and leaned back.

"I hope it's sturdy," Murray said with a laugh.

Our next stop was the electronics store, where Paul picked out and paid for a flat-screen television. "You are buying this with your own money, from your job at the Holiday Inn," I told him, to help him grasp the relationship between work and money. We both carried the box into his apartment and placed it to display a large picture of a couple watching the television.

"*Open the box! Paul wantsa new T.V.*" he said.

"You agreed to leave it in the box until you move. You can watch the old one until then." I knew it was tough, making Paul look at the picture of his TV for three weeks, but I remembered how he had reacted to moving his bed downstairs. He needed something tangible to motivate him when moving day came, and the television was it.

That evening, the phone rang. It was Paul calling on his cell phone from downstairs. He only had two words to say, but they were enough. "*Night Mom.*"

WE ARE ALL A PRODUCT OF OUR UPBRINGING, and Paul's impeding move made me think about my own journey to independence. I was 18 when I left Calgary and eagerly boarded a train for Ontario, with my parents standing stoically on the platform waving goodbye.

My mother was 60, the same age I would be in a few months. I cried all the way from Calgary to Medicine Hat, not because I didn't want to go, but because I knew my mother was thinking I wouldn't be back. And I knew she was right. It wasn't until she had a heart attack the following December that I began to appreciate how hard my leaving must have been on her.

Paul was only moving across town, but I knew as surely as my mother did that this was the end of our life together as we had known it. I sat with a cup of tea in the living room and thought about how much I'd miss him. In another month, he wouldn't be bursting through the door calling, "*Maaam*" with news about the "*Zamboni*" at the Holiday Inn, or "*Jim, da bus driver.*" And it would be so quiet.

Last week, he had forgotten to take his towels out of the dryer, so the homemaker suggested he use a fleece blanket to dry himself. His laughter had floated all the way up the stairs.

I remembered a passage in the Bible where Jesus said to Simon, "Put out into the deep water and let down your nets for a catch." I thought about how much easier it is for all of us to stay close to the safety of the shore, where the terrain is familiar and the risks are fewer. The *deep* water is unknown, unfathomable, but that's where the fish are.

Even though Paul was leaving our home, he was not going alone. His support workers, and Circle members would help him move into the open water and set his own course. Forty-two years ago, my mother had loved me so much she had let me go. I was prepared to do the same for Paul.

"It is not an easy art, to do the loving thing," said Daniel O'Leary in his book, *Travelling Light, Your Journey to Wholeness*. And "the profound poet Rainer Maria Rilke was well aware of this truth."

> For one human being to love another human being
> that is perhaps
> the most difficult task that has been entrusted to us
> the ultimate task, the final test and proof,
> the work for which all other work is merely preparation.

Paul's last Circle meeting in our home was scheduled for February 20, 2010, and the finality of it made me cry out. My head, neck, and shoulders felt as though someone had tightened a winch between them; my back ached and my head throbbed. "Breathe deeply," I kept telling myself, pressing my fingers into my temples.

Paul was excited about the meeting, and he enthusiastically greeted each person at the door, waving them into his apartment. "*Hello Juudee!*" he said grabbing her arm. And then "*John Perkins!*" arrived with a tribute "*AIIIYEEE!*" Sarah and Dick came and so did "*Best Buddy Alex.*"

Theresa sent Paul a pair of red Olympic mitts, and Judy complimented them with an Olympic scarf with *Canada* in big white letters. Paul immediately put the scarf around his neck and kept the mitts on until the cookies were passed. Every person was here for Paul, and he knew it. I watched it all unfold, no longer as the conductor, but from a new place, somewhere in the orchestra.

The next evening, I was going up the stairs as Paul was coming down. He looked so grown-up, so self-assured. "How am I going to manage without you?" I asked. "Do you think I'll be all right?"

"*Yeah,*" he muttered, brushing past me. His response was typical of *any* young person moving on with their life.

"I think you're right," I called back from the top of the stairs.

I thought I was ready to let go of Paul, but the universe must not have been so sure. It's the only explanation for what happened next. It was eight days before moving day, and that evening I had attended a show of photographs destined for the hospital's new emergency department.

It had been a typical winter day of mixed precipitation. When I drove up the driveway to the house, I noticed the green garbage pail by the front door and that Paul's apartment was in darkness; he had gone to bed on his own. Murray was out, so I clipped Molly's leash onto her collar and picked up the garbage can in my right hand. I didn't know there was a thin layer of ice under the snow, any more than I knew the outer edges of my smart red patent boots were worn down to the white plastic.

Molly may have tugged on her leash, I'm not sure. All I remember is becoming airborne and seeing my legs stretched out in front of me. Then, with considerable velocity and a thud, I landed on my outstretched arm. The pain was instantaneous and intense. "I've broken my wrist," I yelled into the empty night.

I lay on the cold asphalt clutching my arm and considered my options. There was only one. Murray and the Emerge doctors were at the art show, and that's where I needed to be. I drove back downtown with all the windows open, praying that I would make it. The head of the emergency department came outside, touched my arm, and said the words I wanted to hear. "I'll call and tell them to expect you."

Despite the efforts of the attending physician to reposition the bones, I had to have a titanium rod inserted in my wrist. I had never broken anything before and had to ask myself, "Is this what it took for me to make a break with Paul?" The only answer I could come up with was, "Probably." I now had no choice but to step aside and make room for others.

A few days later, Paul and I were sitting morosely in the living room. My fingers were swollen like sausages, and he looked like he had lost his best friend.

"Are you worried about your move?" I asked him.

"*Yes*," he said, nodding emphatically.

Instead of telling him everything would be fine, I drew on the conversation we'd had with the psychologist and said, "I know this must be scary for you. It's scary for anyone to move for the first time. Let's talk about the times you were brave. Do you want to do that?"

"Yes Mom, Paul wantsa talk about that."

"You were brave when you got over your fear and went into the mall with Joel. Remember when you were little, and went to camp all by yourself? You were brave when you went snowmobiling with Uncle Eric, and when you rode the bus for the first time all by yourself. Remember when you were afraid to go to the Stage Café because it was too loud, and now you're okay with it? I think you are very brave and strong. Can you tell me that?"

"*Paul's brave 'n strong*," he replied. His head lifted.

"Remember, you will come back here every Sunday to see me, Murray and Molly."

Then I named the familiar support people who would still be in his life, ending with the pièce de resistance – "Alex will be staying with you overnight for the first little while."

"*Pardon Mom?*" his eyes brightened. "*I wanna see Best Buddy Alex!*" he said, jumping off the couch. "*What times he comeen?*"

"When you move, Paul, in four more days."

—⁂—

With my arm in a cast, I had time to reflect on how far Paul had come since leaving school and some of the reasons why. He had been doing HANDLE exercises for the last three years, activities designed to create new pathways and crossovers in the brain for people with learning or life difficulties. As a result, Paul's fine motor skills had improved, he had stopped drooling, and he no long recoiled when an electric razor touched his face. At long last, his chin was dry and smooth.

Another factor in his progress was not being around kids with "behaviours" all day. His role models now were people in the community: bus drivers, "Dan the Man" and the staff at the Wellness Centre, John Perkins, and co-workers at the Holiday Inn who valued Paul for his contribution.

I took a deep breath and thought about the plans we had made with Jeremy's parents and Steve over the last six months. We were ready. It was grounding to know that Paul's weekly activities would remain the same; he would just be doing them in a different location. Steve, as coordinator, had put a good support team in place. He had arranged for young men to take turns sleeping overnight in Paul and Jeremy's living rooms for a few weeks, until they were ready to stay on their own. The Red Cross homemakers would continue in the mornings, and Steve would make sure Paul got to his new bus stop, transferred at the terminal, got to where he was going, and found his way back to his new home. He would also supervise Paul's workouts three times a week, to build his endurance and connections in the community.

Barb, who had worked with Paul for two years, would do the menu planning for the month, and then spend time every week helping Paul shop for groceries and prepare two meals. She would do the same thing for Jeremy, so there would be plenty of nutritious food in each of their fridges. Other supporters were scheduled to help the guys with dinner preparation, prompt them to do their laundry, clean their apartments and settle in each night. Paul and Jeremy would share the evening staff and split the cost. Cost-sharing was the key to both guys having their independence.

On the weekend, we began the process of emptying one apartment and filling up another. Barb and her son came to help pack and move boxes; they added four strong arms to my one. Murray picked up Paul's couch, chair and rug from the furniture store and delivered them to the new apartment. "*Paul's new chair!*" he exclaimed when he saw it. Murray had made an oak television cabinet especially for Paul's new place. "Where does it go?" Murray asked, as it was carried into the apartment.

"*Over there*," Paul said, pointing to the wall across from the sliding doors." At that moment, a ray of sunshine touched the cabinet doors, turning them to soft gold. Murray's cabinet was truly a labour of love.

—m—

The next day, Monday, March 5, 2010, was the one we had been working toward for years. "Hop in the car so you'll be at your apartment when Murray arrives with the rest of your furniture," I said to him. We were half way there when I realized Paul had been in such a hurry, he was still wearing his bedroom slippers. He stood in the middle of his new apartment waving in each item like an eager traffic cop. "*Here we go Murreee*," he said as the television finally arrived in its new home.

With a sigh of satisfaction, Paul plopped onto his lazy-boy chair, flipped up the foot rest and stretched out.

"Will you help put your CD's away?" I asked him.

"*O.K. Mom*," he said, closing the foot rest with a bang.

"This is your very own apartment, Paul. What do you think?" He looked around the room, then raised both arms over his head in a symbol of victory. His actions said it all. This was Paul's moment of glory and he had worked harder for it than any of us will ever know.

By suppertime, we had finished the unpacking and putting away. Steve had asked Barb to make a crock-pot meal for Paul and Jeremy's first night in their apartments so they would feel the immediate benefit of their newfound independence.

Murray and I looked around the apartment and at one another. There was really nothing left for us to do. I looked at Paul, who was giving me that "are you still here" look. I knew it was time to go.

"Well done, Paul," Murray said clapping him on the back.

Paul beamed. Murray's approval meant so much to him.

"See you Sunday. Phone me if you want..." I said from the hallway, as Paul closed his apartment door.

Murray and I walked to the car in silence. It was almost surreal. I had looked forward to this moment for so long, planned it for months, and it had just happened. Paul had moved into his own apartment with the support he needed. A glow of contentment flowed into my heart; a new chapter had just begun, not just for Paul, but also for Murray and me.

"Well, sweetheart, how shall we celebrate?" he asked, holding the car door open.

"I'd love to pop a cork, but all I really want to do is go home to bed," I replied as a blanket of fatigue enveloped me. "Can I have a rain check?"

Before long, I was under the covers. "Good night Paul, God bless you," I whispered before slipping into a long, uninterrupted sleep.

The next morning, I was listening to a program on CBC radio about "Boomerang Kids." The announcer said they are adult children, 19 to 29 years of age, who continue to live at home. Apparently, 30 is the new 20. He explained that many young people today are taking more time to explore possibilities in work and relationships, and as a consequence, they continue to live under their parents' roofs.

I thought about Paul, who had just moved into his own apartment at 24, disability and all. I recalled the conversation I'd had with his paediatrician, 20 years earlier, about Paul being "developmentally delayed," and whether or not he would ever catch up. I wanted to phone him and say, "You know what, I think Paul just has!"

IN PREPARATION FOR PAUL'S MOVE I read Ian Brown's prize-winning book, *The Boy in the Moon*, about his son Walker, who lives with multiple disabilities. Brown had traveled to L'Arche communities in Canada and France in his quest to understand the meaning of his son's life. There, he found insight into community life integral to the L'Arche experience: assistants, people without disabilities, live along-side those with severe physical and intellectual impairments in complete equality and reciprocity. Brown writes that the experience creates a "collective intelligence" that is more sophisticated than either group could produce on their own. This helped to explain the effect Paul had on people with whom he had close relationships. They wanted to be with him, not out of a sense of duty, but because together they experienced something unique.

During his time at L'Arche, Brown also came to understand the difference between weakness and fragility. His son, like so many living with a disability, has a body that is fragile, but he is anything but weak. People with disabilities have an inner strength and resilience that helps them survive in a world that is not designed for them.

Paul showed how much strength he possessed, and how important others were to his success. That first week, he didn't call home once. He was surrounded by a team of caring supporters committed to helping him achieve as much independence as he could manage. He knew from his experience at camp, and the times Murray and I had been away, that he could trust others to look out for him.

Some mothers report feeling melancholy when their kids leave home, but I'd processed those emotions and felt relief, knowing Paul could get along without me. That didn't mean I wasn't excited to see him the following Sunday. I drove to his apartment in record time, pressed the buzzer inside the entrance, and waited for him to pick up the phone.

"Hi, Paul, will you let me in please?" I asked.

"*What?*" he replied, obviously confused by how to do that.

It wasn't a problem; we had installed a lock-box inside the front door with his keys in it, so I was able to let myself in. After some training, he was more successful when I buzzed his apartment two weeks later.

"*Who is it?*" he replied to my request to let me in.

"It's your mother, for heaven sakes!" I started to laugh.

"*Your mother,*" he echoed, as though he was meeting me for the first time. After a few tries, Paul pressed number nine on his phone, and the lock on the lobby door clicked open.

Before long, it was evident that Paul and I had both moved on emotionally. For the first time in a long time, I woke up feeling rested.

For the past six months, Steve, Terry, Shannon and I had been having planning meetings every Friday afternoon at Command Central, our kitchen table. We continued the practise to find out from Steve how the guys were doing, and to pass on parental advice; we couldn't help ourselves. Murray and I were amazed at how quickly Paul adapted to living on his own, and how readily he grasped the idea that "the buck stopped with him." He didn't have us, particularly me, to whine or complain to, so he had stopped. "Why didn't I figure this out before?" I asked myself.

"Paul and Jeremy have accomplished things in weeks that I thought it would take them months to learn," Steve said.

"You could always depend on Paul to rise to a challenge," Murray replied, "and he's proved that once again."

"Do you think this is just a honeymoon phase, and that problems might arise later?" I asked.

"It's possible, but I don't think so," Steve said. "It feels really firm."

—⁓—

Lately, I've been asked to share the story of Paul's move with parents who are exploring options for their son or daughter, but it's not easy to condense 13 years of preparation into 20 minutes. It didn't happen just because an affordable housing unit had become available.

The process we went through with Paul is like building a house. One of the things Murray enjoys most about constructing a new home is building the foundation. He'd come home worn out and covered in mud, so I didn't fully understand the attraction until now. Murray knows the foundation must be level and square, otherwise errors are compounded as the house is built. It requires planning and accuracy in the beginning for the home to be structurally sound in the end.

For the first time ever, the only people who came into our home were people who were invited. In the morning, it didn't matter what I wore or didn't wear around the house; I didn't have to rise early and unlock the front door for the homemaker; and I didn't have to find a replacement if a support worker called in sick. For the first time in 24 years, I was no longer on call 24-7. Murray and I found it was the little things that made a big difference. We could now spontaneously accept an invitation for dinner, go to a movie, or hop on our bikes.

"Why?" we'd ask ourselves.

"Because we can!" we'd reply in unison.

We had a trip planned to celebrate our newfound freedom, but Murray's Dad became seriously ill and we had to cancel. I didn't realize how tired I must have looked after Paul's move, my broken wrist, and managing an Art and Healing fundraiser until I went to the hospital to visit him.

"I'm here to see Lloyd Leadbeater," I said to the nurse in ICU. "Are you his wife?" she asked.

"He's 87 years old! Good grief, I'm his daughter-in-law." By the time Lloyd recovered, I was using a new face cream.

For some much-needed rest, I returned to the Spirituality Centre on the shores of Lake Ontario, the one I had retreated to the year I turned 50. I opened the door to the same room I'd had 10 years earlier, stretched out on the little bed in front of me and fell asleep. I roused myself for meals, but slept for a total of 14 hours.

The next day, Sister Alma, the Spiritual Director, counselled me. "Be open to surprises and to why you are here. Be careful not to fill up your time with reading, writing or sleeping. Take time to listen to God." I took her advice and enjoyed silent walks on the beach and times of quiet meditation.

Before I left home, I'd read an article about the nesting behaviour of robins, and to my delight, I discovered a robin's nest in front of a tiny window near my room. Inside it, a mother robin was feeding her newly hatched chicks. Their scrawny heads sprouted wispy afros, their hungry beaks gaped wide.

I carefully moved a little closer to the glass and watched as the mother swallowed something from the nest, then picked up a piece of broken blue shell and flew away, just like the article said she would. She too would nurture her young until it was time for them to leave. It's an integral part of mothering.

—m—

At long last, I was just Paul's mom. Now that we were no longer butting heads on a regular basis, I was able to enjoy the young man others said was so much fun. On Sunday mornings, we went to our church's contemporary service, where everyone sat in a semi-circle instead of a pew, and sang to the upbeat music played by his friends Emily, Chris and Christian. Paul strode into the Parish hall, called out their names, and then raised his right arm in a salute and greeting, "*Good morning, Father Gordon!*"

"Good morning, Paul," he replied, obviously delighted.

"Paul lights up the room when he comes in," Gordon told me later. "I'm so glad he is here; he brings a smile to everyone's face."

Paul isn't encumbered by analyzing whether or not God exists; his life expresses God's love, unconditionally.

When we got home, Paul began talking about what he wanted to do next.

"*Wouldja like take Molly for a walk?*" "*How bout a bike ride Lakefield?*"

Paul was our man in motion. On Sunday afternoons, he was either doing something active outside, or moving through the living room to the beat of his Walkman, pressing his hands against the window as he went. I'd discover the imprint on the glass the next day; it reminded me of the painted handprint he brought home from kindergarten on Mother's Day. He'd left a little something of himself behind.

Generally things were going well until, four months later, I was awakened out of a deep sleep by Molly barking and the phone ringing. Murray jumped out of bed to answer it. I rolled over and looked at the clock; it was 4:22. "Go to bed Paul!" I heard him say, before slamming down the phone.

"What, what did he want?" It wasn't like Paul to call at any time, let alone wake us up.

"I don't know," he mumbled and rolled over.

My heart was pounding as I scrambled to find the phone. It took a few seconds before it dawned on me to turn on the light, and a few more to steady my shaking fingers. Paul's phone rang and rang. "Pick it up, pick it up" I said between clenched teeth.

Click.

I pressed redial. "This is Paul's phone…" It was my own damned voice: he had turned his phone off. I jumped into my clothes and ran down the stairs to my car. Even though the streets were empty, I drove carefully. I entered Paul's hushed apartment building feeling like an intruder, using the keys in the lock-box to get in. I knocked softly on his door and inserted the key. The dog down the hall barked once.

Inside, all the lights were on, the drapes were drawn, and there he was, dressed in the same clothes he was wearing the night before. A movie was playing on the flat-screen television; it had probably been playing since the night before. We had been at a Homes for Life barbeque, and Paul had helped himself to at least two, maybe three cans of Coke. The caffeine had likely revved his brain, and it had become stuck on rewind. His phone call was a plea for help.

"Hand it over," I said pointing to the DVD. My voice was commanding, but my heart was mush with relief that he was all right. "You'd better get going on your night-time routine. And don't forget to set your alarm clock; it's going to go off in three hours. It's Monday and you have to go to work."

He shot me a baleful look and headed for his bedroom. I closed the apartment door behind me. Paul was finding out that being independent includes making mistakes and facing the consequences. He was learning important life lessons, and I didn't want him to miss out on any of them.

When I was 16, I could hardly wait to get my driver's license and experience the freedom of being able to go places, preferably without my parents. Paul will never be able to drive; his ticket to independence is the bus. And it now stopped half a block from his apartment.

He loved talking about the route to the Holiday Inn. "*George North, transfer Collison, do the loop.*"

"The loop" meant Paul was on the bus 30 minutes longer so he didn't have to cross a busy street. For him, the longer the bus ride, the better.

Once Paul mastered catching the bus to work, his supporter Jenn suggested he expand his repertoire and learn how to transfer to a new bus. She showed him the route on the map, and they talked about where he would get off. She thought she had everything coordinated with the bus driver, but somehow their wires crossed, and when she met Paul's bus, he wasn't on it. He had gotten off at an earlier stop. Jenn backtracked and found him standing in the pouring rain, with the bus driver beside him. He had walked Paul across the road and was waiting for Jenn; the bus's four-way flashers greeted her arrival.

I was delighted to know that people in our community were watching out for him; what more could a mother ask for on her 60th birthday? Other than a glass of champagne, of course.

AUGUST MARKED PAUL'S 14TH YEAR AT CAMP WANAKITA. When we picked him up he was full of his usual excitement about driving "*the pontoon boat and the Johnson.*" This year he added, "*Paul drives the Raangeer*" his voice rising as he named the brand of the ATV they drove between the cabins.

Paul's counsellor Hal walked us to the car with stories of how Paul made everyone laugh. "Everyone likes Paul's dog jokes. He makes jokes about no dogs on the boat, no dogs in the CORE, in the campfire, in the kai-boe, on the Ranger. One night, we were all sitting around the cabin making music and Mike found the dog-barking button on the keyboard. Paul started to laugh and pretty soon everyone in the cabin was on the floor."

Paul reliving the moment, cheered with his arms over his head, an expression of unbridled joy on his face.

"Why don't you tell your parents what happened on the dock," Hal said.

"*Paul threw water a Neil!*" He said, barely able to contain himself. "*Good gracious!*"

"Then Neil threw one over you," Hal said. "As if that wasn't enough, Paul pushed another counsellor Justin off the dock, and laughed so hard he got the hiccups."

When we got to the car, Hal thanked *me* for bringing Paul to camp. "Wasn't it just yesterday that it was the other way around?" I said to myself.

"See you next year," he said to Paul, tapping on the car window.

Paul barely waved; he knew he wouldn't see his friends for another year. Half-way down the camp road an idea came to him that lifted his spirits. "*Hey, Murree, see Grandpa Lloyd atta coddage, go fora boa ride?*"

Paul was, and still is a boy of summer. When it's over, he has to press the re-set button, and return to his routine. The fact that he's able to do it while living on his own gives me insight into how much his apartment means to him. It also demonstrates how much the support staff contribute to his success.

"We're a team," Barb said to me one day, with pride in her voice. "We have responsibility and are given credit for our ability to make good decisions. We can text or call Steve on his cell phone and get an immediate response – it keeps the communication channels open and makes it all work."

Every Sunday evening, Paul willingly returned to his apartment – with one exception. He'd been home over the Labour Day weekend and enjoyed the comforts of home a little too much. When I drove him to his place, he stayed rooted in the front seat of the car and said, "*Paul's not going to apartment. I wan stay home.*"

I knew I was in trouble. I could hardly drag him out of the car and down the hallway, so I recited the litany he had heard many times before: "Your apartment is your new home, we'll see you next Sunday, I'm proud of how mature you are ..."

He just looked at me.

"Paul, do you remember the dark red vacuum cleaner Mary Gareau gave you? We put it in your closet beside the black one."

"*Pardon, Mom?*"

I was gaining ground; he wanted to hear it again.

"Let's go inside and see if that new vacuum cleaner works."

He perked up at the prospect and he jumped out of the car. I touched my index finger to my lips and drew a line in the air – chalk one up for "*da Mom.*"

Later that month, Murray, Paul and I were having supper at dusk on the screened-in porch, the one I had wished for 15 years earlier. We only had a few minutes left before the early autumn chill would take us inside. Paul was still at the table; ordinarily he ate and ran, but tonight, he was eager to talk about what he was doing on Monday.

"*Whatcha doing tomorrow Mom?*" he began.

"Do you mean what are you doing tomorrow?

"*Yes.*"

"Then why don't you tell me."

He recited his schedule and then he asked the question that had been on his mind for years: "*What time is the 9:20 bus?*"

"What time do you think?" I replied.

Paul looked at me, a gleam came into his eyes, and he announced, "*It's at 9:20!*"

"He finally got it," Murray laughed.

"You are absolutely right!" I said. "Independent living has made you smarter."

We all continue to learn and grow as we age, and Paul was no different.

—∽—

In November, there was a federal election and Paul's soccer coach was a candidate, which gave him a good reason to exercise his citizenship rights. "Do want to vote for Coach Betsy?" I asked

"*Yes I do.*"

Even though Paul didn't understand politics, he knew his coach was a good person and he was proud to put his X beside her name. I drove him back to his apartment, and as we approached the building, I asked him if he wanted me to let him off at the back door of the building, or at the front.

"*Front door,*" he said without hesitation.

We drove around the circular driveway to the main door, and Paul jumped out. I watched him pull his key chain out of his pocket, carefully choose the right one, and open the door to the lobby. With the confidence of a young man and the sweetness of a boy, Paul turned and looked at me. For the first time in his life, he placed his left hand over his mouth, and with a sweep extended his arm toward me. His kiss landed exactly where he intended it – on my heart.

—∽—

The year sped by like a movie on fast-forward; it was time to celebrate Paul and Jeremy's first anniversary. We gathered in Jeremy's apartment with the Booths, the staff and members of Paul's Circle, to raise our glasses to these two young men, and acknowledge how far they had come.

Paul grinned and jumped up and down in response to the praise and attention. We had bubbly wine, cheese and presentations: a medal for Steve, engraved with "For going above and beyond the call of duty;" and one each for Paul and Jeremy with their names on one side, and the word "Independent" engraved on the other.

Murray presented Paul with his medal, saying, "Paul, you've made me very happy." I laughed at the understated significance of his remark.

All the talk about Paul being independent must have gone to his head. It was as if he was thinking, "If you think I'm independent now, watch this!"

It was Monday morning, and his female supporter called to say he hadn't shown up for work. She had waited for almost an hour, but he wasn't answering his phone. She didn't have a car, and it was Steve's day off.

Previously, he'd taken off to the mall on his own so I called there, but the security guard hadn't seen him. I drove to his apartment without any luck, and kept calling his cell phone, but it just rang and rang.

On my way down Lansdowne St, a block before the mall, I spotted him. He was standing at the curb wearing his blue Holiday Inn shirt with his royal blue backpack over his shoulders. He looked like any young man waiting for a bus, except there was no bus stop in sight. I wheeled into the parking lot beside him and rolled down the passenger's window.

"Where do you think you're going?"

"*To Canadian Tire.*"

"This is Monday morning. You're supposed to be at work at the Holiday Inn!" I was truly ticked. "Get in the car and I'll drive you to work."

With some reluctance, Paul got in the front seat. There were crumbs lingering on his chin and white streaks down his pant leg which, if sent to forensics, would probably have revealed remnants of a Boston cream donut.

"Have you been to Tim's?" There was one half- a- block away.

"*No, Mom,*" he replied without conviction. He wasn't going to give me any more ammunition.

Paul's supervisor wanted to be contacted when we found him. While we were waiting for her, I said to Paul, "You could lose your job, you know." He turned pale. This was something that never crossed his mind.

"It's important to treat Paul the same as every other employee," I said to his supervisor.

"Then I'll write this up for his file. I'll meet you later in my office," she said, looking at him. "We were all worried about you."

The reprimand from his employer shook Paul up. It shook me up too, but it was what he needed. It's difficult to teach Paul how to be responsible; he had to learn it through a real-life situation. If he wanted to have rights, he had to live up to his responsibilities.

"Some people would call in sick, if they didn't feel like going to work on a Monday morning," my friend Joanna said. "Paul doesn't know how to do that, so he tested the limits in his own way."

That put things into context for me. As much as Paul relied on routine, he also wanted the freedom to do what he wanted. His actions showed he needed help making good decisions; they also revealed he was thinking clearly. He knew where the donut shop was and had figured out which bus to take to get there. And if he had walked further up the street to the bus stop, he would have made it to Canadian Tire.

—⁂—

There was a reason why Paul's brain was clearer. The previous spring, he and I met with his neurologist to discuss whether or not Paul could come off the last of his seizure medication. Dr. Munn put the question back to me.

"Some people would say everything is fine the way it is, so leave well enough alone. Others could argue, why not take the risk? It's up to you."

Many years earlier, I had read about a teenage boy in the States with Tuberous Sclerosis who had come off all drugs and was seizure-free. At the time, it had seemed impossible; Paul was taking 2,900 mg of anti-convulsants in 14 pills every day. Nevertheless, the idea stuck in my head – someone had proved it could be done.

"Paul's been swallowing pills for 25 years," I told the doctor. "Let's go for it!"

"Then proceed gradually and reduce his pills over the next six months," he said.

Paul's pills were cut into halves and then quarters until it was hard to find the fragment in the dish. On the first of January 2012, I said to him, "You don't have to take pills anymore. You're finished."

"*That's it!*" he replied.

When I told the pharmacist, he looked at me in disbelief. "It's like a miracle," he said.

"That's exactly what it is!" I wanted to jump over the counter, the one Paul had run behind many years ago, and give him a hug.

"Paul's an example of what is possible," I told him. "Sometimes, all we need is for someone to show us the way."

Paul was making a lot of gains but he was still vulnerable. Before driving him back to his apartment, I checked his wallet. His change purse was totally empty – not one thin dime or copper penny remained. He should have had at least $20 in his wallet, but there was only a $5 bill.

"Did someone ask you for your money, Paul?" I said.

"*Yes.*"

"Who?"

"*A lady.*"

"Where was the lady?"

"*At Kawartha Dairy.*"

"That lady was fine – you were paying for a milkshake. If someone, a stranger, says to you, 'I want some money,' what do you say?"

"*Yes.*"

"No, Paul, not if you don't know them."

"*Mom. Can I stay Lacinda's house tonight?*"

He'd been home over the Thanksgiving weekend, sleeping in his old room, enjoying the company of his cousins, and having Mom cook his meals. The novelty of looking after himself was obviously wearing a little thin.

Fortunately I had another ace up my sleeve. "You can't get the bus to the Holiday Inn from the house, and tomorrow is Monday." In a flash, he put his iPod in his backpack and was at the front door waiting for a ride to his apartment. There was no way he was going to miss going to work on the bus.

Driving back home, the pain in my left shoulder intensified. At first I thought it was computer related, but then I realized it's where I hold Paul. When he moved, I gave up control, but not my concern about his future.

"At times, I can't get him out of my head." I told Murray. "This letting go is a complex process."

"I don't know how you do it," he replied. "I can't begin to understand it."

Paul stopped asking to stay at home overnight. He made a new request; to go to Toronto on the Greyhound bus, by himself to see his cousins.

"Paul wantsa go CN Tower, ride streetcar and subway. See Carelin an Laura."

Jeremy had gone to Toronto by bus to see his brother, and now Paul was eager to do it too. Gone were the days when Paul was afraid of the traffic noise, the crowded sidewalks and the steep steps going down to the subway on his way to doctors' appointments. His cousins, the same ones he went camping with 15 years ago, were looking forward to the day as much as Paul. Rain was forecasted, but this time, no one needed to buy a tarpaulin!

—⁓—

Paul's second anniversary of independence coincided with a trip Murray and I took to Nairobi, Kenya, to meet our foster son. I had corresponded with Bernard for ten years and eventually put him through university in mechanical engineering. When we finally met, I said to him, "I helped you through university because of Paul. He wasn't going on in school, so I decided to give you that chance. You wanted it so much, and your faith and persistence were qualities I admired."

My heart had been open to Bernard's request for an education, just as John Perkins had been open to my request to take Paul swimming, so many years ago. They seemed to be isolated events at the time, but they revealed a thread of loving kindness that had woven our lives together. Jean Vanier captures this connection beautifully: "Love your neighbour as yourself means your neighbour is yourself, and that recognition of oneness is love."

In his book, *God Has a Dream: A Vision of Hope for our Time*, Archbishop Desmond Tutu encourages us to see the world and people in it with the eyes of the heart, not just the eyes of our head. These are the eyes Paul has. He isn't concerned about someone's appearance or their social standing, but with their essence. Paul allows people to be who they truly are and responds with unrestrained joy.

This is his gift to the world.

Epilogue

Paul had been living in his apartment for almost three years when a situation developed that brought me to my knees. The Booths, Steve and I had been meeting regularly for 37 months, and meeting-fatigue had set in. As parents, we wanted to get on with our own lives and were lulled into the misconception that you can maintain relationships and solve problems through email.

Not surprisingly, communication between all of us started to unravel. I had tried to move away from having an active role in Paul's life, and it wasn't going well. The staff had assumed responsibility, and the more suggestions I made, the more I was perceived as interfering.

"You're Paul's mother," my friends said to me, but I no longer knew what that meant. I was plagued with a question I didn't know how to answer: "How do I ensure that Paul continues to have a meaningful life, and still let him go?" It's a dilemma that weighs on parents whose adult sons and daughters have a disability.

I wanted Paul to find his own voice and learn to make decisions without me. At the same time, I wanted his support team to continue to raise the bar and provide him with opportunities to experience all that life has to offer. The rational part of me knew they wanted that too, but communication had broken down, and my emotional side took over. It felt like a tug-of-war.

Each of us has a unique story about our family of origin and how they have influenced who we are. When Paul moved, he had seven different support workers, and each one brought their own way of doing things into his life. He did well adjusting to the personalities and approaches of people on his team; in fact, he was better at it than I. For the dynamics to work, Steve and I needed to meet regularly, but for a variety of reasons that wasn't happening.

There is a segment of our culture that believes mothers of sons need to withhold affection so that an adolescent boy can grow to become "a man." The author and researcher Marni Jackson offers a feminist perspective on mothering. She believes the more affectionate mothers are with their sons, the stronger their sense of self will be, and that this will help protect them from sexual exploitation.

From the moment Paul came into my life, I never withheld my affection for him – even when his birth mother could have snatched him from my arms. His developmental delay was a balm to my mothering nature; he was my little boy for longer than most. He wanted to sit close "*bye sie me*," and hold my hand when we went for a walk. I'd read to him at night on his bed, massage his feet to help him sleep, and lie beside him if he was frightened by a nocturnal seizure. When his father left, it was just me and Paul.

He and I had been through so much together, and even though my head wanted to let him go, it wasn't easy for my heart to cut the tie.

Once Paul was established in his apartment, neither the staff nor I knew how to sustain our relationship over the long haul. We shared the intimacy of a quasi-family, but without a common heritage. The situation reminded me of my early days as a stepmother.

As we drifted farther apart, I felt increasingly vulnerable. My reaction was to try and regain control; Steve's was to become defensive. Our communication problems deepened, and he and I had a disagreement that threatened to split Paul's world apart.

Paul was not immune to the tension around him; he had one cold after another, took off to Tim's for coffee instead of going to work, and on Sundays he sat in the big chair in our living room with tears streaming down his face. He knew something was wrong, but he didn't know what it was.

Jennifer, my Spiritual Director was in Florida, so I had to imagine what she might say to me: "Every time there is conflict with another person, there's an opportunity to learn something about yourself." She never let me off the hook, and I couldn't let myself off either. If I wanted to follow a spiritual path, I had to do the hard work of looking within, to confront my "Shmutz," as Jennifer called it, and respond with an emotion other than self-pity, blame and anger.

I prayed for God's light to enter my heart and the lives of Paul's supporters, and an image came to me through the words of Leonard Cohen. There is a crack in everything: that's how the light gets in.

Maybe this needed to happen, maybe something good would emerge if I held firm. I clung onto that hope. To still my racing heart, I returned to the Meta meditation of loving kindness I had repeated so many times in the past. In Henri Nouwen's teachings I found wisdom and perspective: "Help us to hold the candle that illuminates today, rather than expect a beam which will illuminate the future."

It didn't happen quickly, but gradually, there was a shift inside me and in the situation; the positive energy that was going into the world was coming back. The right people appeared at the right time, including the members of Paul's Circle, who surrounded us with insight, encouragement and support.

Barb, Paul's long-time supporter, said to me, "You and Steve want the same thing; I wish you could find someone, perhaps a mediator, to talk to." I thought carefully about her suggestion, knowing it had come from her heart, and contacted Judith McGill, the woman who helped us establish roles prior to Paul's move. Judith created a safe environment that allowed Steve and me to be honest with one another and admit that we'd made mistakes. We acknowledged that what we were doing was so new, no one in our community had done anything like it before, and we were learning as we went.

The communication channels began to open as Steve and I listened deeply to one another, making sure we understood what the other had said. Murray participated too, offering his perspective and, at the end, his gratitude for all Steve had done to foster Paul's independence.

We learned a lot about each other, and I learned a lot about myself. I realized I had been so focused on Paul that I hadn't paid enough attention to changing how I related to his supporters. I needed to back off and trust Steve to direct the staff.

Along with that, I had to admit to myself that perhaps, just maybe, I'm a perfectionist, especially when it comes to Paul. My ability to make things happen had served him well, but it was time to ease up and allow space for people with different perspectives. To do that I needed to move out of my head and risk letting others see my heart.

We had survived a crisis, and I wanted to make sure I learned as much from it as possible, so it would never happened again. My role had been illuminated. I would always be Paul's mother, maintaining responsibility for his overall health, but the concerns of day to day living belonged to the staff.

Steve and I are partners in Paul's life, and as good partners, we agreed to hold space for communication between us. Murray is the "silent partner;" he makes sure we continue to listen to one another, plus he's the perfect counterbalance to my exacting nature. "Don't worry, Paul will be fine," he reminds me when I make a fretting comment.

Each of us wanted an outcome that was best for Paul. We achieved that, and more. We came close to losing it all – not because we didn't care, but because Steve and I both cared so much. Letting go is a multifaceted process for any mother, and especially so if your child has a disability. It requires belief in their future and trust. It helps that Paul's Circle is there to encourage him to explore new horizons and find his voice.

Circumstances in Paul's life will change, that's one thing I know for sure. And when they do, his Circle, and his support team and are there to help him figure things out.

Not so very long ago, Paul asked to stay overnight at the house, but he no longer makes that request. On a long weekend, when he *could* sleep here, he insists on going back to his apartment. That is where he lives; it's his home.

It's taken a few years, but I've finally come to appreciate that letting go doesn't just happen once, twice or three times, it's a lifetime's work. Paul is now 28, and I think that's exactly what he wants me to do.

Notes

1. Jean Vanier, *Becoming Human* (Toronto: The House of Anansi Press Inc., 2003) p.59
2. Tim Dansel, *In the Midst of Life's Hurts You Can Choose Joy* (Colorado Springs, Colorado: Cook Communication Ministries, 1985)
3. Keith Ellis, *The Magic Lamp* (New York: Three Rivers Press, a division of Random House Inc., 1996) p.21
4. Sharon Butala, "Seeing," in *Dropped Threads: What we Aren't Told*, ed. Carol Shields and Marjorie Anderson (Toronto: Vintage Canada, 2001) p.217
5. Henri J.M. Nouwen, *The Inner Voice of Love: A Journey Through Anguish to Freedom* (Colorado Springs, CO: Image Press, 1999)
6. A "thin place," in J. Phillip Newell, *Listening for the Heatbeat of God; A Celtic Spirituality*, (New Jersey: Paulist Press, 1997)
7. Francisco Varela, cited in Joseph Jaworski , *Synchronicity, The Inner Path of Leadership* (San Francisco, CA: Berrett-Koehler Publishers Inc., 2011) p.179.
8. Jean Vanier, *Finding Peace* (Toronto: House of Anansi Press, 2003)
9. Darcy Elkes Consulting, West Chester PA. www.darcyelkes.com
10. Rabbi Harold S. Kushner, *When Bad Things Happen to Good People* (Toronto: Random House of Canada Ltd., 1981)
11. John McKnight. The Asset-Based Community Development (ABCD) Institute for Policy Research, Northwestern University, Illinois: www.northwestern.edu/IPR/ABCD.HTML. In Canada, ABCD is taught at the COADY Institute at St. Francis Xavier University in Nova Scotia. www.COADY.stfx.ca
12. "The aim of movements is not to adapt to suit society, but to expand notions of what counts as acceptable." *The New Normal*, The Walrus Magazine, March 2013, p. 37
13. Al Condeluci, Author and Speaker, Pittsburgh, PA. www.alcondeluci.com
14. On December 9. 2013, the Ontario government delivered an apology to all the people who lived and suffered at Huronia. Documentary by Michael Enright, DOC: *The Gristle in the Stew*. September 21, 2013 www.cbc.ca/thesundayedition/documentaries.
15. Judith Snow, *The Thirteen Chapters of the Book of Judith* (Toronto: www.bookofjudith.com, 2011)
16. Jack Pearpoint, *From Behind the Piano: The Building of Judith*

Snow's Unique Circle of Friends (Toronto: Inclusion Press, 1998)

17. Shafik Asante, *When Spider Webs Unite* (Toronto: Inclusion Press, 1996)

18. Rumi, *"A Voice Out of the World," Rumi: Fountain of Fire* translated by Nader E Khalili (California: Cal-Earth - California Institute of Art and Architecture, 1994)

19. Eckhart Tolle, *Oneness With All Life* (New York: Penguin Group, 2008)

20. Information on the Services and Supports to Promote the Social Inclusion of Persons with Developmental Disabilities Act, Ontario 2008. http://www.mcss.gov.on.ca/en/mcss/publications/developmentalSe rvices/servicesSupportSocialInclusion.aspx

21. Joseph Jaworski, *Synchronicity, The Inner Path of Leadership* (San Francisco, CA: Berrett-Koehler Publishers Inc., 2011)

22. David Bohm, cited in Joseph Jaworski , *Synchronicity, The Inner Path of Leadership* (San Francisco, CA: Berrett-Koehler Publishers Inc., 2011) p.81

23. David Pitonyak, Finding new stories for people who experience disabilities, www.dimagine.com

24. Judith McGill, Independent facilitation, consulting and mediation, www.lifepathtraining.ca

25. Daniel O'Leary, *Travelling Light: Your Journey to Wholeness* (Blackrock County Dublin: The Columbia Press, 2009) p.42

26. The unique HANDLE approach has been shown to effectively address a wide range of learning, behavior, and developmental issues. www.handle.org

27. Ian Brown, *The Boy in the Moon* (Toronto: Vintage Canada, 2010) p.227

28. Desmond Tutu, *God Has a Dream: A Vision of Hope for our Time* (Colorado Springs CO: Image, Doubleday, a division of Random House, 2005) p.141

29. Marni Jackson, "Tuck me In: Redefining Attachment Between Mothers and Sons," *Dropped Threads: What We Aren't Told*, ed. Carol Shields and Marjorie Anderson (Toronto: Vintage Canada, 2001) p.66

30. Joan Borsyenko, *A Pocketfull of Miracles, Prayers, Mediations and Affirmations to Nurture Your Spirit Every Day of the Year* (New York: Time Warner, 1994) p.60

31. Henri J.M. Nouwen, *Can You Drink This Cup?* (Notre Dame Indiana: Ave Maria Press, 1996)

Resources

Inclusion

1. Reach for the Rainbow. Integrated summer camps in Ontario: www.reachfortherainbow.ca
2. Individualized Funding Coalition for Ontario: www.individualizedfunding.ca
3. Ready, Willing and Able: www.readywillingandable.ca This initiative is designed to increase labour force participation of people with intellectual disabilities, and thereby advance economic productivity and social inclusion in Canada.
4. iBelong, designed to help young adults develop friendships: www.ibelong.ca
5. Inspirational training modules for the intellectually disabled workforce: www.openfuturelearning.com
6. Articles and ideas on inclusion and belonging that can empower individuals, families, and communities: www.johnlord.net
7. Advocacy support and creating friendships for persons living with disabilities: www.citizenadvocacy.org
8. Inclusion Press for workshops and books on Circles, Planning, School Resources, Building Relationships, Creating Community and more: www.inclusion.net

Planning

1. Planned Lifetime Advocacy Network. Books, seminars, strategies - a valuable website: www.plan.ca
2. *Safe and Secure: Six steps to creating a good life for people with disabilities*, Al Etmanski: www.plan.ca
3. PLAN Toronto provides support, seminars, resources www.plantoronto.ca
4. Supported Employment Training Project (SETP), University of Kentucky, Lexington Kentucky. http://www.hdi.uky.edu/setp/
5. *Make a Difference: A Guidebook for Person-Centered Direct Support*, John O'Brien and Beth Mount, Inclusion Press. www.inclusion.com
6. Families for a Secure Future is dedicated to serving adults with developmental disabilities and assisting them to take up their full citizenship in the community. www.familiesforasecurefuture.ca

7. Judith McGill, independent facilitation, consulting and mediation, www.lifepathtraining.ca

Support

1. Family Support Institute of British Columbia: designed to strengthen and support families who have a member who has a disability: www.familysupportbc.com
2. LIGHTS – a blueprint for success for individuals who want to live outside the family home: www.lights.to
3. My Voice. *Talk Rocket Go* an app that makes talking easy; *Rocket Keys* is a talking keyboard app: www.myvoiceaac.com
4. Canadian Association for Child and Play Therapy believes in the value of play therapy and its contribution to an individual's mental, emotional, social and psychological well-being: www.cacpt.com
5. Community Living Toronto: www.communitylivingtoronto.ca; Community Living Ontario: www.communitylivingontario.ca; Canadian Association for Community Living: www.cacl.ca
6. Tuberous Sclerosis Canada: www.tscanada.st.ca. Tuberous Sclerosis Alliance in the U.S.: www.tsalliance.org

Housing

1. Scarborough Residential Alternative – a family group seeking housing solutions: www.sralternatives.weebly.com
2. Nabors – A Community of Circles, building non-paid relationships: www.nabors.ca
3. Vela – Microboard Association, the creation of a small non-profit board to address a person's planning and support needs: www.microboard.org
4. L'Arche intentional communities: www.larche.org; L'Arche Daybreak in Ontario: www.larchedaybreak.com
5. Deohaeko Family Group, co-op housing and natural supports: www.deohaeko.com
6. Durham Association for Family Respite, including facilitation: www.dafrs.com
7. Home of Our Own. Community Living Peterborough: www.communitylivingpeterborough.ca
8. The BLEND Partnership program provides housing options for seniors and people with disabilities www.buronhicks.ca

Health

1. A good way to organize health information for your wallet: www.sickkids.ca/myhealthpassport
2. Good to Go Transition Program when moving from the child-friendly to the adult health system: www.sickkids.ca/good2go
3. Canada's Physical Activity Guide for Children and Youth: www.phac-aspc.gc.ca/pau-uap/paguide/child_youth/index.html
4. Parent Resources from the Department of Psychology: www.sickkids.ca/Psychology/Resources/index.html
5. Sibling Support Network: www.siblingsupport.org/
6. Healthy Transition, moving from pediatric to adult health care: www.healthytransitionsny.org
7. Special Needs Opportunity Window (SNOW) for information on technology, alternative formats, workshops on autism, developmental disabilities, behaviour disorders and learning disabilities: www.snow.idrc.ocad.ca/index.php

Additional Reading

1. Caroline Myss, *Defy Gravity: Healing Beyond the Bounds of Reason* (Canada: Raincoast, 2009)
2. Caroline Myss, *Anatomy of the Sprit, The Seven Stages of Power and Healing* (New York: Three River's Press, 1996)
3. Anne D. LeClaire, *Listening Below the Noise: A Meditation on the Practise of Silence* ((New York: Harper Collins, 2009)
4. John O'Donohue, *To Bless the Space Between Us, A Book of Blessings* (New York: Doubleday, 2008)
5. John O'Donohue, *Anam Cara, A Book of Celtic Wisdom* (New York: Harper Collins, 1997)
6. Henri Nouwen, *Adam, God's Beloved* (Maryknoll, New York: Orbis, 1997)

Acknowledgements

When I began writing this book, I was surprised that my voice had become buried in the lives of others. My heartfelt thanks to the following people who helped me find and refine my true voice.

To the spiritual teachers in my life: Jennifer (Jinks) Hoffmann, and the Rev. Michael Wright; and my Anam Cara, Joanna Taylor. Thank you for believing in me, and for your wise counsel. I am also grateful to my writing teachers: Mary J. Breen, Nora Zylstra-Savage, and Beth Kaplan, for their encouragement and help in bringing my story to life. Beth also provided incisive and invaluable editorial feedback; copy editing credit goes to Terry Poulton.

My inspiration, and my challenge, for the last twenty-eight years has been my son, Paul. He has taught me not to take anything for granted, to appreciate the little things in life, and to accept people for who they are—I'm still working on that one.

My heartfelt thanks to those who read the manuscript in whole and in part, and offered their perspective and insights: Mary Smith, Jean Elliott, Judy MacIntosh, Ruth Strunz, John Perkins, Sister Sue Mosteller, Eva Marsh, Cheri Davidson, Judith McGill, Jean Vanier, Dr. Daune MacGregor, and Alison Wearing.

And, it would have been impossible to reach the finale of this project without Murray's unconditional love—and his cappuccinos. His kindness pulled me away from the computer and into the sunshine, at just the right moments.

Support Circles
Gillian Chernets

WHAT: A Circle is a group of citizens who come together to support and share a relationship with a person who is vulnerable because of having a disability. People who have disabilities are always at risk of becoming isolated and surrounded by people who are paid to be in their life. Together, people in a Support network/circle develop a shared vision of a safe and secure present and future for the individual.

WHO: Circles have a variety of citizens as members: The individual, family members, friends, neighbours, former teachers, community members and former or current support staff. The ideal circle has a variety of members who bring different perspectives and ideas.

WHY? Circles provide:
- Companionship, relationships, fun and celebration. All this helps the individual feel loved and connected.
- Practical support by offering assistance in many ways.
- A forum for commitment and security – people who know and care will be there over time to make sure the person is supported and safe. Circle members are listeners they ensure the individual's voice is heard they encourage people to dare to dream.
- Help to individuals to make plans for their future and support, strategize and assist good decision making.
- Advocacy in ensuring the individual is treated well and receives the support to which he/she is entitled.
- Assistance, at times, to help the individual manage support funds and staff.

Circle members support the individual who has a disability but frequently the circle also becomes a forum for circle members to support each other. (mutual support)

HOW to begin a Circle:
Consider the network of connections which exists already - who knows the person. Who are the friends and family members they think they would feel comfortable being included in a circle? Some people do not think they have anyone they could ask. If that is the case; sit down with a close friend and do some brainstorming. What does the individual like to do? Are there activities that he/she does where she meets people who could be potential circle members?

Who should do the asking? This varies from family to family. Some parents want to ask people themselves. For some parents the asking is very difficult – the fear of rejection or imposing on people is very hard to overcome. Perhaps a close friend could invite people to an initial gathering.
If you don't feel comfortable asking a friend, you can look for a staff person such as a family support worker to assist.
NOTE: It is important that the person who is inviting people to the circle knows the individual and sees the person as valued and not as a client who needs to be fixed.
The asker can phone, write an invitation or speak to people directly- any way that they feel comfortable doing the "asking" They are doing it on behalf of the person and their family.

What does the asker say? There are many ways to approach people and to some extent it is what the asker feels comfortable in saying.
a) Introduce yourself as a friend of 'Joe' and his family.
b) That 'Joe' and his family have decided to create a circle of support around him to assist with planning and supporting him to have a good life.
c) That we are having a meeting on (date) to come together to learn more about a support circle, to listen to 'Joe's' life's story and to share our own stories about 'Joe.'
d) I'm asking you to join us because you are a person 'Joe' and his family value and respect.
e) This first meeting is an opportunity for you to meet some other people in 'Joe's' life and for you to decide if you would like to be part of an ongoing circle of support.

The first meeting:
a) Space and environment should be welcoming. Ideally held in a home, your own or a friend's or family member's. or a welcoming community setting.
b) It's best if there is a facilitator that is not the parent.
c) Food is a helpful component. Hospitality, a meal, or refreshments sets a tone of welcome.
d) Start with introductions-include how each person knows 'Joe.'
e) Tell 'Joe's' story; what his life looks like; what he and his family hope for in the future.
f) Some discussion can take place about who's in his life, and how you know him.
g) Leave space for people to ask questions and to get clarifications.
h) Set a date for another meeting. Facilitator gives phone numbers out and says she will call people before that next meeting to answer any questions and to discuss their further participation in the support circle and if people feel comfortable.

How do you maintain support circles over time?
a) Circles need to feel empowered.
b) Circle members need to feel valued.
c) Circle members need to celebrate together.
d) People in circles share both the good and bad times.
e) Circles need to come together; although the frequency varies in each situation. Regular meetings for a new circle help people get to know each other and secure the commitment to the process.
f) Circles need to feel meaningful for all the members. Circles are not on the sidelines of activity. Circle work ebbs and flows just as life does.
g) There is no magic number of circle members. Membership evolves over time into a good working number.

Once a circle is working together there is a great comfort in knowing that there are other people who know and care about your family member with a disability and would offer support if and when you – the parent – are not able. Gillian Chernets